ALSO BY EDUARDO PORTER

The Price of Everything

American Poison

AMERICAN POISON

How Racial Hostility Destroyed Our Promise

EDUARDO PORTER

ALFRED A. KNOPF
New York
2020

Library of Congress Cataloging-in-Publication Data
Names: Porter, Eduardo, author.
Title: American poison : how racial hostility destroyed our promise /
Eduardo Porter.
Description: First Edition. | New York : Alfred A. Knopf, 2020. |
"This is a Borzoi book published by Alfred A. Knopf." |
Includes bibliographical references and index.
Identifiers: LCCN 2019030765 (print) | LCCN 2019030766 (ebook) |
ISBN 9780451494887 (hardcover) | ISBN 9781524731588 (ebook)
Subjects: LCSH: Racism—United States—History. | Race awareness—
United States—History. | United States—Race relations.
Classification: LCC E184.A1 P658 2020 (print) | LCC E184.A1 (ebook) |
DDC 305.800973—dc23
LC record available at https://lccn.loc.gov/2019030765
LC ebook record available at https://lccn.loc.gov/2019030766

Jacket design by Carol Devine Carson

To Mateo and Uma

There has to be a better deal.

—LYNDON JOHNSON

Contents

American Poison

American Poison

In the early summer of 2015, I could not imagine that immigration had the power to deliver somebody to the White House. Just 7 percent of Americans believed immigration was the nation's most critical challenge, according to Gallup. Three in four thought it was good for the country. Only a third said we should admit fewer immigrants. This was half the share who thought so in the mid-1990s, when California's governor, Pete Wilson, ran for reelection by whipping up fears of an illegal alien invasion. Indeed, it was the lowest share since the 1960s.

Illegal immigration was, after all, pretty contained. There were 1.2 million fewer unauthorized immigrants in the United States in 2015 than there had been in 2007, when the implosion of the housing bubble wiped out the construction jobs that many of them relied on. The economy was growing briskly, after its painful slog out of the Great Recession, and the unemployment rate was falling fast, reducing what competition there might have been between immigrants and American workers for available jobs.

Then Donald Trump decided to run for president. He promised to protect the homeland from the rapist thugs streaming illegally into the United States from Mexico. He pledged to build a wall, to once and for all bring America's sieve-like southern border under control. All of a sudden the fear of immigrants that was lying dormant in America's subconscious propelled Trump to the presidency. It may change the United States for good.

There's a public park in Brooklyn a few blocks from where my son, Mateo, used to go to school. It's named, in true Brooklyn style, after a Beastie Boy: Adam Yauch. In the days after the election, somebody painted swastikas on the playground equipment, alongside an exhortation: "Go Trump."

I was born of a Mexican mother and an American father and grew up mostly in Mexico. I consider myself both Mexican and American. At home I speak mainly Spanish, hoping it will encourage Mateo to embrace his Mexican side too. On the day after the election, we were riding the subway when he leaned into my ear and whispered, "Dad, perhaps we shouldn't speak Spanish in public anymore?"

One might read this moment in American history as an aberration brought about by a uniquely racist political entrepreneur, or explain it as the product of specific economic circumstances. You've heard the argument: working-class voters frustrated by decades of wage stagnation lashed out at the cosmopolitan class that ignored their plight for so long.

There is some truth to this. Many of Trump's voters are among the losers of America's economic transformations. He won white voters without a bachelor's degree by a thirty-nine percentage point margin over Hillary Clinton. The 2,584 counties that Trump won in 2016 generated only 36 percent of the nation's GDP, according to research by Mark Muro and Sifan Liu of the Brookings Institution's Metropolitan Policy Program. They include most of rural and small-town America—depopulated, aging, in seemingly terminal decline. The 472 counties that voted for Hillary Clinton, by contrast, accounted for 64 percent of America's economic output. This lopsided pattern can be made to fit the view that the "us" who were left behind by progress voted the smug beneficiaries of America's prosperity out of power.

But that is hardly the whole story. It would be a historic mistake to gloss over the critical, defining role of xenophobia in America's choice. It was not a freak event, not a bug in the system. The mix of contempt and resentment across frontiers of religion, race, ethnicity, and citizenship that anchored Trump's seduction of sixty-three million voters has distorted American politics since the birth of the nation. It defines who we are.

You may call our condition racial hostility or simply racism. From America's slaveholder past through the Civil War and beyond, in the form of legal segregation across the Jim Crow South and de facto segregation across the urban North, the poll tax deployed to keep blacks from the polls, and campaigns against imagined voter fraud to purge blacks from the rolls, "ethnic divisions"—to give them a tamer name—have conditioned every turn in the development of the American state. Standing in the way of social trust, blocking solidarity, they have made us decidedly poorer. Upon those injustices we have built the most exceptional country, one in which the most extreme wealth coexists comfortably with deprivation that has no place in the industrialized world.

Trump's election might have exposed America's ethnic divisions to the unforgiving glare of the klieg lights, but the uncomfortable questions raised by a president who likens immigrants to rapists ready to come for our women, who blocks Muslims from entering the country, who offers understanding to white supremacists marching torches in hand, coiled at the ready for a Nazi salute, have been lying in America's political underbrush for a long time.

The very image of the United States as a melting pot—forged by the likes of Ralph Waldo Emerson and Henry James to evoke an exceptional culture, built of a multiplicity of immigrant experiences bound into a national American identity—was ultimately a blinkered concept. Emerson might have dreamed of America as an "asylum of all nations," where Africans and Polynesians contributed to create a new race, a new religion, and a new literature to replace the old Eurocentric paradigm. In fact, the crucible smelted only Americans of European stock.

The term "melting pot" made its way into the American vernacular through Israel Zangwill's homonymous play, which opened at the Columbia in Washington, D.C., on October 5, 1908. It's an ersatz *Romeo and Juliet* in which a Jewish Russian immigrant and a Christian Russian immigrant, in New York, overcome the vast historical and cultural chasm between them. "Germans and Frenchmen, Irishmen and Englishmen, Jews and Russians—into the crucible with you all!" trumpets the main character, David Quixano. "God is making the American." At the premiere, President Theodore Roosevelt, to whom Zangwill had dedicated the drama, is said to have shouted, "That's a great play."

The indigenous communities living in the United States before all those Europeans arrived were not invited into the pot, though. Nor were the descendants of African slaves or the brown Catholic Mexicans from whom the United States had acquired about a third of its territory sixty years before. The American alloy certainly had no place for Chinese immigrants, who were prohibited from gaining American citizenship under the Chinese Exclusion Act. In 1924, sixteen years after the debut of *The Melting-Pot*, Congress passed restrictions limiting legal immigration from Asia, Africa, and Latin America. They would remain on the books until 1965.

Over the last half a century or so, however, these disparate peoples once excluded from the crucible have come to define the de facto American. As a response, all those Americans of European stock who melted over the years into the contemporary concept of non-Hispanic white ditched the crucible metaphor and replaced it with a different organizing principle: to each his own. For years they circled the wagons, hoping to bar the nonwhite from the benefits of citizenship. When the Civil Rights Act stripped them of this ability, they set out to sabotage the collective American project. Donald Trump is merely a natural step in this progression.

One of the most notable features of President Trump's victory was its whiteness. Sixty-two percent of white men chose him, compared with 32 percent who voted for Clinton. He won a plurality of white women, beating the first female presidential candidate from a major party in history by a margin of 47 to 45 percent. He opened a new divide in American politics, a split between the mostly white homogeneous culture of small-town America in slow but steady economic decline and the messy mix of the nation's vast urban hubs.

The urban-rural cleavage is just an old wound in a new place. In 2016 rural whites voted in lockstep to preserve what privilege they could despite their demographic stagnation. Their choice was an extension of whites' long-standing effort to preserve for themselves what America has to offer.

Consider the Fourteenth Amendment, passed in 1868. It's the one stating that people born in the United States are automatically citizens, entitled to the full complement of constitutional rights. It's also the one President Trump has called to repeal. The amendment came into being eleven years after the Supreme Court's infamous decision in *Dred Scott v. Sandford*, which denied citizenship to African Americans, whether free or enslaved. The amendment didn't mention race, but as the historian Eric Foner has written, it "challenged legal discrimination throughout the nation and broadened the meaning of freedom for all Americans." As soon as it was passed, this tool for the protection of equal rights was deployed in the service of, uh, butchers.

New Orleans butchers ultimately failed to convince the

Supreme Court that Louisiana's regulation of slaughterhouses unconstitutionally abridged their citizenship privileges. Still, the ludicrous deployment of an amendment designed to protect African Americans from disenfranchisement was but the beginning of a trend. For the Supreme Court's *Slaughterhouse* decision further limited blacks' rights. The Fourteenth Amendment, it decided, covered only a narrow set of federal citizenship rights, like habeas corpus. Everything else fell under the domain of the states.

To this day, the Fourteenth Amendment has been used as often to limit the rights of the descendants of the four million people freed from slavery as it has been to protect their place as Americans.

Justice Samuel F. Miller in the *Slaughterhouse Cases* tried to remind everybody of the purpose of the Thirteenth, Fourteenth, and Fifteenth Amendments, which abolished slavery, guaranteed birthright citizenship, and ensured citizens' right to vote regardless of their race. "The one pervading purpose found in them all, lying at the foundation of each, and without which none of them would have been even suggested," he wrote, was "the freedom of the slave race, the security and firm establishment of that freedom, and the protection of the newly made freeman and citizen from the oppressions of those who had formerly exercised unlimited dominion over him."

Few were listening. From time to time, the Court has deployed these amendments to serve these goals, most notably in the 1954 *Brown v. Board of Education of Topeka* decision, which made school segregation illegal. But the Fourteenth Amendment was ultimately powerless to prevent even the most blatant racial discrimination. Just thirty years after its passage, the Supreme Court decided that the "separate but equal" doctrine that underpinned racial segregation in the Jim Crow South did not abridge African Americans' rights as citizens. Its infamous decision in the *Plessy v. Ferguson* case of 1896 argued that shunting blacks to separate railcars did not, in fact, impute their racial inferiority. Whites were also expected to stay on the white side of the line. The law of separation applied to both races alike.

In its 1978 decision in *Regents of the University of California v. Bakke,* the Court eviscerated the idea that affirmative action was meant to grant long-oppressed minority students a leg up, ruling that it deprived a white applicant to medical school of his Fourteenth Amendment rights. In 2018 a conservative group launched a class action against Harvard University, arguing that its efforts to enroll black and Latino students violated the Fourteenth Amendment rights of Asian applicants.

If it eliminated all consideration of race and other variables, Harvard pointed out, the African American share of its freshman class would decline to 5 percent from 14 percent and the Hispanic share would decline to 9 percent from 14 percent. "The Supreme Court appears, once again, to be poised to turn the Fourteenth Amendment away from its original purpose of protecting against discrimination and providing equal opportunity for African Americans and people of color who were long excluded from colleges, universities and other opportunities because of their race and ethnicity," wrote the legal scholar Theodore M. Shaw. In 2019, Harvard, surprisingly, won.

It's not just the Fourteenth Amendment whose spirit has been distorted. Many of the gains achieved by African Americans through the civil rights movement of the 1960s are being chipped at relentlessly. The 1965 Voting Rights Act, anchored in the Fifteenth Amendment, was designed to protect blacks' right to vote against the shenanigans deployed by electoral authorities in the South to keep them away from the polls. In 2013 the Supreme Court ruled that the blatant racism that justified giving the Justice Department oversight power over the voting rules in nine states and parts of six others was no longer widespread. So it ended it. It has become decidedly more difficult for blacks to vote since then.

Following the ruling in *Shelby County v. Holder,* many juris-dictions have started requiring voters to present official identifi-cation. Others have purged voter rolls, culling mostly nonwhite voters. They have reduced polling locations in poor minority neighborhoods and curtailed early voting. Many have required documentary proof of citizenship, which poor black and brown voters often lack.

The Brennan Center for Justice in New York has estimated that one in nine Americans lack a government ID. Often born at home rather than in hospitals, names slightly misspelled on birth certificates issued often far away and decades ago, the poor and the old face unfathomable hurdles to procure them. Eric Holder, President Obama's first attorney general, argued that new voter-ID requirements were designed to do the same job as the poll taxes deployed across the Jim Crow South: to prevent blacks from voting.

White Americans are also doing their best to keep black and brown kids out of their children's schools, carving their more affluent neighborhoods out of larger urban school districts in order to protect their exclusivity without breaking the law. Decades after the Fair Housing Act, affluent white neighbor-hoods and cities still deploy zoning rules against multifamily dwellings and rental housing to prevent poorer nonwhite resi-dents from moving in.

The story is old. In the throes of the Great Depression, Pres-ident Franklin D. Roosevelt proposed the New Deal to cover Americans with a society-wide insurance policy that rested on a sense of collective sacrifice for the good of all. What the many cheerleaders of Roosevelt's program fail to acknowledge is that it had very narrow borders, clearly circumscribed by race. Its initiatives and agencies—think of Social Security or the Federal Housing Administration—excluded the nonwhite at every turn.

The political scientist Ira Katznelson called the New Deal affirmative action for whites. When the Civil Rights Act let nonwhites into the tent, the political consensus that set America down the path toward social democracy, underpinned by a robust safety net, collapsed. Shocked by the diversity on its streets, the white majority turned away from the New Deal's goals.

George Wallace, the Alabama governor who blocked the enrollment of two African American students into the state's flagship university, understood this well. He received thousands of congratulatory notes for his defiance of federal law, from below and above the Mason-Dixon Line. "They all hate black people, all of them," he concluded. "Great God! That's it! They're all Southern."

Running for president in 1968, Wallace figured out that he couldn't run an overtly racist campaign. But he appreciated the value of stoking whites' fears of blacks moving "into our streets, our schools, our neighborhoods." In *White Rage: The Unspoken Truth of Our Racial Divide*, the historian Carol Anderson reports that in 1966, 85 percent of whites were sure that "the pace of civil rights progress was too fast."

What white melting-pot Americans fail to understand is that their efforts to exclude the brown and the black from the benefits of citizenship are causing untold damage to white America too. Blacks and Latinos may suffer disproportionately when they can't vote, their kids are banned from good schools, and they are barred from homes in middle-class neighborhoods. But by turning their backs on an understanding of collective goods that requires sharing with their nonwhite sisters and brothers, whites have impoverished American society. They too are suffering the consequences.

I was in Harlan County, Kentucky, just before the midterm elections of 2018, at a town hall with Governor Matt Bevin. Harlan is legendary in Appalachia's coal country, the site of a yearlong strike by the United Mine Workers in the 1970s to improve wages and working conditions. Over 95 percent of the population is white and not Hispanic. About four in ten live under the poverty line. The income of a typical household in Harlan is about $24,000, less than half the national median, and most of that comes from federal assistance. Barely a third of Harlan's adults hold a job. It is one of only eleven counties in the United States where government assistance adds up to more than half of families' income.

Harlan faces a destitute future. Coal mining is in inexorable decline; these days it supports six hundred jobs in the county, down from twenty-nine hundred in 1990. There is no obvious industry to take its place. Still, when Governor Bevin railed at the abuse of government welfare, the five dozen or so beleaguered residents gathered at the old courthouse gave him a standing ovation. They buzzed with outrage as Bevin told a story about a lazy bum who lounged on the couch in his poor mother's home, living off government benefits.

Medicaid benefits amount to some 17 percent of the personal income of Harlan's residents, on average. Still, those gathered at the town hall gave a round of applause to Bevin's plan—frustrated by the courts—to require thousands of able-bodied Medicaid recipients of working age to get a job, enroll in a training program, or perform community service for twenty hours a week.

When the governor unveiled his plan, roughly half of the 350,000 able-bodied Medicaid beneficiaries in Kentucky failed to meet the work requirements. His administration estimated that the new rules would cull some 100,000 people from the rolls within five years; those who stayed on would have to pay for their health care. Bevin called for a premium starting at $1 per month for extremely poor families living on up to one-quarter of the federal poverty line—who, I was amazed to discover, do exist in Kentucky. It rose to $15 for those who manage to stay above the poverty threshold. Overall, the governor estimated his proposals would cut the state's spending on Medicaid by $2.4 billion over five years.

Bevin is a bit of a firebrand, a Tea Party favorite who won the governorship over the opposition of Kentucky's Republican establishment. But his proposals fit well within the mainstream of the Republican Party.

Two decades ago, Kentucky eagerly embraced the nation's latest attempt at "welfare reform" when the poor's entitlement to federal assistance dating back to the New Deal was replaced by a set of fixed grants to the states. States, under the legislation, were freed to impose whatever requirements they saw fit to limit the pool of beneficiaries. Kentucky took full advantage of the opportunity.

The state's poverty rate hasn't budged much since then. It stands just above 17 percent, making it the fifth poorest in the nation. But the number of families getting cash assistance under Temporary Assistance for Needy Families, the program known as TANF, which replaced the federal entitlement for the poor, has plummeted by two-thirds. TANF provides benefits to fewer than one in five poor families in the state, less than half the share it covered at its inception in 1996. Forced to jump through multiple hoops to get a benefit that tops out at $262 a month for a family of three, even some of the poorest families have decided it's not worth it.

Kentucky is hardly the meanest state. In sixteen states, anti-poverty cash benefits reach fewer than one in ten poor families with children. Like Bevin, Republican governors across the country rushed to save on Medicaid too, taking advantage of the Trump administration's offer to let states experiment with the program. By the summer of 2019 sixteen states had asked the federal government for permission to attach work requirements to Medicaid, according to the Kaiser Family Foundation. Twelve had requested co-pays and power to limit benefits. Fifteen had asked to impose other eligibility and enrollment restrictions. Only a few of these requests had been blocked in court.

These proposals are invariably justified as mechanisms to

encourage poor Americans to get a job and prosper, free from the clutches of the welfare state. And yet if culling government programs was meant to somehow enhance Americans' well-being, it failed. Welfare reform did lead many poor people to get jobs, but they never earned enough to pull their families out of poverty. The loss of welfare payments pretty much canceled out their earnings from work. With little education and virtually no access to training, they got stuck in the low-wage labor market that has taken over so much of the American economy.

The efforts to limit Medicaid benefits amount to playing with people's lives. In 2005, just across Kentucky's southern border, Tennessee removed 170,000 people from the Medicaid rolls to save money, almost one in ten Medicaid beneficiaries in the state. People started delaying visits to the doctor, according to one study. Some stopped going to the doctor altogether. Many reported suffering more days in bad health and incapacitated, and they ended up more often in emergency rooms, which are required by law to care for all comers regardless of their ability to pay. One study found that culling the Medicaid rolls led to delays in diagnosis of breast cancer, which led to more such cancers being detected at a later stage. Women who lived in low-income zip codes were 3.3 percentage points more likely to receive a diagnosis of late-stage cancer than women living in high-income zip codes. They were also more likely to die.

Kentucky is the state with the most cancer deaths in the nation, and the most preventable hospitalizations. It is forty-fifth out of fifty in terms of its death rate from diabetes, second in deaths from septicemia, and forty-first measured by deaths from heart disease. What will happen when the sick poor of Kentucky can't afford a doctor's visit? A review of recent research published in the *Annals of Internal Medicine* concluded that the odds of dying for non-elderly uninsured adults are between 3 and 29 percent higher than if they had health insurance. A study by the economists Katherine Baicker, Benjamin Sommers, and

Arnold Epstein calculated that covering 176 additional adults with Medicaid would prevent one death per year. Culling thousands of people from the Medicaid rolls would, correspondingly, shorten their lives.

I have no direct evidence linking overt racism to Harlan's residents' rejection of the government they so rely on. There are only 723 blacks and 243 Hispanics in the entire county. Harlan's 26,000 non-Hispanic white residents could go through their lives without ever seeing an ethnic minority. And yet this book proposes that racial hostility is, indeed, what blocked the construction of an American social welfare state.

"Welfare queens" and other racial stereotypes peddled over decades by the political foes of redistribution have become enmeshed in the national conversation about the role of the government in America. Amplified by the media, repeated relentlessly by the champions of small government, they ultimately convinced white Americans that people of color are undeserving moochers from the public purse.

This point of view short-circuited the understanding that a healthy society must inevitably deploy the resources of the fortunate to help give a leg up to the disadvantaged. Taking comfort in their race-based interpretation of the ills of the welfare state, white voters marginalized by the same economic forces that wreaked havoc in many communities of color could not figure out that they were shooting themselves in the foot.

The hardened attitudes toward welfare of the people of Harlan echoed those recorded in 2012 by my colleague from *The New York Times* Binyamin Appelbaum in Chisago County, Minnesota, where the guy from the tattoo parlor complained that people were using government checks to pay for tattoos, and the guy who retired from the Department of Corrections thought that the "big thing" ailing the nation is "the country is full of people who think that the government owes them something."

Racial mistrust is never far from the surface. What but xenophobia could explain Harlan's voters' enthusiastic embrace of Trump's appeal to blood and soil? Almost nine out of ten voters in Harlan voted for Trump. His promise to build a wall along the Mexican border somehow resonated in a county where only 189 persons—0.7 percent of the population—were born in another country.

This is not unique to Harlan. Eighty-one percent of the population of Fremont, Nebraska, is non-Hispanic white. Only 8 percent of its residents were born in another country. Still, in 2010 and again in 2014 the residents of Fremont voted for the toughest municipal ordinance against illegal immigrants in the country, barring landlords from taking them as tenants and employers from hiring them.

The people of Fremont were driven by abstract fear: fear of Hispanics, who more than tripled their share of Fremont's population since the turn of the century to 15 percent; fear of a colossal chicken-processing plant built by Costco, which is expected to draw thousands of nonwhite workers to the area. Similarly, the people of Harlan's aversion to the safety net is motivated by otherness. At the Pine Mountain Settlement School, just over the mountain from Harlan, I met a young assistant director, Preston Jones, who offered a considered rejoinder to both welfare and immigration. "We can't even support the people that are here now," he told me. "How will we be able to support new people coming in?"

The political scientist Rodney Hero has carefully studied the link between race and attitudes toward government spending. The increasing social and economic distance between whites and nonwhites, he finds, is not only eroding support for the social safety net. His research with colleagues Morris Levy and Brian Yeokwang An found compelling evidence that rising income inequality between racial groups reduces local spending on public goods like police and fire departments. White taxpayers are more reluctant to fund public spending when such spending will benefit the nonwhite, so they vote in candidates campaigning against public spending of all types. "These results re-affirm and clarify the nature as well as the persistent and fundamental importance of race and of class in U.S. society and its politics and policies," they wrote.

Voters don't need to experience minorities to mistrust them. Under 4 percent of Kentucky's population were born outside the United States. Still, in the month running up to the midterm election of 2018, 27 percent of the political ads aired in Kentucky stoked fears about immigration, according to the Wesleyan Media Project. In a national survey by the Brookings Institution and the Public Religion Research Institute in 2016, only 22 percent of Americans said immigration was changing their local community, but 39 percent said it was changing American society as a whole.

So it is with attitudes about race. Only 8 percent of Kentucky's population are black. Still, the people of Kentucky rank just after the people of West Virginia and Mississippi in searching for the word "nigger" on the Internet. The data scientist Seth Stephens-Davidowitz argues this is a pretty good indicator of racial animus. "Google data, evidence suggests, are unlikely to suffer from major social censoring," he wrote. People are more honest in the privacy of their Internet searches.

In hindsight, Trump's electoral victory should not have been such a shock. His platform built on resentments of race and class was just what the disgruntled white voters who made up the Republican base wanted to hear. What is more surprising is how well President Trump's policy agenda meshed with the long-standing Republican project. Sure, his attempts to ban people from Muslim countries and deport more unauthorized immigrants might not have served the objectives of pro-business

Republicans, who tend to welcome immigrants as a source of labor. His wanton protectionism also strained against corporate interests. But on every other front, Trump's domestic agenda hewed closely to the standard GOP wish list.

President Trump's tax reform of 2017 was a dream come true for even the most zealous antitax evangelists on the Republican right. By the end of 2018, federal tax revenues had dropped to 16.7 percent of the nation's gross domestic product, according to White House estimates, a full percentage point less than in the last year of the Obama administration.

On the spending side, his administration did not just allow states to cull beneficiaries from the Medicaid rolls. It has been working to cut food stamps, too. In April 2018 the president signed an executive order instructing all government agencies to reform their welfare programs by "encouraging work and reducing dependence," tightening work requirements for non-disabled Americans of working age "to the extent current law allows." By the White House's own estimates, this new requirement could affect up to thirty-four million people. Ultimately, the president is proposing a narrow safety net that is useless to those who most need it.

Trump's strategy dovetails smoothly with the federalist agenda—the demand for state control of government policy that was championed since Reconstruction across the South in an effort to hamstring federal programs that might provide for African Americans. "By separating national and local authority, American federalism allowed local communities to override national majorities on basic matters of citizenship," wrote the political scientists Robert Lieberman and John Lapinski. "Even (and especially) in parts of the South where blacks were a majority."

Politically, Trump owes his victory to the continued process of racial sorting that began over half a century ago, when white southern Democrats responded to President Johnson's civil rights agenda by defecting to the Republican Party. Over the years, the process transformed the GOP into the defender of white privilege, eager to protect America from the demands of the colored. It also transformed the South into a safe Republican enclave for generations.

In 2016, race-based voting proved decisive beyond the South. Nonmetropolitan areas across the country turned out for Trump by margins exceeding 40 percent, on average. Small cities and towns also voted decisively for him: There are some 380 metropolitan areas in the United States. In 31, Trump won by a margin of at least fifty points. Their average population: 180,000 people. More than three out of four residents were non-Hispanic white. By contrast, Hillary Clinton took only 7 metros by margins above fifty percentage points. But they were bigger, with an average population of 1.2 million. Six out of ten of their residents were people of color.

This racial sorting has accelerated sharply over the last decade. In 2008, white voters without a college degree split their political allegiances roughly equally between Democrats and Republicans. By 2015, they favored the GOP by a margin of 24 percentage points. It poses a direct threat not only to the liberal agenda but to America's ability to thrive in an open, globalized, multiethnic era. Since the 1960s at least, the liberal ethos has rested on the dream of a grand progressive alliance: working men and women, the poor, immigrants, and racial and other minorities coming together in a coalition to counter conservatives and their corporate allies. The 2016 election, in which whites without a college degree voted for Trump over Hillary Clinton by thirty-nine percentage points, drove an unforgiving stake through these expectations.

In her insightful book *White Working Class: Overcoming Class Cluelessness in America*, published just after the election, Joan Williams proposed that blue-collar white voters turned against welfare programs because they saw them as tools designed by urban liberals to help the urban poor. "All they see is their stressed-out daily lives, and they resent subsidies and sympathy available to the poor," Williams observed.

Struggling middle-income families do not understand that welfare programs are so meager that the poor hardly get any help, she wrote. They seethe at a safety net that allows a poor single black mother to stay at home while offering nothing to a hardworking couple tag-teaming day and night shifts to care for their children. They view it as a scheme to hand over goodies to the black and brown designed by an elite that looks down upon less educated white workers with barely concealed contempt.

The dream of a grand alliance breezed too easily over the ideological chasm between a socially conservative working class and a liberal urban agenda where transgendered bathrooms have a spot on the priorities list along with better jobs. And yet, to my mind, the liberal challenge is much steeper than Williams suggests. Crafting a platform that might draw blue-collar whites into a multicultural tent is not simply a matter of prioritizing the class struggle over other elements of the liberal canon; it requires rebuilding solidarity—reclaiming the proposition that paying taxes to fund public goods for all is indispensable to maintaining a healthy society. That will require bridging a racial divide that has been centuries in the making. The challenge will remain even after President Trump leaves office: How to build social trust across the breach cloven by racial hostility? The Right isn't interested. As far as I can tell, the Left isn't brimming with ideas either.

The demolition of public housing in Chicago starting around the turn of this century offers a sobering take on the continuing political power of race. A dozen housing projects run by the Chicago Housing Authority were demolished between 2000 and 2004. They housed some twenty-five thousand people, more than ninety-nine out of a hundred of whom were black. Several were very close to predominantly white neighborhoods.

According to the political scientist Ryan Enos, after they were demolished, the turnout of white voters living nearest to them dropped by ten percentage points. What's more, they became more liberal. The researcher concluded that having blacks living nearby drove whites to circle the wagons. Or, as he put it, "the white voters in Chicago were threatened by a spatially proximate, yet segregated, out-group." Once the projects were flattened and the blacks removed, whites could afford a more generous stance. Racial fear even colored their presidential choices. In the general election of 2008, white voters near projects that had been demolished were more likely to vote for Obama than white voters living near projects that were still standing, other things being equal.

It is not an exaggeration to say that today racial fear is one of the main drivers of the country's choices. Stephens-Davidowitz argues that racial animus in the United States cost Obama roughly four percentage points of the national popular vote in both 2008 and 2012. The voting public is also evaluating policy through a racial veil.

The political scientist Michael Tesler concludes that voters' feelings about race shaped their attitudes toward the Affordable Care Act, the fiscal stimulus deployed by the Obama administration to combat the Great Recession, and even tax rates. Whites who expressed the most racial resentment—who believe that whites suffer unfairly from antidiscrimination policies, think blacks are to blame for their own misfortune, and so forth— were consistently less likely to support government-provided health insurance.

America's first black president widened the gap. Between December 2007, toward the end of the George W. Bush administration, and November 2009, when Obama had been in office for ten months, the share of racially resentful whites who argued that responsibility for health care should be left to individuals jumped from 40 to 70 percent. "The declining support for government health insurance during Barack Obama's presidency was driven by racially conservative defections," Tesler concluded.

During the Clinton administration African Americans were 26 percent more likely to support government-provided health insurance than whites. In the early years of the Obama administration, however, the gap in support widened to 45 percent, driven both by increased support among blacks and less support among whites.

Even framing an increase in top tax rates as an Obama policy activated racial resentment and reduced white support. As Donald Kinder and Allison Dale-Riddle noted in *The End of Race?*, no matter what President Obama said about society and government, or about the nation's problems and policies, "at the end of the day, every time American voters caught a glimpse of him, he was black."

Racial prejudice colors Americans' take on democracy. Back in 1980, Paul Weyrich, the conservative activist who founded the American Legislative Exchange Council, argued, "I don't want everybody to vote." Republicans, he noted, tend to do better "as the voting populace goes down." So ALEC, as the council was known, set out to draft voter-ID legislation that, invariably, made it more difficult for citizens of color to vote.

Racism in America may be as old as the hills. But there is still something particularly unsettling about our current moment. Well into the twenty-first century, we have come to expect that even avowedly racist Americans understand their racism is not welcome in public discourse. Racist views, we thought, could only be expressed these days veiled by subterfuge. Obviously, this understanding is wrong.

In the election campaign of 2012, Mitt Romney's political ads relied on racial cues. Writing about Romney's campaign strategy, Thomas Edsall in *The New York Times* said that the Republican candidate had nowhere else to go. "Faced with few if any possibilities of making gains among blacks and Hispanics—whose support for Obama has remained strong—the Romney campaign has no other choice if the goal is to win but to adopt a strategy to drive up white turnout," he wrote.

The Republican contender accused President Obama, misleadingly, of gutting the work requirements attached to welfare in the 1996 reform—a coded appeal to the common trope among whites that blacks are lazy takers hoping to live on the taxpayer's dime. He also asserted that the president was taking hundreds of millions from Medicare, whose beneficiaries are overwhelmingly white, to pay for medical benefits for the disproportionately minority population of uninsured.

In 2016, the racial appeals did away with the smoke screens. Trump's path to the presidency relied even more heavily on less educated white men. Only 38 percent of women, 27 percent of Hispanics, and 7 percent of black registered voters leaned Republican, according to the Pew Research Center. Only 41 percent of college graduates supported the GOP. Trump's shot at the presidency depended on white men without a college degree. So he discarded the subtly coded dog whistles about lazy blacks and replaced them with overt appeals urging whites to save America from the black and brown in their midst.

His voters were already there. The Tea Party, which rose to prominence in the early days of Obama's presidency, was ostensibly motivated by concerns over the budget deficit and focused on cutting taxes and slashing public spending. But Tea Party rallies often featured photoshopped portraits of the president and his wife, Michelle, blended in with images of apes. Tea Party posters referred to Obama as the "primate in chief." When the National Association for the Advancement of Colored People passed a resolution branding the Tea Party a racist organization, Mark Williams, leader of the Tea Party Express in California, penned a mock "letter to Abe Lincoln" in which "We Coloreds" argued against emancipation: "Freedom means having to work for real, think for ourselves, and take consequences along with the rewards. That is just far too much to ask of us Colored People and we demand that it stop!"

The political scientists Nicholas Valentino, Fabian Guy Neuner, and L. Matthew Vandenbroek published a study in 2018 trying to understand why overtly racist rhetoric had become more acceptable in mainstream political discourse. They suggested a couple of dynamics. For starters, the great sorting of voters set off by the Civil Rights Act in the 1960s is pretty much complete. As the GOP has become dominated by whites hostile to minorities, the political cost for Republicans to express overtly racist views has declined.

At the same time, whites' loss of demographic clout compared with fast-growing minority groups has produced an embattled white consciousness. Obama's rise to the presidency allowed many white voters to convince themselves that racial discrimination against African Americans was a thing of the past. Affirmative action and other programs to help minorities get ahead were no longer needed. By 2016, this feeling had evolved into a sense that it was the working-class whites of stagnant small towns and Rust Belt metros who needed protection from others.

Romney's defeat in 2012 inspired a bout of soul-searching within the GOP. A widely circulated postmortem argued that to remain relevant the party had to reach out to women and people of color. There weren't enough white men in America to keep them in power. But by 2016 Republicans had, evidently, forgotten about all that. They chose a different path.

Trump won the presidential election. The next year white supremacists marched through Charlottesville, Virginia, defiantly wielding their torches and Confederate flags. "We suspect that the norms of acceptable racial rhetoric in American politics have shifted dramatically," Valentino and colleagues wrote.

"The distinctive power of implicit versus explicit racial cues may have diminished as an increasingly large group of citizens no longer reject explicitly hostile appeals." This is scary. What happens when overt racial hostility takes over the national debate about social welfare, immigration, or even national security? What happens when it spills over from political rhetoric to the physical world?

There is something sadly ironic about racism's renewed impetus. It comes on the cusp of an era in which white Americans will be forced to rely on others like never before. White Americans are getting old. The median white is forty-three years old. Four in ten are over fifty-two. By contrast, the median age for Latinos is only twenty-eight. As the demographer William Frey notes in his book *Diversity Explosion*, "The older, largely white population will need the future minority-dominant adult population to be productive workers, taxpayers, and consumers if the nation's economy is to continue to grow and produce revenues and services that benefit both the young and the old."

The Pew analysis noted how immigration has padded the labor force for years. Immigrants and their children accounted for more than half the growth of the population of twenty-five- to sixty-four-year-olds over the last two decades, according to its analysis. They will account for more than the entire labor force's growth over the next two.

Baby boomers are retiring, leaving a big hole in the labor supply. If the United States were to cut off the flow of new immigrants, the study noted, its working-age population would shrink to 166 million in 2035 from 173 million in 2015, even as the number of elderly Americans mushroomed.

The United States doesn't just need foreign computer programmers and other highly skilled immigrants, by the way. It needs lots of less educated immigrants too. The Conference Board projects that the working-age population with no education beyond high school will shrink over the next ten years.

But Department of Labor projections suggest that the occupations that will add the most jobs over the next twenty years will require no more than a high school certificate. We will need an additional 800,000 personal care aides over the next decade alone, and 600,000 more workers in food preparation.

The economists Pia Orrenius and Madeline Zavodny recommend policies to increase legal immigration, including an expanded temporary work visa program for low-skilled immigrants who could serve fast-growing industries. Good luck with that. Whatever happens to Donald Trump, American politics are unlikely to transition smoothly from debating an "impregnable" wall to offering a job to all those brown foreigners we now want to keep out at any cost.

America's ethnic divisions pose a monumental test for its ability to engage with an open market economy in the throes of relentless technological change. The critical insight by the economist Dani Rodrik comes to mind: the countries most successful in dealing with globalization are the ones that have the richest, most robust safety nets. As he points out in his book *The Globalization Paradox*, markets and governments are not substitutes but complements. To the extent that racial animus prevents the United States from building a sufficiently robust government, it will prevent it from engaging productively with the rest of the world.

Over the last half a century or so, the prevailing economic orthodoxy in the United States held that any constraint on the worldwide flow of goods and capital had to be a bad thing: inefficient. But the Republican critique that welfare amounts to sand in the economic cogs—encouraging low-income (mostly black) people to lie back, cash their government checks, and have children out of wedlock—has surely been proven irrelevant. The social safety net, including what Americans call welfare, is the tool rich societies use to allow workers to cope with economic risk. America's populist upheaval has proven that whatever its cost to efficiency, it is a small cost to bear. Because without such a safety net, workers are unlikely to accept the kind of disruption globalization carries in its wake. No political democracy can bear the disruptions that unfettered efficiency brings about.

And that's not even my main concern. What keeps me up at night is what the new America of open racial conflict means for the future of my children: Mateo, newly wary of speaking Spanish in the open, and my daughter, Uma, who has an equally complex ethnic heritage. The United States will need them, as much as any other young American, but that's no guarantee that they will be accepted into the melting pot. The ethnic animosity driving American politics and policy may drive them out.

Thirty-five years ago, in his outgoing presidential address to the Population Association of America, the prominent demographer Samuel Preston sounded an alarm over the failure to invest in America's children. American mothers were having more babies out of wedlock. Measures of school achievement had slumped. Though the poverty rate among the elderly was falling, child poverty was on the rise. By neglecting its children, warned Preston, the United States was putting its future at risk.

This neglect, I would argue, was largely motivated by race. One critical factor blunting "any outbreak of altruistic behavior towards other people's children," Preston observed, was that "they are increasingly drawn from minorities with whom the majority may have trouble identifying." He had scathing words for such a myopic understanding of our collective well-being. Whites who viewed the problems of childhood as confined to African Americans should know that "there is not a single trend that I've talked about that does not pertain to both races," he wrote. Indeed, some troubling trends, like the growing numbers of single mothers, were advancing faster among whites. American children, he lectured, are "a group that includes all races."

America's political class evidently had no patience for such lecturing. The income of the average American is nearly 50 percent greater than it was when Preston made his speech, after accounting for inflation: almost $60,000 per year. Still, nearly thirteen million children live in poverty, only 600,000 fewer than in 1984. The share of babies born to single mothers is about twice what it was back then.

Whites already account for less than half of all American children. Preston's warning about the risk incurred by all Americans by failing to invest in the young holds as true now as it did then. Indeed, in the course of this book I hope to convince you that persistent barriers of racial mistrust and hostility running through the American experience have prevented "any outbreak of altruistic behavior," not only toward our children, but across all of American society. And I hope to convince you that such racism has, again and again, done harm to us all.

In 1940, a time when Jim Crow laws imposed discrimination at work, segregated schools, and clove neighborhoods, the median black man earned the same as a white man at the twenty-fourth percentile of the white earnings distribution. In 2014, following over half a century of laws and court rulings designed to end such discrimination, the median black man's earnings had climbed all the way to the twenty-seventh percentile of white men.

The economist Raj Chetty and his colleagues at Opportunity Insights have found that African Americans living in areas with a large black population experience particularly low levels of economic mobility. And this portends ill for the future of social insurance.

But whites are not unscathed. Reconstruction's Black Codes, which aimed to reinstate something akin to slavery by shackling black workers to their jobs, also depressed the wages of poor whites. The poll taxes designed to keep African Americans from the voting booth disenfranchised poor white voters too. So the miserly modern state the United States has built for itself—hemmed in by whites' unwillingness to extend a hand across its tribal walls—is condemning the nation's future.

CHAPTER 2

Welfare for Whites

You couldn't tell from the rows of dolled-up brownstones hugging the western bank of the Hudson River in Hoboken, New Jersey, but that bedroom community to Manhattan's thriving financial economy, only a short ferry ride from the trading floors of Wall Street, provided communism with a toehold in America.

This middling city of some sixty thousand played a central role in the fast industrialization that overtook the United States in the wake of the Civil War. Hoboken was home to the dry docks of the great nineteenth-century shipbuilder W. & A. Fletcher and Company, designer of the first steam turbine engine in the United States. It housed cherished icons of America's industrial past—Tootsie Rolls, Twinkies, Maxwell House coffee, the zipper. Its docks provided the setting for one of America's most iconic stories of corruption in the workplace, immortalized by Marlon Brando in Elia Kazan's *On the Waterfront*. What's less known is that Hoboken was also the home of Friedrich Adolph Sorge, a German immigrant who, in the words of Selig Perlman, labor historian of the late nineteenth and early twentieth centuries, was "the father of modern socialism in America."

Hoboken's docks were an important gateway for hundreds of thousands of Germans who made their way into the United States in the second half of the nineteenth century. By 1890, just before the Immigration Act of 1891 gave the federal government authority over immigration, immigrants accounted for some 40 percent of the city's population, half of them from Germany.

Sorge arrived in the United States in 1852, fleeing a death sentence at home for his role in the republican uprisings that shook the German principalities in 1848 and 1849. Following sojourns in Switzerland, Belgium, and London, he crossed the Atlantic, docking in New York in June. He moved across the Hudson to Hoboken, married a young German immigrant woman, and devoted the next fifty-four years of his life to teaching music and instigating the class struggle among the workers of New Jersey.

Sorge cofounded with Joseph Weydemeyer the Proletarian League in 1852. He launched the Communist Club in New York in 1857, affiliating it to the First International, conceived by Karl Marx. He led the strike by the silk workers of Paterson, New Jersey. He organized the International Labor Union of Hoboken. And he became the secretary to the Central Committee of the International Workingmen's Association in America. In *Socialism and the Worker*, a pamphlet first published in 1876, Sorge wrote, "He who declares himself an enemy of Communism declares himself an enemy of common interest, an enemy of society and mankind!"

He failed, of course. For all the social ferment in post–Civil War America—where a large urban labor force serving a burgeoning industrial economy demanded higher wages, shorter hours, and better working conditions—efforts by Sorge and his fellow German expatriates to fuel the flames of the class struggle gained little traction. America's industrial working class showed no interest in the dictatorship of the proletariat.

Historians have proposed different hypotheses to explain this lack of revolutionary spirit. Perhaps the United States' democratic politics and its lack of a feudal past defanged calls for a violent overthrow of the capitalist system. Maybe it was the influence of Yankee reformers, who burdened the cause of workers' rights with a grab bag of aspirations including women's rights, land reform, racial equality, and spiritualism. Unlike Europeans, American workers were enjoying relatively widespread prosperity, on the back of a fast-growing economy protected by high barriers against imports. The brisk pace of economic mobility would temper workers' desire for equality by offering them a plausible shot at higher incomes down the road.

Sorge befriended both Marx and Friedrich Engels at the 1872 congress of the International in The Hague. From then on Engels kept up a regular correspondence from his base in London with his comrade in arms. He offered a different take on his comrade's failure.

Engels argued that second-rate German socialists in the United States couldn't keep their priorities straight. Anarchists battled pro-labor-union Marxists, who were at war with social democrats. More incisively, he remarked on a unique feature of the American experience that set it apart from Germany and other European nations: ethnic and cultural diversity. Immigration, Engels wrote, "divides workers into two groups: the native-born and the foreigners, and the latter in turn into (1) the Irish, (2) the Germans, (3) the many small groups, each of which understands only itself: Czechs, Poles, Italians, Scandinavians, etc. And then the Negroes." To form a single party out of these groups would require "quite unusually powerful incentives," he argued. "The bourgeois need only wait passively, and the dissimilar elements of the working class fall apart again."

The rubble of the old Soviet bloc, where the dictatorship of the proletariat held sway for three-quarters of a century, suggests American workers were wise to ignore Sorge's efforts to bring communism across the Atlantic. Still, Engels's analysis of his old friend's failure to ignite class solidarity in the United States more than one hundred years ago underscores an existential American weakness: the inability to extend solidarity across racial, ethnic, and cultural borders. It is a weakness that erodes the United States' social fabric to this day. The ethnic hostility that kept communism at bay also kept America from building the institutions that could shield the nation's vulnerable from the turmoil of rapid economic change.

In *Socialism and the Worker*, Sorge offered an expansive panoramic of the virtues of communism. Whoever wanted to destroy it, he wrote, would have to destroy roads, schools, and more: "He will have to destroy the public gardens and parks, he will have to abolish the public baths, the theaters, the waterworks, all the public buildings; for instance town halls, courts, all the hospitals, the alms-houses; he will have to destroy the railroads, the telegraphs, the post office!" These public goods, he said, "belong to Communism."

The list today seems hopelessly naive, at odds with a memory of communism in which gulags are at least as prominent as public gardens. Still, his remarks have proven prescient. Americans didn't just reject the notion of collective rule by the working class. Americans rejected the notion of collective solutions, period. Race is, indeed, the culprit.

The Workingmen's Party in Philadelphia, perhaps the first political party committed to represent the interests of the working class, offers a telling example. The party platform, established in 1828, had laudable goals: the ten-hour workday, for instance, and putting an end to debtors' prisons. It demanded public support for free public education and denounced chartered monopolies, the liquor industry, and public lotteries.

Class solidarity, however, was reserved for whites. The party had no space for darker hues. In *The Free Black in Urban America, 1800–1850: The Shadow of the Dream*, the historian Leonard Curry quoted one of the ten thousand free blacks in the City of Brotherly Love. If a man of color had children, he said, "it is almost impossible for him to get a trade for them, as the journeymen and apprentices generally refuse to work with them, even if the master is willing, which is seldom the case." As the historian Rayford W. Logan pointed out, "The first large-scale exclusion of Negroes by private organizations in the postbellum period was the handiwork of organized labor."

American unionism was born segregated. The National Labor Union, one of the first national union federations—lineal ancestor of the American Federation of Labor—was all white. On the morning of August 18, 1869, a skilled black caulker named Isaac Myers addressed its convention in Philadelphia to ask that black workers be accepted too. "The white laboring men of the country have nothing to fear from the colored laboring men," he told them. Three days later, after much deliberation, the white representatives at the convention voted no: if blacks wanted to be represented by a union, they would have to form their own. Neither the National Labor Union nor its affiliated unions had any plans to organize them. "The white worker did not want the Negro in his unions," commented the sociologist and historian W. E. B. Du Bois. It wasn't simply a matter of tactics or strategy, he argued: the white man didn't want the black man inside the tent because he "did not believe in him as a man."

The railways were among the earliest battlegrounds for class warfare, opening the paths along which industrial America sank its roots. Operating unions representing workers in train and engine services fought for collective bargaining as early as the 1880s, and they became some of the strongest unions in the United States. But these champions of the working man had little to offer men of different color. A fireman on a railroad in Texas quoted by the labor historian Eric Arnesen put it in terms Engels could understand: "We would rather be absolute slaves of capital, than to take the negro into our lodges as an equal and brother."

From the late nineteenth century through the New Deal, almost all the major railroad unions had constitutional provisions barring African Americans from many jobs. Blacks were banned from the unions that represented boilermakers, machinists, and blacksmiths. And organized labor didn't hesitate to take industrial action in favor of its racist policies. In 1909 white unionized firemen called a strike to force the Georgia Railroad Company to discharge its black firemen and exclude them from future jobs. When the railroad refused to meet their demands, whites who lived along the railroad lines mobbed trains operated by black firemen. Ten years later, the Railroad Administration agreed to new regulations benefiting white trainmen at the expense of African Americans. One rule provided that "Negroes are not to be used as conductors, flagmen, baggagemen, or yard conductors."

Government control of the railways limited outright discrimination during World War II. But even wartime mobilization couldn't end racial tension in the workforce. As the district organizer of the International Association of Machinists in Seattle warned the Boeing Corporation, workers had already been asked to make many sacrifices for the war effort. Allowing blacks into the union was a sacrifice too far.

Once the war ended, efforts to exclude blacks from the labor movement picked up pace. In the 1940s, the firemen's union negotiated agreements that openly cut out blacks. And discrimination was not limited to some few industries. It "involves many unions in a wide variety of occupations in manufacturing industries, skilled crafts, railroads and maritime trades," wrote Herbert Hill, who was the labor secretary for the National Association for the Advancement of Colored People from the early 1950s through the late 1970s.

The Seafarers International Union, which operated union-controlled hiring halls in Great Lakes ports such as Duluth, Chicago, Detroit, Cleveland, and Buffalo, dispatched only black workers for menial jobs as mess men in the galley departments of ships operating under the collective bargaining agreement. The United Brotherhood of Carpenters and Joiners, one of the most important building trades unions, would import white workers from neighboring cities before sharing working opportunities with local blacks.

Well into the 1960s, after the Civil Rights Act ended officially sanctioned discrimination, race still trumped class solidarity in workplaces across the American economy. As Hill wrote, "Trade union discrimination is the decisive factor in determining whether Negro workers in a given industry shall have an opportunity to earn a living for themselves and their families." In 1960, there were still no blacks in Local 26 of the International Brotherhood of Electrical Workers in Washington, D.C., which controlled all hiring for electrical work in the nation's capital. Following protests from civil rights organizations, one black electrician, James Holland, was allowed to work in a government installation. Organized labor, concluded Hill, was "the institutional expression of white working-class racism."

Unions did not exclusively discriminate against blacks, by the way. On the West Coast, they systematically excluded Chinese workers from jobs. "The most important single factor in the history of American labor," wrote Selig Perlman, was excluding "Mongolian labor" from the workforce. From the end of the nineteenth century and well into the twentieth, the journal of the United Mine Workers of America would warn about the "yellow peril" and the "hordes of black, brown, yellow and striped workers . . . who have not the slightest idea of the meaning of organization."

The American Federation of Labor, the largest labor organization in the first half of the twentieth century, founded in 1886 as an alliance of craft unions, worked strenuously to secure the adoption of the Chinese Exclusion Act of 1882, the first racist immigration law in American history. The federation's president, Samuel Gompers, argued that the Chinese "as a race were cruel and treacherous." With the act due to expire in 1902, Gompers reminded participants at the annual convention of 1901 of what was at stake. "Every incoming coolie means the displacement of an American, and the lowering of the American standard of living," he said. The Chinese were "utterly incapable of adaptation to the Caucasian ideals of civilization." American workers, he added in his speech to the convention in 1904, already had enough problems "without being required to meet the enervating, killing, underselling and under-living competition of that nerveless, wantless people, the Chinese."

Unsurprisingly, blacks had trouble embracing the labor organizations that worked so hard to exclude them. In 1902, W. E. B. Du Bois, a prominent activist for the rights of African Americans, observed that forty-three national unions had exactly zero black members. Three years later he and other black intellectuals formed the Niagara Movement, precursor to the NAACP, which condemned labor unions' practice of "proscribing and boycotting and oppressing thousands of their fellow-toilers simply because they are black."

During the 1920s blacks were only too eager to play the role of strikebreakers to break into the railway industry. They crossed picket lines to gain jobs as blacksmiths and electricians, car men and machinists. Though union rules still kept them from better-paying jobs as conductors or engineers, by the end of the decade blacks had doubled their share of jobs in many industries related to the railroads.

Employers exploited the racial mistrust. The United States Steel Corporation aggressively deployed race to prevent the American Federation of Labor's attempts to organize the steel industry after the end of World War I, recruiting tens of thousands of African American and Mexican workers eager to have a shot at the previously forbidden jobs to cross the picket lines and help break the Great Steel Strike of 1919.

The Congress of Industrial Organizations, which seceded

from the AFL in the 1930s, did better by black America. Unlike the craft-based guilds affiliated with the AFL, CIO unions mostly organized workers with few specific skills toiling on the assembly lines of a new American economy of mass production. Blacks made up a significant part of this workforce. Organizing them imposed a dose of racial egalitarianism on the labor movement. There were 150,000 organized black workers in 1935, at the time of the CIO's creation. By the end of World War II there were 1.25 million. "Probably no movement in the last thirty years has been so successful in softening race prejudice among the masses," said Du Bois.

Yet racial prejudice remained rampant in industrial unions. In 1935, the National Urban League and the NAACP were extremely skeptical of the Wagner Act, which established workers' right to form labor unions to bargain collectively with management, worrying it would allow racist unions to lock blacks out of many jobs. Even after 1955, when the AFL merged with the CIO, unions in the new confederation often excluded blacks outright, or segregated them into all-black locals. They established separate seniority lines by race in collective bargaining agreements and excluded blacks from apprenticeship programs. Blacks reciprocated: In 1960, thirty-one hundred workers at the Savannah River Atomic Energy Project in Aiken, South Carolina, held a vote on whether to be certified by the National Labor Relations Board as a bargaining agent of the metal trades department of the AFL-CIO. The six hundred black workers voted as a bloc against certification, dooming organized labor's effort to get in the door.

As Engels predicted, the hostility between African Americans and labor only served their foes. Consider the Philadelphia Plan, the first federal affirmative action program in the country. The plan, originally implemented during the administration of Lyndon Johnson, required construction contractors working for the federal government to prove their workforce included minorities to match the ethnic composition of the area. Labor leaders hated it. So President Nixon embraced it enthusiastically. Nixon's adviser John Ehrlichman acknowledged in his memoirs that the plan would drive an effective wedge between two pillars of the Democratic Party's national coalition, creating "a political dilemma for the labor union leaders and civil rights groups."

This tactic fit into a broad political strategy that has shaped Republican thinking to this day. Alongside his well-known "southern strategy" to convert white Dixie Democrats into Republicans by exploiting racial animosity, Nixon's strategy for the North relied on driving a wedge between two traditional Democratic constituencies: African Americans and labor.

If there is anything wrong about Engels's analysis, it is its narrowness. Racial divisions haven't merely stood in the way of class consciousness; they have blocked solidarity writ large. The great paradox of the American experience is how its exceptional diversity—ethnic and racial, religious and linguistic—a well of inexhaustible vim and unparalleled creativity, has also stunted its development as a nation. It has undermined its unions and undercut its government. It has shaped the most meager social safety net in the club of advanced nations. And it has paralyzed its politics, bringing policy making to a standstill.

In 1938, in the depth of the Great Depression, the Carnegie Corporation commissioned the Swedish sociologist Gunnar Myrdal to do a study of the condition and prospects of American Negroes. There was no shortage of competent American social scientists at the time, Carnegie's president, Frederick Keppel, acknowledged, but the corporation wanted somebody who would not be caught up in America's entrenched conflicts over race, somebody who could bring fresh eyes to a problem "for nearly a hundred years so charged with emotion." Scandinavia, a region of rigorous intellectual standards yet no tradition of imperialism, "which might lessen the confidence of the

Negroes in the United States as to the complete impartiality of the study and the validity of its findings," was a natural place to look.

Six years later, in a tome that ran to more than fifteen hundred pages of tight, urgent print, Professor Myrdal offered his conclusion: "The Negro problem in America represents a moral lag in the development of the nation." Myrdal couldn't tell, at the time, how heavily this moral shortcoming would weigh on America's future. But seventy-five years later it hasn't loosened its grip, building perhaps the most uncaring, least empathetic state in the Western world.

In *When Work Disappears: The World of the New Urban Poor,* a book published during the presidency of Bill Clinton in the 1990s, the eminent sociologist William Julius Wilson argued that racial attitudes dating from the era of Jim Crow still shaped public policy. "White taxpayers saw themselves as being forced, through taxes, to pay for medical and legal services that many of them could not afford to purchase for their own families," he wrote.

And so they allowed their society to wither. Take a pick of virtually any measure of social progress over the last four decades, and you will find that for all its claims to greatness the United States in fact lags the rest of the industrialized world. It may still be the undisputed leader in terms of military might, economic growth, and technological innovation, but when it comes to measures of social health and cohesion, the portrait of the American experience is alarming.

It is well known that the United States spends more on health care than any other country. It is less known that it ranks in fifty-first place in the world in terms of infant mortality, roughly in the same place as Croatia. Whether it is the incidence of diabetes and obesity, the death rate from parasites and other infections, or years lost to premature death, the United States invariably lags pretty much all other rich nations. "On nearly all indicators of mortality, survival, and life expectancy, the United States ranks at or near the bottom among high-income countries," lamented a report published in 2013 by the National Research Council and the Institute of Medicine with the depressing title "U.S. Health in International Perspective: Shorter Lives, Poorer Health." It has gotten worse since then. The life expectancy at birth for white males fell in both 2015 and 2016.

A fifth of American children live in poor homes, compared with only 3 percent in Denmark. Teens have more babies in the United States than in most of the developed world—almost three times as many as teenagers in France. More than one out of every four children in the United States lives with a single parent, the largest percentage by far among the industrialized nations of the globe.

What's most perplexing is how America lost so much ground. Among the thirty-six countries that today compose the Organization for Economic Cooperation and Development, a group of leading industrialized nations, the life expectancy of girls born in the United States fell from thirteenth place in 1980 to thirtieth place in 2017. While older Americans, aged fifty-five to sixty-four, have the third-highest college graduation rate in the OECD, their juniors, aged twenty-five to thirty-four, have slipped to twelfth place as educational attainment among many of America's peers has grown much faster.

Much of this is simply a consequence of America's entrenched poverty, the deepest recorded among advanced nations. White babies born to married mothers with a college education have similar mortality as those in advanced European countries. It's the babies of poor, less educated women who die prematurely. In Marin County, California, one of the wealthiest corners of the country, women's life expectancy at birth is eighty-five years, among the highest in the world. In Perry County, Kentucky— just north of Harlan, where empty storefronts and mothballed coal mines tell the brutal story of Appalachia's precipitous decline—baby girls are expected to live only to seventy-four. That's less than in Algeria and Bangladesh. Deprivation is not only confined to communities of color. Nine out of ten residents in Perry County are non-Hispanic whites.

It's startling how poverty has been given such a free hand to rip through American society. Barriers of class and, critically, race have prevented the construction of a safety net that might mitigate social dysfunctions. In *Fighting Poverty in the US and Europe: A World of Difference*, the economists Alberto Alesina and Edward Glaeser applied statistical techniques to figure out how differences in racial, ethnic, linguistic, and religious composition might affect public spending in western Europe and the United States.

Europe has a decidedly more generous approach to welfare. Even after the Affordable Care Act expanded health insurance to tens of millions of previously uninsured Americans, public social spending in the United States—pensions, unemployment, health insurance, antipoverty programs—eats up less than 19 percent of the United States' gross national product. The French government, by contrast, spends over 31 percent of its gross economic product on these sorts of social goods; the Germans, 25 percent; the Swedes, just over 26 percent. Professors Alesina and Glaeser concluded that about half the public spending gap between Europe and the United States could be explained by America's more diverse racial and ethnic mix, standing in the way of solidarity.

The stinginess of America's social contract is evident beyond its threadbare welfare programs. The federal minimum wage has sunk to decade-long lows. American labor regulations do little to protect workers from employers eager to squeeze the last penny out of them, while labor laws designed to prevent collective bargaining deprive them of voice. Poor and minority students are deprived of opportunity by a segregated public-school system that devotes vastly more resources to their white, richer sisters and brothers. Even physical infrastructure—roads and ports and public transportation networks—has been left to rot in a nation uninterested in investing in the common good.

Americans are not necessarily less generous than Europeans. Indeed, charitable spending is much more robust in the United States. But philanthropy is not quite the same as funding public goods. Donors get to choose which goals and which people are worthy of their largesse. They often prefer to finance stadia at their alma maters over housing for the urban poor. They finance pet theories about social well-being—charter schools, a universal basic income—rather than supporting the public institutions grounded in democratic choice that most advanced countries rely on to build cohesive societies. And private largesse is also gummed up by racial hostility. Research by the economist Daniel Hungerman found that all-white congregations in church become less charitably active as the share of black residents in the local community grows.

Racial and ethnic biases are not, of course, an American invention. In the 1990s, the economists William Easterly and Ross Levine, then working at the World Bank, published a seminal essay in which they traced the dismal economic performance of countries in sub-Saharan Africa to the impact of ethnic fragmentation on social polarization. "Polarized societies will be both prone to competitive rent seeking by the different groups and have difficulty agreeing on public goods," they wrote. Not only were they likely to get stuck with poor public schooling, bad public infrastructure, and weak public finance, but stability and growth would be stymied as competing groups jockeyed to capture economic rents at the expense of their rivals.

The Balkan state of Yugoslavia was not a large country. Its population peaked at around twenty-five million. But in 1991, a few months before the formal demise of the Soviet Union, the power that stitched eastern Europe together, the multiethnic, multicultural republic exploded into a succession of nationalistic wars pitting Orthodox Serbs against Catholic Croats against Muslim Bosnians against Albanians. After a decade of bloody ethnic conflict, it ultimately splintered into seven distinct countries—Serbia, Croatia, Bosnia and Herzegovina, Slovenia, Montenegro, Kosovo, and North Macedonia.

Ethnic diversity has not always led to war, but it has inevitably left its stamp on government. The economists Jan-Egbert Sturm and Jakob de Haan studied more than a hundred countries in every region of the world, assessing the relationship between the ethnic and linguistic fractionalization of the population and the magnitude of government redistribution, measured by how much taxes and government transfers reduced income inequality. Market economies with relatively homogeneous populations experienced more income redistribution, they found. Regardless of the system of economic organization, more diverse countries redistributed less.

Buying into welfare requires a society-wide sense of solidarity. How else can one accept paying taxes in order to finance a program for somebody else's less privileged kids? The point hammered home by Alesina and Glaeser's research is that this solidarity is hard to sustain across ethnic and racial borders, and the United States has more of those borders than more homogeneous countries like France and Sweden.

At its most basic, racial divisions can destroy empathy. The economist Erzo Luttmer has systematically analyzed surveys of people's attitudes toward redistribution, census tract by census tract. His conclusion is straightforward: people mostly want to help people who look like them. "An additional black welfare recipient in one's tract reduces support for welfare by nonblack respondents but has little effect on black respondents," he finds. "Conversely, an additional nonblack welfare recipient reduces black support for welfare but has little effect on non-black support."

This racial obstacle to generosity has shaped America's institutions. One study from the early years of the twenty-first century by Alesina and his colleague Eliana La Ferrara found that racial diversity in American communities reduces participation in all sorts of groups, from churches to youth clubs. The share of local government spending on public services—sewage treatment, trash clearance, education, roads, libraries—is also generally lower in more diverse American cities and counties. As Alberto Alesina, William Easterly, and Reza Baqir wrote in another study a few years earlier, "Ethnic conflict is an important determinant of local public finances."

Years ago, the veteran economist James Poterba found that spending on public education declined in municipalities with an aging population, not a hugely startling find. It makes sense that older people with no children would have little use for public schools. They would probably prefer their tax dollars to be spent on, say, health care for the elderly. What was surprising about the Poterba study was that spending on education fell most in places where the elderly were of a different ethnicity than the school-age population.

Another notable study, by Alesina, Baqir, and Caroline Hoxby, analyzed how the diversity of political jurisdictions, municipalities, schooling zones, and such might affect their size. A larger school district enjoys many benefits of scale. It can spread its administrative costs over a larger footprint. Its libraries and sporting facilities will serve more students. But size can also come at a cost: different people often have different preferences. In crafting curricula and teaching methods, larger school districts will have to navigate the disparate demands of a broader set of families. The more diverse the population, the more difficult these compromises will be.

Voters, the economists confirmed, are less likely to buy

into the benefits of size when they live in more diverse areas, preferring to live in a small homogeneous city than in a larger diverse one. And of all the variables they studied—income, religion, race, ethnicity—the one that mattered most was race. "It appears that people are willing to sacrifice the most, in terms of economies of scale, in order to avoid racial heterogeneity in their jurisdiction," they wrote.

The political scientists Rodney Hero and Morris Levy have added a couple of twists to the analysis. Using census data from 1980 to 2010, they found that, other things being equal, rising inequality between racial groups reduces support at the state level for welfare programs that redistribute income from the haves to the have-nots. A one percentage point increase in the share of income inequality accounted for by inequities between races was associated with a drop in annual spending under Temporary Assistance for Needy Families, the nation's main cash welfare program, equivalent to some $150 per person in poverty.

Widening social distance between America's ethnic groups isn't just sapping its tolerance for welfare. It is undermining Americans' support for a broad array of public goods, eroding its belief in a shared commons. In a subsequent study with Brian Yeokwang An, Hero and Levy found that municipal spending on hospitals, cops, firemen, parks, and so on also took a hit when racial inequality rose. "Clearly, there is a link between local-level inequality and the provision of public goods that are not as well known to be racialized and whose stated purpose is not to redistribute income."

That puts America in a particular quandary. Because half a century after the Civil Rights Act, income inequality between racial groups has not budged, it will be difficult to build a nation of shared purpose on such a lopsided distribution of opportunity.

· · ·

It is no secret that racial hostility has shaped the residential geography of contemporary America. Four million blacks escaped the South between 1940 and 1970, seeking jobs in the more industrialized North and West. The exodus raised the black share in northern and western cities from barely 4 percent in 1940 to 16 percent in 1970. It also persuaded many whites to leave town: the median city outside the South lost 10 percent of its white population over the period. The economist Leah Platt Boustan estimated that each black arrival in cities outside the South led to 2.7 white moves from urban cores into the surrounding suburbs.

This reconfigured the geography of opportunity. Many public goods, including, notably, primary and secondary education, are locally financed in much of the country. Residential segregation automatically shaped the provision of education along racial lines. Though federal and state governments were supposed to top up the limited local resources available to poor urban minorities, racial hostility again muted the government's response.

Consider Bill Clinton's famous promise during the 1994 presidential campaign to "end welfare as we know it." As I mentioned earlier, welfare reform ended the poor's legal entitlement to government aid, replacing the federal antipoverty program created by Franklin D. Roosevelt in the depth of the Great Depression with a block grant to the states, which were given the freedom to set their own programs, with their own criteria and limits, to grant whatever assistance they deemed proper.

This is not to impute racist intent to President Clinton, who had a solid base of support among black voters. But the overhaul of welfare did have racial undertones, motivated in large part by the belief that government assistance to needy mothers discouraged both work and marriage among African Americans and encouraged black mothers to have babies out of wedlock.

The policy change shortchanged blacks across the South. The political scientist Richard Fording concluded that the racial composition of states directly influenced the conditions imposed on the distribution of aid: states with large shares of black welfare recipients were much more likely to attach tough work requirements on government assistance, impose tight caps on how long people could get benefits, and include provisions to stamp out the "irresponsible" behaviors of the poor.

Temporary Assistance for Needy Families, the program that replaced the New Deal–era entitlement for the poor, is decidedly less generous in states with larger black populations. In Louisiana, for instance, in 2014 only 4 percent of poor families received benefits under the program. In Vermont, 78 percent did. In Mississippi, TANF benefits top out at $170 a month for a family of three headed by a single parent, one-sixth of the maximum benefit in New Hampshire. Scholars at the Urban Institute found that the benefit ceiling is 6 percent lower in states where the African American population is five percentage points higher than average, other things being equal. In twenty-five states that are home to 56 percent of the African American population but only 46 percent of America's non-Hispanic whites, TANF payments reach less than one in five families in poverty.

People tell each other stories to justify their preferences. An experiment run by the political scientist Martin Gilens asked people for their impressions of a mother on welfare. Would she try hard to get a job, or would she have another kid to get a bigger welfare check? Half of the people in the survey were told the mother was black; half that she was white. Unsurprisingly, people were much more likely to call the black mother lazy, ready to abuse the welfare state. The very words "welfare" and "food stamps," Gilens found, prime white Americans to think of blacks.

This has blocked the construction of an American welfare state. John Roemer, an economist and political scientist, argues that some voters oppose government transfers to the less fortunate because they see recipients as undeserving. But even voters who otherwise believe in redistribution might vote for antiwelfare Republicans because they share Republicans' racial mistrust.

Together, these biases tip the political odds in favor of the Republican Party and against efforts to raise taxes to finance government spending. In a study written with the Korean economist Woojin Lee, Roemer estimated that between the mid-1970s and the early 1990s voters' racial hostility reduced the Democratic share of the vote by somewhere between five and thirty-eight percentage points. It also reduced the income tax rate by somewhere between eleven and eighteen percentage points.

This bias didn't just hurt poor blacks. It hurt every American. In an essay titled "*E Pluribus Unum:* Diversity and Community in the Twenty-First Century," the sociologist Robert Putnam observed that racial divisions directly undermine trust across the population. "In more diverse settings, Americans distrust not merely people who do not look like them, but even people who do," he wrote. "Diversity seems to trigger not in-group/out-group division, but anomie or social isolation." This happens in poor and rich neighborhoods, in high-crime and low-crime communities.

Critically, racial hostility deprived not only black Americans from needed government assistance but also poor whites who could do with the government's help. An entrenched aversion to public goods deeply rooted in racial mistrust deprived *all* Americans of the public assistance that is commonplace among the advanced market democracies the United States considers its peers.

Opposition to social welfare spending is not just about race. The United States has lagged other rich countries in providing cash assistance for the poor and social insurance for the middle class since the early nineteenth century. It was the latest country in the developed world to offer compensation for workers hurt on the job. It was late to provide pensions to the elderly and insurance to the unemployed. And it has never offered truly universal health insurance, a common institution across the developed world.

From the end of the Civil War through much of the twentieth century, the American working class demanded little government assistance because America's dynamic economy offered a clear shot at prosperity. In Sorge's day, even Engels acknowledged that workers—white workers at least—had a greater opportunity to escape their lot in the United States than in Europe, where a rigid, long-standing class structure erected a formidable wall against social mobility. Millions of impoverished immigrants from Europe reinforced this point, sailing across the Atlantic to give their children and grandchildren a shot at a better life in the land of opportunity.

Americans preferred public education. Their firmly held Protestant ethic supported a meritocratic view of virtue based on personal effort. And the United States did not suffer Europe's feudal past, with an attendant landed aristocracy adamantly opposed to a system of public education that could offer serfs better opportunities off the land in a burgeoning industrial economy.

The poor in 1950s America might not have enjoyed the same opportunities as the rich, but compared with the old continent it looked like a paragon of equality. In 1958, upper-class Americans were five times more likely to attend university than their country folk from the lowest class. But in Germany the rich were sixty-one times more likely to go to college than the poor. In Sweden, they were twenty-six times more likely.

The very forces that supported education as a tool to improve the lot of the poor rejected government welfare as a path to dependency and sloth. Having a greater shot at opportunity, even impoverished Americans were less likely to support taxing the rich to finance social benefits if they believed they might eventually hit the jackpot themselves.

While much of Europe had to contend with socialist worker parties proposing alternatives to the market economy, unfettered capitalism in the United States never had much to fear from the ideological Left. It didn't have to contend with a French Revolution next door, as Britain did, offering the dispossessed the option of rebellion as an alternative to the status quo. American leaders never faced the risk of social upheaval that persuaded the German chancellor Otto von Bismarck to launch the world's first social security programs in the late nineteenth century, including old-age pensions, and insurance against sickness and injury in the workplace. The workers' revolution that produced the Soviet Union on Europe's eastern flank was, to Americans, little more than an unpalatable abstraction.

Unchallenged by alternative forms of social organization, American capitalism flourished in its most uninhibited form. Here, the arguments that compelled European countries to build robust social safety nets never gained much traction. Steeped in racial hostility, the case against a robust redistributive state prevailed.

There are few greater heroes to American liberals than FDR, the architect of the modern American welfare state. His New Deal, a break with the penny-pinching government of his predecessor, Herbert Hoover, deployed the power of the government to fight the devastation caused by the Great Depression and laid the foundation upon which to reformulate the very idea of government as a guarantor of the well-being of the governed.

Until then, Americans lived their lives without much of a net to speak of. By 1920, forty states had established mothers' pensions to provide for fatherless children. Most states had some form of compensation for injuries on the job. But these were hardly generous programs. Even after the end of World War I, public welfare was mostly the job of cities and private charities. Relief was conceived as a deterrent: sending the poor to the almshouse was considered a tactic to prevent "pauperism." Federal welfare of the kind that today ignites bloody ideological battles over the purpose and limits of government didn't exist.

When the Great Depression struck, Hoover's strategy to mitigate the effects of the crashing economy was to deport "Mexicans," roughly anybody with a Mexican-sounding name, ostensibly to open jobs for American workers.

Then came the New Deal. President Roosevelt's brainchild put millions of destitute Americans back to work, building roads for the Works Progress Administration or dams for the Tennessee Valley Authority. The National Labor Relations Act passed on his watch established workers' rights to form unions, strike, and engage in collective bargaining. The Fair Labor Standards Act established the first national minimum wage. The Social Security Act not only guaranteed pensions for the elderly; it offered compensation for the unemployed and federal matching funds for state initiatives on public health, maternal and child welfare, and assistance to the blind. Fifty years after its passage, the Democratic Speaker of the House, Thomas P. O'Neill, said that "without such protection, half of these people would be living in poverty." In 1932, the year before Roosevelt assumed the presidency, federal government revenue amounted to 2.8 percent of the nation's gross domestic product. By 1941, before the United States entered World War II, it had grown to 7.5 percent. In 1945, when the president died in office, it hit 19.9 percent of GDP—roughly the size it is today.

Yet for all its promise, even that seminal period in the history of American progressivism was stained by racial mistrust. That racism stymied the first great liberal leap in policy making sticks in the craw of American liberals. It offends believers in the grand alliance of working men and women, immigrants, and racial and other minorities, coming together to confront conservatives and their corporate allies. But race shaped the New Deal.

Consider the mass expulsion of Mexicans. As the Great Depression set Americans in search of someone to blame for their misery, hundreds of thousands of people of Mexican origin—up to two million by some counts—were expelled from the United States starting in 1929. Agents raided workplaces and public squares, rounding up and deporting people who looked Mexican—shorter, Spanish-speaking, brown. Social workers would knock on the door of Mexican Americans, threaten them with withdrawing whatever meager public assistance they received, and offer them tickets to go "back home."

Hoover was under enormous political pressure to offer some relief for soaring unemployment. Because he was unwilling to increase federal spending to stimulate the economy, blaming the brown seemed like a reasonable alternative. In their book *Decade of Betrayal: Mexican Repatriation in the 1930s*, Francisco Balderrama and Raymond Rodriguez wrote about how William Doak, President Hoover's labor secretary, "instigated a personal vendetta to get rid of the Mexicans." His motivations were political, however: "to create a diversion to counteract organized labor's hostile attitude" toward the administration.

In an interview with NPR in 2015, Balderrama noted that "whether they were American citizens, or whether they were Mexican nationals, in the American mind—that is, in the mind of government officials, in the mind of industry leaders—they're all Mexicans. So ship them home." They continued shipping them home until 1936, well into the presidency of FDR.

Rural blacks were treated better. As the Swede Myrdal pointed out, "Of all the calamities that have struck the rural Negro people in the South in recent decades—soil erosion, the infiltration of white tenants into plantation areas, the ravages of the boll weevil, the southwestern shift in cotton cultivation—

none has had such grave consequences, or threatens to have such lasting effect, as the combination of world agricultural trends and federal agricultural policy initiated during the thirties."

Blacks were an afterthought when the Agricultural Adjustment Administration decided to pay landowners to take land out of cultivation—a last-ditch attempt to raise farm prices and keep indebted farmers afloat. Some 40 percent of African American workers at the time made a living from the land, as sharecroppers and tenant farmers for white landowners. Their parcels were taken out of production first. Between 1933 and 1934, the Agricultural Adjustment Administration's policies forced more than 100,000 black tenants off the land. Though the federal government offered compensation, the white landowners mostly kept it for themselves.

Racial divisions snaked their way through every New Deal initiative. The Federal Housing Administration, created in 1934, is celebrated for expanding homeownership by offering federal guarantees to insure mortgage loans of Americans of limited means. But it also contributed to the "redlining" of America, refusing to back loans in predominantly black neighborhoods and barring blacks from the American dream of homeownership.

The Civilian Conservation Corps, which offered unskilled young men nature conservation jobs on government lands, maintained camps segregated by race. The labor codes established by the National Recovery Administration allowed businesses to offer whites a first crack at jobs and authorized lower pay scales for blacks. NRA officials argued it was for blacks' own good. If blacks demanded the same treatment as whites, they contended, blacks would be left without a job.

Blacks were not entirely excluded from relief. By 1935, one-third of all blacks, some 3.5 million people, were receiving aid from the Federal Emergency Relief Administration, established in 1933 to offer means-tested work relief programs, direct assistance to the poor, transient care, and various other programs. A government study in the early 1930s found that blacks constituted 20 percent of all Americans on the welfare rolls, even though they accounted for just 10 percent of the population.

Harold Ickes, a former leader of the Chicago chapter of the NAACP who was drafted into FDR's cabinet as secretary of the interior to oversee many of the New Deal programs, poured federal funds into black schools and hospitals in the South. He stipulated that the agency's federal contractors had to hire a percentage of blacks at least as big as their share of jobs recorded in the 1930 occupational census. The Works Progress Administration—the largest of the New Deal agencies, which employed millions of mostly unskilled men building roads, bridges, museums, and playgrounds—strove to include black workers and, in the North, even hired black supervisors. In 1939, the National Urban League's magazine *Opportunity* noted that in the North the WPA gave blacks their "first real opportunity for employment in white-collar occupations."

Blacks reciprocated. In 1936, only 28 percent of African Americans voted for the Republican ticket, half the share that had voted for the Republican Herbert Hoover against FDR four years before. "Armies of unemployed Negro workers have been kept from the near-starvation level on which they lived under President Hoover," noted *The Pittsburgh Courier,* a black newspaper, in January 1936. Discrimination against black sharecroppers and other workers persisted. But, said *The Courier,* "what administration within the memory of man has done a better job in that direction considering the very imperfect human material with which it had to work"?

There is little to suggest that FDR shared the bigoted views prevalent among the white southerners who made up the core of the Democratic Party. First Lady Eleanor Roosevelt remained a forceful voice against racial discrimination throughout his presidency and after his death. Still, dependent on the vote in Congress of white southerners to pass his proposed legislation, the president only reluctantly challenged their bigotry. New Deal programs that offered opportunities to African Americans in the North routinely discriminated against them in the South, offering them lesser jobs and paying them on a lower scale. As the historian Harvard Sitkoff pointed out in his book *A New Deal for Blacks*, the "Roosevelt Administration perpetuated more of the discrimination and segregation inherited from previous decades than it ended." Blacks eventually got the message: only the threat of mass mobilization would move the president to openly support their cause.

The armed services discriminated openly: In 1940 there were forty-seven hundred blacks in an army half a million strong. There was not a single black in the U.S. Marines, the Tank Corps, the Signal Corps, or the Army Air Corps. Blacks were trained in segregated camps and assigned support duties, like digging ditches and cooking. When Roosevelt aired the possibility of desegregation, George Marshall, the army chief of staff, responded that it was "not the time for critical experiments which would inevitably have a highly destructive effect on morale." Frank Knox, the secretary of the navy, once flatly told the president that desegregation was impossible in the navy because whites and blacks would have to share the cramped quarters of a ship. "In our history we don't take Negroes into a ship's company," he said.

Defense companies also closed the door on African Americans, limiting hundreds of thousands of jobs to whites only. In Kansas City, Standard Steel informed the National Urban League, "We have not had a Negro worker in twenty-five years, and we do not plan to start now." Even government training programs excluded black workers on the grounds that trying to train them would be a waste of time and money.

German bombs were raining on Britain in 1940 when Roosevelt finally agreed to deploy the industrial might of the United States to produce wartime matériel for America's beleaguered ally across the Atlantic. It was the most massive industrial buildup the country had ever seen, credited today for finally putting a definitive end to a decade of economic depression. To participate in this unprecedented opportunity, black leaders would have to play hardball.

They tried nicely at first, politely requesting a meeting with the president. But they changed tactics when Roosevelt ignored their case: A. Philip Randolph, the charismatic labor leader who rose to national prominence by organizing the black sleeping car porters, caught the president's attention by threatening to bring 100,000 blacks on a march on Washington on July 1, 1941. "We want something concrete, something tangible, positive and affirmative," he demanded when the president finally agreed to a meeting. Randolph didn't get all he wanted: the armed forces remained segregated. But he did get President Roosevelt to sign Executive Order 8802, which aimed to ban discrimination in the defense industry. To Roosevelt's great relief, he called the march off in the nick of time.

Blacks faced a formidable foe: Democrats in the South. So scared was Roosevelt of alienating southern whites that he refused to lend the power of his office to end one of the most barbarous legacies of America's slave-owning past: lynching. More than forty-seven hundred people, the vast majority of them black, were lynched in the United States between 1882 and 1968, according to the NAACP. In 1933 alone, twenty-eight blacks were murdered, hanged, or burned at the stake by angry white mobs. Yet in 1934, Roosevelt failed to stick his neck out for an antilynching bill that had the support of the Senate Judiciary Committee. "The Southerners by reason of the seniority rule in Congress are chairmen or occupy strategic places on most of the Senate and House committees," he told

Walter White, who headed the NAACP. "If I come out for the antilynching bill now, they will block every bill I ask Congress to pass to keep America from collapsing. I just can't take that risk." Instead, he let southerners in the Senate squelch it by refusing to bring it up for a vote. The United States never passed such legislation. Since 1882, in fact, Congress has tried and failed dozens of times to pass a law against lynching. In December 2018 the Senate passed a bill making it a federal hate crime. The House, however, did not follow through.

How much should we fault FDR for condoning racial injustice, accepting racial violence, and perpetuating racial inequity? Race was a scary thing to touch in the 1930s. Just ending segregation in the defense industry caused a burst of social unrest as northern whites rioted to resist blacks moving into their cities seeking the newly available jobs. In 1943 black families moving into a housing project near a Polish neighborhood in Detroit sparked two days of fighting that yielded thirty-four dead, twenty-five of them black.

As he saw it, Roosevelt's choice was between fighting for racial equality and building a welfare state within the constraints of a racist political system. While history may forgive his reluctance, race has no doubt hemmed in Roosevelt's legacy. Reluctant to cross racial boundaries, he built a welfare state that remains ensnared to this day in the prejudice he failed to stare down.

Controversy hangs over why the most critical programs established by the Social Security Act of 1935 and the Fair Labor Standards Act passed three years later excluded both domestic workers and those toiling on the nation's farms. Some scholars have argued that it would have been unrealistic to include workers whose workplaces were so hard to police and whose earnings were so hard to track and tax. Still, as the NAACP forcefully argued at the time, this decision excluded some two-thirds of black workers. As Charles Houston, a member of the board of the NAACP, told the Senate Finance Committee, Social Security looked "like a sieve with holes just big enough for the majority of the Negroes to fall through."

The thought could be applied to every step in the construction of the social safety net. Take Aid to Dependent Children, known as ADC, a program created by the Social Security Act to support single mothers, widows, and their kids. Southern states were eager to get their hands on the federal money. They were less eager to give the federal government a say on how the money was to be spent. So Congress stripped the Social Security Board's supervisory controls. States got to decide which people were "suitable" to get aid. Southern blacks, of course, got less.

In one study, the political scientists Robert Lieberman and John Lapinski noted that ADC coverage in the Black Belt—heart of the rural South, where African Americans were most concentrated—was lower than in the rest of the country: "Although whites received coverage at essentially the same rate in the Black Belt as in the rest of the South, black coverage was nearly one-third lower." Drawing on a Social Security survey and an account by the State Department of Public Welfare, the Swedish demographer Richard Sterner found that in 1935, 14.4 percent of white eligible families in Georgia but only 1.5 percent of the black eligible families got aid under the program. This inequity has prevailed across time. As Ira Katznelson notes in his book *When Affirmative Action Was White: An Untold History of Racial Inequality in Twentieth-Century America*, federal programs that were not explicitly racist turned out to be racist in practice because they gave states control over federal money.

In its first inception, the School Lunch Act would have barred giving federal funds to states with segregated school systems. Southern Democrats "saved" the program from certain legislative defeat by eliminating the nondiscrimination clause offered by the Harlem Democrat Adam Clayton Powell Jr., one of the few blacks in the House. Non-southern Democrats found it impossible simultaneously to "fight for an enhanced federal role and against Jim Crow," Katznelson wrote. "Liberal whites understood they had to choose. And they regularly made the first of these aims their top priority."

That's ultimately why agriculture was exempted from the Fair Labor Standards Act of 1938, which established a minimum wage rising from twenty-five to forty cents an hour, reduced the working week to forty hours, and prohibited child labor. Southern members of Congress opposed a minimum wage that would have required paying blacks the same as whites. "There has always been a difference in the wage scale of white and colored labor," noted Representative James Mark Wilcox of Florida. "So long as Florida people are permitted to handle the matter, the delicate and perplexing problem can be adjusted; but the Federal Government knows no color line and of necessity it cannot make any distinction between the races."

Some of the holes in the New Deal's safety net were subsequently closed. In 1950, Social Security was extended to cover all workers. Farmworkers were covered by the Fair Labor Standards Act in 1966. In 1948, President Harry Truman ordered the full integration of the armed forces. By 1954, a year after the end of the Korean War, they were officially integrated.

But the million or so African Americans inducted into the forces during World War II were shortchanged, again, when the nation rewarded its heroes. The GI Bill of 1944, celebrated as one of the great levelers of opportunity in American history, providing a subsidy to go to college for veterans from all walks of life, again dealt a short straw to the nonwhite.

Ostensibly color-blind, the bill offered subsidies to go to college for blacks and whites alike. But blacks in the South ran into a problem: segregation in public higher education remained a legal mandate, and at the end of the war there were only about a hundred educational institutions in the South that would take them, twenty-eight of which were classified as sub-baccalaureate teachers colleges or junior colleges and did not offer a bachelor's degree. While the GI Bill produced unquestionable benefits for whites and blacks in the North, in the South, GI Bill benefits increased racial educational disparities.

Few black veterans were able to make use of the housing provisions of the GI Bill either, because banks wouldn't offer mortgages in black neighborhoods, while deed covenants coupled with informal racism kept African Americans from purchasing homes in the predominantly white neighborhoods in the suburbs.

As black workers joined the industrial working class, political support for labor rights buckled too. Democrats who had been eager to support the pro-labor Wagner Act in 1935 proved critical in passing the Taft-Hartley Act of 1947, which opened the door to union-free shops across the South. "As labor unions began to enjoy increasing, unexpected success in the South, and as non-southern New Deal liberals pressed to create a more expansive federal administration to advance labor interests without relenting where race intersected with labor, southerners in the House and Senate closed ranks to consider labor questions defensively," Katznelson wrote.

For the second half of the twentieth century, the American safety net came to be defined by its exclusion of nonwhites: white Americans would pay taxes to finance a public network of social supports as long as the supports were pretty much limited, by law or practice, to the white majority. When these constraints were challenged by the civil rights movement, when President Lyndon Johnson invited blacks into the white schools and the voting booths, when he expanded government programs to help the most downtrodden of Americans, most often people of color, whites' political support for a social safety net they had grown to think of as their own started to crumble. FDR achieved the consensus needed to build the first stages of an American welfare state by limiting its benefits to white America. By bringing colored people into the net three decades later, civil rights legislation challenged the narrow solidarity upon which the New Deal was built.

Minorities still get a raw deal from Social Security, typically receiving more meager payouts than whites, even though they are more likely to suffer poverty in old age. Blacks die younger than whites, so draw benefits for a shorter time. They are more likely not to marry, so gain less from Social Security's spousal benefits. Hispanics, on the other hand, are younger. The system they contribute to is less generous than the one that uses their payroll taxes to provide benefits to mostly white retirees. Many are immigrants who won't be able to draw any benefits unless they work and pay into the system for at least ten years. Adding up these factors, researchers at the Urban Institute concluded that white Americans, as a group, get more money from Social Security than they contribute to the system through payroll taxes. African Americans and Hispanics, by contrast, get less. This holds even after considering that minority children may receive more benefits from the system because their parents are more likely to die earlier. Social Security is redistributing money from poorer minorities to richer whites.

Maybe that is why Social Security is one of the few programs in the federal government's arsenal that whites support unreservedly. According to a poll by the Pew Research Center, two-thirds of whites would prefer a smaller government that delivered fewer services. This compares to only a third of blacks and about a quarter of Hispanics. But when a panel of the National Academy of Social Insurance surveyed Americans on whether they would accept raising taxes on working people in order to preserve Social Security, 81 percent of whites (and 90 percent of blacks) said yes.

The consensus underpinning the case for a broad-based safety net started to unravel before the ink on civil rights legislation was dry. President Johnson didn't know it at the time, but the creation of Medicare and Medicaid in 1965—offering public health insurance for the old and the poor—amounted to the last part of the project started thirty years earlier to build an American safety net. By 1968, Richard Nixon would campaign for president on the argument that "doubling the conviction rate in this country would do far more to cure crime in America than quadrupling the funds for [the] War on Poverty."

Nixon won that election. Though he didn't immediately put an end to welfare, he refocused government on a new national priority: the war on drugs. Over the coming decades, as more African Americans were taken from the streets and put into prison for violating drug laws, the American consensus in favor of social welfare spending unraveled, and the construction of the safety net stopped. The next watershed moment in its evolution was President Bill Clinton's campaign against welfare.

The United States was not always the most miserly rich country on earth. In 1965, a year after Congress passed the Civil Rights Act, taxes raised by federal, state, and municipal governments in the United States to pay for everything from defense to Medicaid added up to some 23.5 percent of the nation's gross domestic product. It was not far behind the tax revenue raised in other industrialized nations: the average for the countries in the Organization for Economic Cooperation and Development was 24.8 percent.

The gap has widened since then, however. In 2017 the average tax take across the OECD amounted to 34.2 percent of GDP. The French and the Danes contributed 46 percent of the economy to public coffers; Canadians, 32 percent; the British, 33 percent. They used the money to pay for rich networks of social assistance. In the United States, by contrast, the total tax take by all levels of government remained at 27 percent of the economy, putting the country in thirty-first place among the thirty-six industrialized nations in the group.

The barrier Friedrich Engels identified in the nineteenth century standing in the way of a working-class movement in America also blocked the construction of a true welfare state in the twentieth and, so far, the twenty-first.

CHAPTER 3

From Welfare to Prison

Americans are going softer on crime. In 2009, 1 out of every 135 Americans was locked up in a federal or state prison or in a local jail. By 2018, the rate was down to 1 out of every 143. Many states have embraced criminal sentencing reforms, offering alternatives to incarceration for low-level felons to preserve space in prison for violent and chronic offenders. In December 2018, President Trump signed the First Step Act, the most drastic easing of imprisonment and sentencing laws in a generation, designed to trim the ever-growing population of Americans behind bars.

But let's not get too excited about America's apparent change of heart. The new push for leniency is motivated less by sympathy for the imprisoned than by state budgets stretched to the breaking point by the high costs of incarceration. Critically, the United States remains the most punishing country in the world: in 2018 there were 2.3 million Americans languishing in prisons or jails. That is over a third more than in China, a country that is four times as populous as the United States and is not known to be soft on crime. It is more than five times the number of prisoners in India, and over three times that in Russia. Only the Seychelles, a former British and French colony in the Indian Ocean that has been run by the same party since a coup the year after it gained independence in 1976, puts a larger share of its citizens behind bars.

To anybody looking in from the outside, America's embrace of prisons never made much sense, at least if the objective was supposed to be crime prevention. The nation's crime rate has declined relentlessly since the early 1990s. By 2017 it was half the rate of twenty-five years before. Still, the population of inmates in America's jails and prisons nonetheless grew continually from 1980 until 2008. Four decades ago, about one of every four hundred fifty Americans was in a correctional institution, about the same rate as in the rest of the developed world. Today, we lock up proportionally more than three times as many.

A report published by the National Research Council in 2016 concluded that the ballooning incarceration rate was due entirely to policy changes. First, they raised the odds that an arrest would lead to prison time. Second, they lengthened mandatory sentences. "Changes in crime trends or in police effectiveness as measured by arrests per crime," it noted, "contributed virtually nothing."

Prison, in the United States, had nothing to do with rehabilitation. Nor did it achieve much in terms of deterrence. Crime rates may be at their lowest level since the early 1970s, but the United States suffers higher rates of violent crime than countries using lighter sentencing policies. In 2015, there were 5 intentional homicides in the United States for each 100,000 Americans, down from 8 twenty years earlier. This is, of course, good news. Still, the American homicide rate remains higher than that of other rich nations: across the OECD, the average is 4 homicides per 100,000 people. In the European Union it was only 1. Many experts have suggested, in fact, that incarceration in the United States seems to be encouraging rather than mitigating crime. It puts too many people with marginally criminal behavior into prisons packed with more serious criminals, thereby minting new felons.

To make sense of America's criminal justice strategy, one must understand it as pursuing an entirely different goal. To put it simply, America's vast ecosystem of jails and prisons was designed, mainly, to lock out of sight the unpleasant human consequences of our social dysfunction. Prison, said the sociologist Bruce Western, came to be conceived as "a last resort for a whole variety of social failures." Whether inmates suffer from mental health issues, drug abuse, or unemployment, he told me, "all the people that slip through the safety net and end up in crime end up in the prison system." Lacking the safety net that could offer the most vulnerable Americans some protection from the shocks delivered by an increasingly globalized world, the United States instead locked them up.

"The criminal justice system," the late sociologist Devah Pager told me, "became the only effective institution that could bring order and manage urban communities." And it is now trying to bring "order" to rural America too. A study by the Vera Institute of Justice in 2017 found that rural counties home to only 15 percent of the American population housed 20 percent of the people in jail. "In the mid-to-late 1990s, incarceration rates in America's biggest cities began to level out, and then fall, while incarceration in both small- to mid-sized cities and rural communities continued to rise," Jack Norton, a researcher at the Vera Institute, told me. "Today, rural communities have the highest rates of both jail incarceration and prison admissions, dynamics that are both driven by and more deeply entrench the lack of access to both geographic and social mobility."

Given the option to erect a robust safety net with fewer cracks to slip through—including, say, universal health care and perhaps a welfare program that did not stigmatize the jobless—the American political class preferred to build prisons. Federal, state, and local spending on corrections jumped nearly fourfold between 1982 and 2015, after inflation, to $87 billion. That is more than the government spent on food stamps that year and two and a half times what it spent on unemployment insurance. The nation's premier antipoverty benefit, the earned income tax credit, cost 25 percent less.

The United States did not always think of criminal justice as a substitute for the welfare state. Beginning in the 1930s, social policy had been imbued by the sense of collective purpose implicit in Franklin Roosevelt's New Deal. Lyndon Johnson's War on Poverty, on the heels of the Civil Rights Act, amounted to a doubling down on the promise of solidarity across lines of race, class, and income. Then something happened. Over the next half a century, putting criminals in prison became a surefire route to political success.

Why did America's policy consensus turn so sharply, losing faith in the safety net while embracing prisons and jails? The turning point is that moment in history when blacks acquired the nominal right to the benefits of American citizenship.

Many scholars of crime trace the origins of America's incarceration spree back to 1974. That's when the government of the state of New York asked the criminologist Robert Martinson to evaluate the effectiveness of programs to rehabilitate criminals, the ostensible goal of the American penal system for a generation. Published in *The Public Interest* as "What Works? Questions and Answers About Prison Reform," Martinson's conclusion came to be known as the "nothing works" thesis. In the left-leaning *New Republic*, he wrote that "the array of correctional treatments has no appreciable effect, positive or negative, on rates of recidivism of convicted offenders." In the conservative *Public Interest*, he wrote that standard rehabilitation strategies "cannot overcome, or even appreciably reduce, the powerful tendency for offenders to continue in criminal behavior." His bipartisan analysis lent itself to one powerful conclusion: all the government could do was remove criminals from society.

Over the next quarter century or so, all fifty states adopted mandatory sentencing laws, specifying minimum sentences. Many also adopted "three strikes" laws to punish recidivists, curtailing judges' power to offer shorter sentences. In 1989, the Supreme Court upheld federal sentencing guidelines that dropped the notion of rehabilitation entirely, and in 1994 President Clinton signed into law the Violent Crime Control and Law Enforcement Act, the most expansive criminal justice legislation in generations. It not only increased the federal budget for prisons; it created entire new categories of crime and enshrined the principle of three strikes and you're out.

Martinson's conclusions remain controversial to this day. Scholars have pointed out that there was too little rehabilitation going on in the 1960s and 1970s for him to arrive at such a stark conclusion about its effects. Prison staff had neither the training nor the incentives. A report by a National Academy of Sciences panel in 1979 argued, "When it is asserted that 'nothing works,' the Panel is uncertain as to just what has even been given a fair trial."

A onetime civil rights "freedom rider" who had spent forty days in the maximum-security unit of Mississippi's Parchman State Penitentiary, Martinson didn't intend his analysis as an argument for more prisons. He was pushing back against the arbitrary sentences of uncertain length imposed by judges based on fuzzy criteria about felons' "attitude," which supposedly indicated whether they were sufficiently rehabilitated. But a political class frazzled at the end of the Vietnam War, sure that America was becoming a drug-addled Gomorrah, seized upon the idea as an opportunity to lock up everyone who worried them for as long as possible.

These were, to be sure, unstable times. Safety was a growing concern for many black and white families across urban America. The homicide rate doubled from the early 1960s to the early 1970s as the first bubble of baby boomers entered adulthood.

The deinstitutionalization that closed psychiatric institutions across the country in the 1960s led to the release of thousands of mentally ill people onto the streets. Fear was inevitably colored by racial mistrust. In 1993, as the national crime rate was peaking, the Reverend Jesse Jackson acknowledged, "There is nothing more painful to me at this stage in my life than to walk down the street and hear footsteps and start thinking about robbery, then look around and see somebody white and feel relieved."

But the white Americans fretting about society careening out of control also had something else in mind: blacks with equal rights. In 1963, Governor George Wallace had stood at the door to the auditorium of the University of Alabama to prevent the enrollment of two black students. By the late 1960s, desegregation had allowed blacks into all sorts of public spaces that whites had long considered their preserve. For the white Americans used to running things—Democratic or Republican—the image of black crime stood in for a broader, deeper unease.

Crime rates had already been declining for several years in 1996, when John J. DiIulio, a political scientist who would go on to head the White House's Office of Faith-Based and Community Initiatives in the administration of George W. Bush, partnered with the conservative politician William J. Bennett—secretary of education under President Reagan and drug czar under the first president Bush—and John P. Walters, Bennett's former chief of staff, to write *Body Count: Moral Poverty—and How to Win America's War Against Crime and Drugs*. It forcefully articulated a case to lock young blacks up. "America is now home to thickening ranks of juvenile 'super-predators'—radically impulsive, brutally remorseless youngsters," they wrote. They "do not fear the stigma of arrest, the pains of imprisonment, or the pangs of conscience."

The super-predators, in this rendition, were a threat to the very essence of America. "As high as America's body count is today, a rising tide of youth crime and violence is about to lift it even higher," wrote Bennett, DiIulio, and Walters. There was no choice but to put them away. "If the question is how to restrain known convicted criminals from murdering, raping, robbing, assaulting and stealing," DiIulio added in an op-ed for *The New York Times*, "then incarceration is a solution, and a highly cost-effective one."

Being tough on crime became a weapon of choice in the battle to capture a political constituency that was up for grabs. Southern Democrats straining to recover the allegiance of whites lost with the passage of the Civil Rights Act took to "law and order" as a rallying cry. Republicans hoping to pry working-class whites from Democrats' grasp did too. "Crime" thus became the code word for racial unease. "The crime debate was racialized to an important degree," Professor Western told me. "The anxieties white voters felt were not just about crime but about fundamental social changes going on in American society." As Michelle Alexander noted in *The New Jim Crow*, super-predators were inevitably inner-city blacks. Being tough on crime became the surefire tactic to woo white voters shocked at the sight of blacks invading public spaces, the schools and the hospitals, the white-only restaurants and the seats at the front of the bus that they had thought of as their own.

In 2016, almost one out of every hundred Alabamans was locked up. Blacks, who make up just over a quarter of the state's population, made up 54 percent of the state's inmates. Their incarceration rate was one in fifty-six. Similar patterns have repeated themselves across the country. In 1980, about 5.2 percent of adult men had a felony record, whether they were in prison or not, according to a study led by the sociologist Sarah Shannon. By 2010, the share was up to 12.8 percent.

Most Americans with a criminal record are black. In 2010, a third of African American men had a felony record. Over 15 percent were either in prison or on parole. Nearly half of all black men and 38 percent of white men will have been arrested at least once by the age of twenty-three, according to a study by the late criminologist Ray Paternoster and colleagues. For low-skilled black men, argue Western and Becky Pettit, going to prison is now more common than serving in the military or earning a college degree.

I'm sure Johnson didn't expect his administration would provide the capstone marking the end of the New Deal era. Johnson understood that the Civil Rights Act of 1964 would cause his party political damage. Democrats "have lost the South for a generation," he famously told his press secretary after signing the act into law. Still, he underestimated the extent of the damage: a couple of generations later, in 2018, Republicans captured 100 of the 152 seats in the House of Representatives from the eleven former Confederate states and their allies, Missouri and Kentucky. Johnson failed to grasp the scale at which inviting people of color into the network of rights and assurances created in the 1930s by FDR to protect the well-being of white American workers would undermine support for the safety net altogether.

President Johnson expanded aggressively on Roosevelt's template. His legislative achievements include creating universal health insurance for the elderly through Medicare as well as more limited health insurance for the poor through Medicaid. He increased Social Security benefits for poor families. He expanded cash aid and subsidized housing. He created the food stamp program to provide what amounted to a nutritional floor to the most destitute families. Federal spending on health, education, employment and training, housing, and income transfers tripled in his administration, reaching 15 percent of the federal budget in 1970.

Johnson worked to ensure the welfare apparatus he created served all Americans. "Many Americans live on the outskirts of hope—some because of their poverty, and some because of their color, and all too many because of both," he declared in his State of the Union speech of 1964. "Our task is to help replace their despair with opportunity." The additional federal funding made available through the War on Poverty gave him powerful leverage to pursue "a continuing assault on discrimination," as articulated in the *Economic Report of the President* that year. He also put relentless pressure on recalcitrant state and local governments, not to mention private actors, to reduce segregation and other forms of racial discrimination.

It is hard to fully comprehend the effect of expanding the access of black Americans to public services. In 1956 Dr. Paul Cornely, a professor of preventive medicine at Howard University, took it upon himself to assess the extent of racial integration at the nation's medical schools and hospitals in Blue Cross Blue Shield insurance plans and in medical societies. He sent questionnaires to chapters of the National Urban League, a civil rights organization, which set out to investigate the state of medical desegregation. Medicine in the North, Cornely found, was relatively integrated: 83 percent of hospitals reportedly offered integrated care. In the South, by contrast, only 6 percent of general hospitals admitted black patients without restrictions. Of the remaining 94 percent, a third did not admit any African American patients, half had segregated wards, and the remainder had other segregated patterns.

The Hill-Burton Act of 1946, which regulated government funding for hospital construction, legalized racial segregation, allowing separate white and black facilities to be built as long as they were of "equal quality." Across the South, equality proved to be a fiction. Even in so-called nondiscriminatory integrated facilities, barring black doctors and limiting black patients' access to certain services remained common.

The Johnson administration pretty much put an end to that. First came the stick. Title VI of the Civil Rights Act of 1964 directly forbade granting federal funds to institutions that discriminated on the basis of race, creed, or national origin. Then came the carrot. In 1965, President Johnson signed into law the biggest incentive that American hospitals had ever seen to comply with federal guidelines: Medicare, which carried the promise of billions upon billions of federal dollars.

Hospitals and clinics had until July 1, 1966, to get their act together. They had to ensure equal treatment for patients, desegregate services, open doors to black doctors, close segregated employee cafeterias, desegregate bathrooms, and put black and white patients in the same rooms. They hurried to comply. In April 1966, 15 percent or less of hospitals in seven southern states were compliant—including only 3 percent in Mississippi. By June 29, however, 31 percent of Mississippi's hospitals abided by the desegregation guidelines. In Alabama, compliance rose from 15 to 36 percent between June 3 and June 29.

It's hard to overstate the impact of these policies on the health of African Americans. One study by the economists Douglas Almond, Kenneth Chay, and Michael Greenstone found that at least twenty-five thousand black infants born between 1965 and 2002 who would have died before they turned one survived due to hospital desegregation. "The gains in black access to hospitals coincide with a striking reduction in black post-neonatal death for causes considered preventable with timely hospital care," they noted. What's more, "the financial incentives of Medicare were crucial to achieving hospital desegregation."

Yet the aggressive use of the federal purse to desegregate government welfare programs had another, more insidious consequence, one that hamstrings the United States to this day. By expanding access to the nation's social welfare programs to blacks and other minorities, civil rights legislation dealt a blow to the political support for government assistance altogether. President Johnson's War on Poverty, which expanded the safety net to help impoverished Americans, undermined its political stability by putting a poor black face on welfare.

As we've seen, in the depths of the Great Depression, Franklin Roosevelt resisted extending the benefits of the New Deal to African Americans because he knew he couldn't get any bill through Congress without the support of white southern Democrats. President Johnson, by contrast, rejected the trade-off. A white southerner who had spent many years in the Senate, he understood the immediate political costs his stand would impose on the Democratic Party, offering Republicans an opportunity to capture the South by attracting disgruntled whites with racist themes. What he couldn't grasp was the enduring impact his project of racial equality would have on the nation's political equilibrium. The nation is still reeling from the collapse not only of Americans' support for the safety net but of their general support of public goods and the entire apparatus of government.

The political scientists Nolan McCarty, Keith Poole, and Howard Rosenthal have devised a measure of political polarization based on roll-call votes in Congress. From the 1930s through the mid-1970s, they concluded, it remained fairly low. There were plenty of conservative white Democrats in the South and a good number of Republican liberals in the Northeast with shared views on a range of issues. That stands in stark contrast with the politics of the present. Since the 1970s, the political distance between Democrats and Republicans in Congress has increased relentlessly year after year, largely driven by Republicans' rightward drift as they have taken a rising share of the seats formerly held by conservative southern Democrats. The southern white support upon which President Roosevelt built the nation's early safety net has evaporated.

. . .

Few figures loom larger in the debate about American poverty than Daniel Patrick Moynihan. A policy intellectual who entered political life as a staunch liberal Democrat and served both in the Senate and in four consecutive administrations, from that of President John F. Kennedy to that of Gerald Ford, Moynihan provided the intellectual foundations for the conservative attack on the welfare state.

Assistant secretary of labor for policy, planning, and research from 1963 to 1965 under Presidents Kennedy and Johnson, Moynihan was tasked with developing a strategy for what would become Johnson's War on Poverty. What he came up with was *The Negro Family: The Case for National Action.* Intended as an evaluation of the scars left by slavery and racism, an argument for affirmative government action to address race-based inequality beyond guaranteeing equal rights, what is now known as *The Moynihan Report* ultimately helped make a case against the social safety net by giving welfare the face of a dysfunctional, irresponsible black family. The psychologist William Ryan famously accused Moynihan of "blaming the victim." The controversy colors the American debate over social policy still today.

The nub of Moynihan's message was based on one critical chart, which social scientists came to know as "Moynihan's scissors." It illustrated how the caseload of Aid to Families with Dependent Children, the nation's principal welfare program set up by Roosevelt through the Social Security Act of 1935, known as AFDC, tracked black unemployment. Until the early 1960s, the two followed each other pretty consistently. But around 1963 the caseload kept rising as black unemployment fell. This led Moynihan to conclude that black poverty was becoming disconnected from the status of the economy. This, he argued, was a consequence of the breakdown of black families who were trapped in a "tangle of pathology" and "approaching complete breakdown." The policy of the United States, *The Moynihan Report* concluded, "is to bring the Negro American to full and equal sharing in the responsibilities and rewards of citizenship. To this end, the programs of the Federal government bearing on this objective shall be designed to have the effect, directly or indirectly, of enhancing the stability and resources of the Negro American family."

In the end, Johnson never did much with Moynihan's analysis. The president drew on Moynihan's ideas in his commencement address in June 1965 at Howard University, one of the nation's leading historically black colleges, where he called for a White House conference to discuss additional steps needed to achieve racial equality after the passage of civil rights legislation. But Moynihan's underlying proposition that something called a black culture was inevitably producing poverty made his recommendations too hot to handle.

The argument never left the public arena, though, picked up enthusiastically by the Right. For the next fifty years, conservatives relied on variations of Moynihan's analysis to justify cutbacks in social welfare projects on the grounds that they fostered dependency and undermined black families' self-reliance. They proposed Moynihan's scissors as proof positive that government intervention is at best pointless and probably counterproductive, unable to help poor black families trapped in a "culture of poverty." They argued that to break out of the poverty trap, black families simply had to get their act together, embrace the white middle class's moral code, and assume responsibility for their lives. Conservatives relentlessly pummeled the AFDC, which they blamed for encouraging the breakdown of black families. They ultimately succeeded in repealing the nation's main antipoverty program with the passage of the Personal Responsibility and Work Opportunity Reconciliation Act of 1996.

Moynihan himself was horrified by this outcome. In a speech delivered in the Senate in September 1995, as welfare reform legislation made progress in Congress, Senator Moynihan blasted Bill Clinton's administration for working to undo the AFDC program, the main plank of support for poor children. "If this administration wishes to go down in history as one that abandoned, eagerly abandoned, the national commitment to dependent children, so be it," he thundered. "I cannot understand how this could be happening. It has never happened before."

Moynihan never supported the standard conservative argument, which simply posits blacks' moral failings as a starting point from which all else follows. He argued that black families' dysfunction was the product of hundreds of years of oppression, from slavery to segregation across the Jim Crow South, and he proposed to harness the energy of the civil rights movement to go beyond the demand for equal opportunity. The goal, he claimed, should be "equality as a fact and as a result."

Just the same, Moynihan earned a place of honor among conservatives hoping to undercut the welfare apparatus. A report on Johnson's War on Poverty commissioned in 2014 by Paul Ryan, the Republican chair of the House budget committee who would rise to become Speaker the following year, fell back on Moynihan to argue that "perhaps the single most important determinant of poverty is family structure." More than a third of families headed by single mothers lived below the poverty line, he noted, compared with only 13 percent of all families.

Welfare reform would probably have happened anyway. Democrats in the 1990s feared that their support of welfare amounted to an electoral liability. "Reform" that tied government aid closely to work, they hoped, might reduce voters' hostility toward antipoverty efforts. Still, Moynihan's analysis was the most direct articulation of welfare's racial handicap. It cemented welfare in the American consciousness as an effort to reward low-income black families for not adhering to white middle-class work and family values. Whether he had this in mind or not, Moynihan's ideas underpinned the political strategy followed by every Republican administration since Richard Nixon's.

Nixon is famous for launching the "southern strategy" with which the GOP took over the South from the Democratic Party by leveraging southern whites' opposition to civil rights legislation. But as I mentioned before, he also had a strategy for the North, to redirect the charged racial politics surrounding the War on Poverty and draw blue-collar white workers out of the Democrats' orbit by leveraging their distaste for a welfare system they perceived as an undeserved gift to blacks. "I intend to begin this administration by telling black Americans and the rest of Americans the truth," Nixon proclaimed in November 1968. "I am going to propose new programs the purpose of which will be to get people off welfare rolls and onto payrolls."

Arthur Burns, Nixon's top economic adviser, presented the president in 1969 with a review of an article in *New York* magazine by the journalist Pete Hamill titled "The Revolt of the White Lower Middle Class." Hamill quoted a man from Brooklyn who asked, "Who feeds my wife and kid if I'm dead?" He answered his own question—"nobody"—and launched into a diatribe against perceived injustice.

"The niggers, they don't worry about it. They take the welfare and sit out on the stoop drinkin' cheap wine and throwin' the bottles on the street. They never gotta walk outta the house. They take the money outta my paycheck and they just turn it over to some lazy son of a bitch who won't work," the man said. "You know what I am?" the man concluded. "I'm a sucker."

In his report to the president, Burns concluded, "The bitterness of the urban white worker, who feels he is supporting Negroes on relief as a result of the machinations of vote-hungry politicians, is a social and political fact of first-rate importance."

The great paradox is that Nixon's overall welfare strategy would have vastly expanded the welfare state. He proposed to replace Aid to Families with Dependent Children with what was essentially a basic income for all poor families—the so-called Family Assistance Plan, or FAP. It wasn't very generous, maxing out at $1,600, but the administration estimated it would almost triple both the number of beneficiaries, to twenty-eight million, and federal welfare's cost, to almost $6 billion. Welfare rolls would expand by 30 to 50 percent in states that already had high welfare enrollment, like New York, and increase by up to 400 percent in some of the stingier states in the South. A third of the population of Mississippi would have received benefits under Nixon's plan.

This seemingly liberal proposal was an ambitious gambit in a time of brooding resentment at the relentless growth of federal welfare rolls. "Mr. Nixon has taken a great step forward," wrote the *New York Times* columnist James Reston after Nixon announced the new policy. "He has cloaked a remarkably progressive welfare policy in conservative language."

But the political beauty of the plan, from the president's perspective, lay in its power to change the color of federal help, shifting the racial composition of welfare recipients away from blacks and toward poor working whites. Welfare at the time was mostly reserved for families headed by single mothers. Forty-six percent of the families on the AFDC program in 1969 were black, up from 43 percent in 1961. "In no state is any federally-assisted welfare available to families headed by full-time working men who earn poverty wages, the working poor," noted Robert Finch, secretary of health, education, and welfare, in congressional testimony. "We have backed ourselves into a situation in which we will help men who don't work, but we cannot help those who do work."

Organized labor deeply resented welfare. Clinton Fair, legislative director of the AFL-CIO, explained this in testimony to the Senate: "One of the most frustrating and discouraging features of all is that a male worker, employed full time, may be worse off than his neighbor, working only part time, but receiving welfare." Nixon worked hard to deepen the rift. In a meeting to discuss a speech about his welfare proposals, he told John Ehrlichman, his assistant for domestic affairs, and William Safire, his speechwriter, that he wanted to speak "not to welfare recipients, unemployed, blacks." He wanted to address exclusively "the working poor, taxpayers."

In the spring of 1970, Nixon's Domestic Council, an advisory body on domestic policy, launched a program of discussions among key members of the White House called "The Problem of the Blue-Collar Worker." In June of that year, George P. Shultz, Nixon's secretary of labor, sent a memorandum on behalf of the group to Ehrlichman, head of the council, recommending that it address the white working class's growing resentment of racial minorities. Welfare, it suggested, would provide a fruitful way in.

Working-class whites "feel the relentless pressures of the minorities in their immediate neighborhoods, at the job site, in the schools, and in the community," argued the memo. "Observing the welfare programs for the poor, they feel excluded and forgotten. As taxpayers they help pay the freight for 'free riders' and get none of the apparent help." Pulling it all together, the working group on blue-collar workers crafted a document underscoring, point by point, the insidious political impact of welfare policy. Work? A typical welfare recipient does "little or none," it stated, while a blue-collar worker "works regularly and hard." A welfare recipient could get up to $4,000 in government aid while a blue-collar worker would get none.

Nixon's stratagem didn't work, though. On April 16, 1970, the Family Assistance Plan passed the House by a margin of 243 to 155, but it never made it through the Senate. Early estimates suggested that minorities would account for fewer than four in ten beneficiaries under the FAP. Still, members of Congress from the South balked at a large universal benefit that would have raised incomes and deprived employers of cheap black labor. Phil Landrum, a Georgia Democrat in the House, opposed Nixon's plan on the grounds that "there's not going to be anybody left to roll these wheelbarrows and press these shirts." Critically, a universal federal system would have deprived southern states of their power to determine who got welfare and who didn't. They couldn't stand for that.

Southern states—and their senators—would not willingly hand over to Washington the power over the welfare machinery. In 1970 only 5 percent of people in the South benefited from federal aid. In New York the share was eight times as large. More than half of Mississippians lived below the poverty line, but only 14 percent got government assistance. The Department of Agriculture estimated there were a million people in Alabama who didn't have enough money to pay for a marginally acceptable diet. Fewer than 300,000 benefited from the department's food assistance program.

The sociologist Jill Quadagno reports how Robert Clark, the first black elected to the Mississippi legislature in almost a hundred years, explained this pattern: "Should you be able to walk or crawl, then you do not qualify for such programs." Across the South, welfare became a tool by which state governments guaranteed planters a stable, cheap workforce: the aid supported farmworkers through the winter, and its withdrawal forced them off the rolls and into the fields in the spring and summer.

Moynihan, who had been appointed to the cabinet by Nixon as secretary of the newly formed Urban Affairs Council, was the main architect of the president's plan. Embittered by its defeat, he lashed out at liberal opponents, whom he accused of being in the pocket of the existing welfare establishment: social workers in northern states, where benefits were more generous, who opposed doing away with the Aid to Families with Dependent Children program. His critique, however, ignores Nixon's political strategy: the president sought to capitalize on white resentments of blacks empowered by their new civil rights.

The political scientist Scott Spitzer believes that Nixon's FAP was the centerpiece of what he calls Nixon's "Northern Strategy" to leverage racial resentment in order to peel off white voters from the Democratic Party. It "was less a response to the problem of poverty, and more a response to the anger and frustration that had been mounting throughout the nation towards the rapidly expanding size of the welfare rolls in the late 1960s," he wrote. It would not just abolish a welfare system that coddled lazy blacks. It would also extend federal assistance to blue-collar whites, redeploying welfare—the cornerstone of liberal policy erected from the administration of FDR to that of Lyndon Johnson—to deliver Republicans a lasting political majority.

Nixon's insight was hardly new. Andrew Johnson, who succeeded Abraham Lincoln to the presidency in the early years after the Civil War, already chafed at the notion of a federal bureaucracy designed to care for "one class of people"—newly emancipated slaves—while ignoring "our own race."

But welfare was just too toxic. In the 1970 midterm elections Democrats expanded their majority in the House by a dozen seats. To contemporary observers, the outcome presents American politics as an oxymoron: Republicans lost an election on the grounds that Nixon supported putting "millions more on welfare." It proved the definitive turning point. The president abandoned his welfare plan in the wake of the GOP's electoral defeat and shifted, instead, to crime. Crime was, hands down, the more effective way to pick up white voters.

"You have to face the fact that the whole problem is really the blacks," noted the president in 1969, according to notes in the diary of his chief of staff, H. R. Haldeman. "The key is to devise a system that recognizes this while not appearing to." Thus the Republican strategy to curry the favor of working-class white voters by redeploying welfare to serve their interests was replaced forevermore by the simpler formula of rejecting welfare altogether. By the end of the presidency of Ronald Reagan twenty years later, the party's overriding goal had moved on from transforming welfare to ending it.

Remember the "welfare queen"? Ronald Reagan introduced her to American voters at a rally during the Republican presidential primary season in 1976. Based on Linda Taylor, a woman from Chicago's South Side who had been arrested for welfare fraud, Reagan's depiction built upon Nixon's race-heavy image of welfare, weaving it into a tale of lavish spending at taxpayers' expense. "She used eighty names, thirty addresses, five phone numbers to collect food stamps, Social Security, veteran's benefits for four non-existing deceased veteran husbands," Reagan said. "Her tax-free cash income alone has been running $150,000 a year."

Linda Taylor was real enough—a serial criminal who did much worse than just steal from the public purse. It goes without saying that she wasn't a typical woman on welfare. Reagan deployed her to create a wildly misleading image of recipients of public aid as thieves bleeding taxpayers dry.

Though he lost that election, defeated in the primary by the incumbent president, Gerald Ford, his depiction of welfare recipients as undeserving females of color, potential fraudsters who should, in any case, be held responsible for their own poverty, proved a powerful motif that would help deliver him the presidency four years later. Riding what was then an unusual voting coalition that included both big business and disaffected working-class whites angry at a government that seemed uninterested in their plight, Reagan successfully blamed the government for working to help blacks get ahead.

African Americans, to be sure, were increasingly on welfare. In 1936, only 14 percent of recipients of Aid to Dependent

Children were black. By 1969, blacks made up 45 percent of the rolls. In 1960 poverty meant a white family in Appalachia. Twenty years later it evoked an unmarried black mom in Chicago. What's more, as riots broke out in Harlem, Chicago, the Watts neighborhood in South Central Los Angeles, and elsewhere, the debate over poverty got enmeshed with the discussions about growing unrest in black communities. Blacks on welfare became easy political targets.

Reagan's attack on welfare wasn't overtly directed at African Americans. But it was the racial hostility among white voters that made welfare such an easy target. The victims of the enormous budget reductions he wrote into the Omnibus Budget Reconciliation Act of 1981 were clear. Benjamin Hooks, executive director of the NAACP, called the cuts "an Alice in Wonderland approach that takes from the poor and gives to the rich" and promised that his organization "will move against this iniquitous treatment."

President Reagan slashed spending on welfare, food stamps, Medicaid, public housing, and job training, even as he promised to protect Social Security, Medicare, and veterans' benefits—which mostly served whites. The Center on Budget and Policy Priorities, a left-leaning think tank, estimated that blacks were three times as likely to participate in the programs for low- and moderate-income families that were cut. The cuts—combined with consecutive recessions in 1980 and 1981—took a toll: by 1982, the Census Bureau reported that almost 36 percent of blacks lived in poverty, the highest rate since 1968; poverty among Latinos shot up too.

It is tempting to understand the racialization of welfare as a product of Republican thinking alone. It would be a mistake. As I mentioned earlier, it was Bill Clinton who in 1996 replaced the poor's entitlement to federal assistance with a set of state-run antipoverty programs that, as a general rule, required beneficiaries to get a job. The political pressure to end a program that served mostly single black mothers had become irresistible. Having lost the House of Representatives in a Republican landslide two years earlier, a Democratic president lent himself to the goal of ending a so-called culture of dependency on the public purse, buying into the idea of welfare as a social scourge that discouraged work, encouraged childbearing out of wedlock, and led to all sorts of bad behaviors among minority families.

Aid to Families with Dependent Children, which had been around in pretty much the same form since the 1930s, was replaced by Temporary Assistance for Needy Families. It consisted of a block of cash delivered to the states with few strings attached other than a five-year limit on benefits. Given ample liberty to craft their own strategies, many states attached stringent work requirements to their assistance and cut it off considerably before the five-year limit. The harshest states turned out to be those with large minority populations.

In *Disciplining the Poor: Neoliberal Paternalism and the Persistent Power of Race*, the political scientists Joe Soss, Richard Fording, and Sanford Schram noted that five years after the reform was enacted, it turned out that six in ten families in the most restrictive welfare programs, with the steepest eligibility rules and the toughest penalties for noncompliance, were black. Six in ten families in the most lenient programs were white. "The only thing we could find that really drove one policy decision after another was the percentage of minority recipients on the welfare rolls at the time," Soss said in an interview with BillMoyers.com. "And when you add those different rules up, what we found was that even though the Civil Rights Act prevents the government from creating different programs for black and white recipients, when states choose according to this pattern, it ends up that large numbers of African Americans get concentrated in the states with the toughest rules, and large numbers of white recipients get concentrated in the states with the more lenient rules."

Clinton's reform did not lead to the spike in poverty many of his critics expected. The red-hot economy fueled by the dot-com revolution in the second half of the 1990s pulled a lot of people out of poverty on its own. What's more, welfare reform was preceded by the expansion in 1993 of the earned income tax credit, which subsidized the earnings of low-income workers. By 2000 the EITC had become the largest antipoverty tool in the federal government's arsenal, at a cost to federal coffers of $31 billion. That was twice as much as it provided in 1992.

Still, Clinton doesn't get a pass. Sure, the EITC helped make work pay, and it was remarkably successful in drawing single mothers into the labor force, but it failed to raise the incomes of families at the bottom of the ladder: for every dollar in wages gained by women who left welfare and went to work, they lost about a dollar in government benefits. Most critically, people without a job were left out in the cold. When the Great Recession hit in 2008, the government was not there. "TANF was not responsive in the Great Recession," wrote the economists Marianne Bitler and Hilary Hoynes. Without it, "extreme poverty became more cyclical," deepening sharply when the economy took a hit.

In 1996, before Clinton's welfare reform, nearly ten million children and five million adults received cash benefits from public assistance programs. Today the rolls have been trimmed to about three million kids and one million parents. Poverty rates, however, have not improved. According to the sociologists Kathryn Edin and H. Luke Shaefer, this has contributed to a 130 percent jump in the number of households with children living on cash incomes of less than $2 per person per day.

The clearest takeaway is that welfare reform did not work as a political strategy to build public support for government programs. Writing a decade after Clinton's program went into effect, Schram and Soss concluded that aid to the poor "continued to be associated with targeted aid to blacks, and white preferences for welfare spending remained tied to stereotypes regarding black effort." Opposition to reducing inequality actually grew. Americans became no more willing to spend on the poor, on blacks, or on welfare. "Welfare has retained its negative connotations," Schram and Soss wrote. All the efforts to cut blacks from welfare were unable to mitigate the racial resentment that delivered the presidency to Donald Trump.

America's working-class white voters seem to have been waiting forever for somebody to articulate their apprehension about this United States that looks so little like that of their youth. Since 1994 the General Social Survey has asked, "Compared to your parents when they were the age you are now, do you think your own standard of living is much better, somewhat better about the same, somewhat worse, or much worse than theirs was?" In his book *Labor's Love Lost*, the sociologist Andrew Cherlin noted how whites lacking a bachelor's degree have become progressively more pessimistic, with the share ticking off "somewhat worse" or "much worse" increasing from 13 to 21 percent between 1994 and 2012. Meanwhile the share of blacks of similar educational background choosing either of these options declined from 19 to 11 percent.

Whites have become more pessimistic about their kids' prospects too. "In the 1990s blacks were more negative than whites in their assessments of intergenerational progress," Cherlin wrote, "but now they are more positive." And so, remarked the law professor Joan Williams, blue-collar whites were ready in 2016 to hear somebody like Donald Trump tell them that the immigrants and the minorities whose footprint on America continues to grow were to blame.

This might strike blue-collar blacks and Latinos as insane, because they have always occupied a lower rung on the ladder of opportunity. They never experienced the prosperity that their white brothers and sisters once did. Still, they remain bound by whites' frustration over a broken American dream, caught in a political argument that pits them as unworthy beneficiaries of a government project that has left whites behind.

There is a great irony in white workers' eager embrace of Trump. Their deprivation has been deepened by a government that all but forgot about its displaced and its poor. The erosion of the social safety net that was justified by recourse to a racially tinged definition of the undeserving ultimately left less educated whites at the mercy of the elements too. Yet the white working poor's response has been to double down on their whiteness and blame the colored moochers for their plight.

Trump's policy objectives came from the same playbook that produced the United States' ineffective safety net. His presidency exploded America's exceptional contradiction: unwilling to share the bounty of state with people of other races and creeds, heritages and colors, real Americans—the white ones—have prevented the erection of a welfare state at all. "If America's policy makers better understood white working-class anger against the social safety net, they might have a shot at creating programs that don't get gutted in this way," Williams writes. Personally, I'm not sure this would turn the white working class around. So far, their anger and despair are anchoring a policy platform that cannot but undermine their own prosperity.

What happens now to the safety net? Trump's first swing of the ax to make America great again was against the Affordable Care Act—the only major expansion of the nation's safety net for poor Americans since Lyndon Johnson's War on Poverty fifty years before. His second was to cut tax rates on corporations and rich Americans, raising them over the long term for many Americans in the middle class.

The battle over Obamacare precedes Trump's rise on the

political scene. In 2010 it was passed into law with zero Republican votes in Congress. Republicans opposed it for typical Republican reasons: it taxes the rich to pay for a government program to help the working class and the poor. But Trump managed to turbocharge Republican opposition to the bill by overtly layering racial and ethnic hostility onto the political platform.

Immigrants are "not going to come in and just immediately go and collect welfare," the president promised, somehow ignoring that legislation passed during the Clinton administration already imposed a five-year wait on most legal immigrants' access to government benefits. Though his facts were spotty, the political tactics were spot-on. Support for the Affordable Care Act might have surged to its highest level ever in the wake of Trump's election, but it still showed a clear racial bias. Three-quarters of blacks and 68 percent of Hispanics supported Obamacare, according to a tracking poll by the Kaiser Family Foundation in November 2018. Only 46 percent of whites approved of the program.

The assault on Roosevelt's and Johnson's legacies may look like the standard Republican platform, but hitched to less educated white voters' fantasy of a better, ethnically uniform past, it has taken a more troubling shape. White voters without a college degree remain the only constituency steadfastly loyal to Trump. They trust he will take their side against their rivals—competitors for attention and resources—on the other side of America's ethnic divides. Poor white America, though, will probably rue the moment it chose Trump as a champion. Because in a society that refuses the very concept of solidarity, poor white Americans lose too.

In his book *Coming Apart*, published in 2012, the conservative writer Charles Murray went out of his way to detail the depth of social dysfunction among working-class whites. He proposed a fictional town called Fishtown, after the blighted neighborhood in Philadelphia. This was the home of white Americans who never got an education beyond high school and worked, at best, in low-level white-collar jobs.

In 2010 three in ten Americans lived in Fishtown, Murray estimated, based on census data. Among them, one in three didn't earn enough to keep a family of two out of poverty. One in five Fishtown kids lived with a single, divorced, or separated parent. Fewer than six in ten families were headed by somebody with a full-time job. A criminal justice system that blacks long suspected was tailored to keep them in jail caught up with poor whites too. In 1974, Fishtown's imprisonment rate amounted to 213 per 100,000 people. By 2004 that had ballooned to 957 per 100,000, and this figure excludes municipal and county jails.

Murray, who wrote from a perch at the American Enterprise Institute, argued that Fishtown is a product of government overreach: Lyndon Johnson's project to relieve poverty and help the working class in the 1960s undermined workers' industriousness and undercut their moral fiber. "When the government says it will take some of the trouble out of doing the things that families and communities evolved to do, it inevitably takes some of the action away from families and communities," Murray wrote. "The web frays, and eventually disintegrates."

I would argue that this is exactly the wrong lesson. Fishtown is what happens when the government turns a blind eye to the plight of its citizens. In the aftermath of the Johnson presidency, successive administrations reshaped the American social contract into a deal that split the deserving from the rest. Designed to cut off black America—a territory to be demarcated from the America of upright whites—the emasculation of the welfare state inevitably came around to punish impoverished white families too. A safety net created in the shadow of racism, built to skirt people of color, to define them as ineligible and deem them undeserving, ended up betraying the white Americans in whose name it was built.

Blacks are by far the greatest victims of America's criminal justice. At the end of 2016, 1,608 out of every 100,000 African Americans were in prison. So too were 856 Latinos out of every 100,000. The imprisonment rate for whites, by contrast, was only 274 per 100,000. This is still, however, a much higher imprisonment rate than that of 190 countries and territories tracked by the Institute for Criminal Policy Research at the University of London. The share of white Americans behind bars is almost three times the share of imprisoned Frenchmen, almost four times that of Germans, and double that of imprisoned Britons. France, Germany, and Britain chose a social safety net.

CHAPTER 4

The Black and the Brown

I landed in Los Angeles with a specific task. It was the year 2000, and demographer types were aflutter about what the decennial census would discover about the changing tissue of America. *The Wall Street Journal* hired me to report on what was anticipated to be the most significant demographic shift of all: a vast increase in the number of Americans like me.

As it turned out, the American Hispanic population increased by 60 percent over the 1990s, to just over thirty-five million at the turn of the century. Just a year later Latinos would surpass blacks as the biggest ethnic minority in the United States, accounting for 13 percent of the population. With so many businesses hoping to sell their wares into this formerly neglected corner of the consumer market, it was only natural for the *Journal*, peerless chronicler of corporate America, to send in a Hispanic to decipher the appetites of the newfound demographic for the rest of the nation.

I jumped at the chance. Having spent most of my career writing for small Latin American publications—a Mexican newswire, then a Brazilian business magazine—this was my chance to start writing in English, in *The Wall Street Journal*, no less. I got to write a story about lard, which was making a comeback on the strength of Mexican culinary nostalgia eroding Americans' fear of saturated fat. I wrote about California's

Milk Processor Board, which commandeered a Mexican legend about a mother who drowns her own children to try to persuade Hispanic teens to drink more milk. I wrote about the Republican Party, so hopeful it could convince Latinos that their conservative Christian upbringing made them Republicans at heart.

Some of the most fun stories were about American companies trying to sell Hispanic pizzazz to mainstream America. The oddest, for sure, was about Liz Claiborne's efforts to create a Latino smell. As Neil Katz, who ran Liz Claiborne's fragrances division at the time, put it to me, the challenge was about "interpreting the idea of a Latino in an American's head." The company commissioned a French *parfumier* to devise a scent for women and a Spaniard to come up with the smell for men. They were inspired, they told me, by Carlos Santana's "Smooth" and Jennifer Lopez's hips, by the sweat of a matador fresh after the bullfight and the image of the Roman Catholic Church. They called it Mambo. I remember Katz telling me it was not, in fact, supposed to evoke the mambo. Clara Rodriguez, a New York–born Puerto Rican sociologist who had written a book about the representation of Hispanics in American media, wondered out loud whether Hispanics were supposed to recognize each other when they wore it.

Of course marketing executives traffic in stereotype. There is nothing unusual about companies approaching consumers as a collection of niches of different tastes and needs: men; women; the old; the young; the married; the single. There is nothing singularly egregious about the concept of a Hispanic market. Yet the construction of such a proper box for Latinos to live in made me uncomfortable. The Latino experience over the years has been characterized by more than a little brutality. There were some lynchings; there were some deportations. Latinos, too, have experienced living on the wrong side of a color line. As African Americans might cringe at cool corporate stereotypes of blackness set against a historical backdrop of unimaginable racial violence, Latinos—most specifically Mexican Americans—might find the contrast between the sleek marketing materials and the bleaker images from the not too distant past a little hard to swallow.

Hispanics are somewhat of a fiction. You can't find them outside the United States. Outside the United States there are Mexicans and Ecuadorans and Salvadorans. They share some traits: Spanish, a common experience of colonization by Spain, the long, overbearing presence of the Roman Catholic Church. But they do not amount to a coherent collective. Like "Latin America," the terms "Hispanic" and "Latino" are labels designed by non-Latinos to manufacture a collective.

Latin America was invented by the French during the empire of Napoleon III, who invaded Mexico and briefly installed the ill-fated Maximilian of Habsburg as emperor of the Second Mexican Empire. To prevent the continent from being semantically engulfed into some greater Spain, France hoped to build a regional identity around a broader cultural root that also included the French. While Maximilian eventually faced the firing squad and France's Mexican aspirations came to naught, "Latin America" lives on, a durable, though imperfect, moniker for the world south of the Rio Grande.

Hispanics in the United States have a different origin. We are the product of Americans' unremitting passion for ethnic categorization. American businesses, politicians, and government officials needed a name for a set of people who were different from both whites and blacks. They wanted a drawer in which to put us—to count us, to sell us stuff, maybe to understand us, whatever "us" means. How otherwise could we feature in the American experience, so precisely determined by the race of its characters? "Hispanic" wasn't just concocted to fence us off from the white American core or its black underclass. The word created us, provided us with a requisite feature to exist in the United States. "Hispanic" does not identify a race, as the Census Bureau patiently repeats every time it surveys us. But it provides a patina of scientific objectivity to our otherness. Inevitably enfolded in the broader identity wars, the word officially invited us into the long-drawn narrative of America's racial conflict.

Many Hispanics have enthusiastically embraced their made-in-America label. It does, after all, convey more power to be part of a fifty-five-million-strong community of Latinos than to be one of two million Salvadorans, five million Puerto Ricans, or even thirty-five million Mexicans. In a nation in which government largesse is commonly apportioned among historically afflicted groups—defined by ethnicity or race, age maybe, gender, or educational attainment—it makes sense to belong to one with the political clout to draw a substantial share of the pie.

Reporting for the *Journal*, I witnessed the redistricting process following the 2000 census. That is when congressional districts are reshaped to adapt to changing demographics, to ensure that every seat in the House of Representatives, state legislatures, and city assemblies represents roughly the same number of people.

I recall standing in a room full of Hispanic political operatives. Art Montez, member of the local school board, hovered over a map of Orange County with Magic Marker in hand. His goal was to maximize the political clout of Latinos' growing population—drawing political boundaries around electoral districts that had just enough of them to elect a Latino to office but not too many that they could deprive a neighboring district of the Hispanics it would need to elect their own too.

Montez barely mentioned the *H* word. In 1993 the Supreme Court ruled that race cannot be a predominant factor to justify reshaping electoral boundaries. Districts, the Court declared, must be based on "communities of interest," a nebulous term that could include everything from educational attainment to homeownership status. "Racial gerrymandering," the Court argued in *Shaw v. Reno*, "may balkanize us into competing racial factions." Attempting to build an electoral majority around Latino identity was a legally vulnerable strategy.

That Supreme Court decision was written by Justice Sandra Day O'Connor, who at the time held the middle of the Court's ideological spectrum. She understood more than most just how tough it is to break through the barriers prejudice has erected across American society. After graduating from Stanford Law School in 1952, she couldn't land a job interview at a law firm and ended up taking a government job as deputy county attorney in San Mateo, California. Still, she made what must count as one of the most disingenuous statements in the history of America's fractious race relations. "Racial classifications of any sort pose the risk of lasting harm to our society," she wrote in the 5–4 decision. "They reinforce the belief, held by too many for too much of our history, that individuals should be judged by the color of their skin."

Evidently, to Justice O'Connor, the discrimination exercised by the institutions of white America against people of other skin tones was a minor issue compared with the potential harms that might flow from allowing minorities to rally around the proposition to push back. Using race to shape voting districts, she said, "threatens to carry us further from the goal of a political system in which race no longer matters." In her view, apparently, institutions that empowered ethnic minorities to defend their civil rights amounted to backsliding from America's inexorable path toward racial harmony.

I was pretty much fresh off the boat, as it were. Though I was born in the United States, I had until then lived most of my life elsewhere, mostly in Mexico. Witnessing Montez's contortions to produce a Latino-heavy congressional district without ever talking about Latinos was my first direct exposure to the chasm between how race is lived and how it is talked about. It was a critical lesson in what became a crash course on the power of race to determine everything in America.

Reporting on Latinos in Los Angeles, I discovered that race is, in fact, everywhere. It determines where you go to school, church, or work; how you dress and talk; whom you marry; how you fare when you run into the cops. Racial boundaries shape American institutions whether we accept it or not. As Pedro Colón, a Latino in the Wisconsin State Assembly, lamented to me about the redistricting process following the 2000 census, "I can't mention race, but that's what I mean."

As I learned about race's power to shape American society, I also learned that its footprint is more complicated than is portrayed by the conventional image of a binary conflict pitting whites against blacks. The terror visited by white America on powerless black communities may amount to racism's deepest wound. But there are other divides inspiring racial mistrust. In Los Angeles, racial hostility was rife between peoples who might have understood themselves as sisters and brothers united against a common oppressor. It arose between Latinos and blacks, and even within the purported Hispanic family. Despite many shared experiences and beliefs, Mexicans and Salvadorans fought over turf like the best of enemies.

This wrinkle in the standard narrative is important, because it clarifies what it will take to overcome America's foundational racism. It is not simply a matter of achieving harmony between whites and blacks. There are other divisions that need to be bridged. The ongoing mistrust between whites and blacks and Latinos and Asians, between Mexicans and Salvadorans and Guatemalans, has shaped American society to an extent few Americans are even aware of, let alone willing to accept. Some social scientists hopefully forecast that race relations in America will improve as its ethnic quilt becomes more complex, incorporating different skin tones, languages, and cultural mores. The past, however, does not justify much optimism.

Los Angeles had experienced its last big riot less than a decade before I got there. It started on the afternoon of April 29, 1992, after a jury of ten whites, one Latino, and one Asian American acquitted four cops who had been caught on camera beating a speeding black motorist, Rodney King. Fifty-two persons died; 2,499 were injured; 6,559 people were arrested.

The riot in South Central L.A. was hardly America's first. Riots amounted then to one of the nation's most nagging leitmotifs. Nearly three decades earlier, thirty-four persons had been killed in the Watts neighborhood of Los Angeles in a disturbance following the arrest of a young African American man for drunk driving. On July 27, 1967, following riots in Newark and Detroit, President Lyndon Johnson established the National Advisory Commission on Civil Disorders to look into the causes of the nation's civil unrest. Led by the Illinois governor, Otto Kerner, its assessment of the riots came to be known as the Kerner Report.

"This is our basic conclusion," it stated, in words that have by now become famous. "Our nation is moving toward two societies, one black, and one white—separate and unequal." The stakes could hardly be higher: "the destruction of basic democratic values." Blacks were openly segregated in employment, education, and housing. Cities were left to decay as whites fled to the suburbs. Blacks found themselves isolated in impoverished, crime-ridden urban ghettos, chewing on unfulfilled expectations built of a civil rights movement that came up decidedly short. What the rioters wanted was only "fuller participation in the social order and the material benefits enjoyed by the majority of American citizens."

While the deepening of racial divisions was not irreversible, "to continue present policies is to make permanent the division of our country into two societies," the commissioners noted. "One, largely Negro and poor, located in the central cities; the other, predominantly white and affluent, located in the suburbs

and in outlying areas." They foresaw "violent protest" by blacks,
"followed by white retaliation, and, ultimately, the separation
of the two communities in a garrison state." The only choice
America had, it argued, was "a policy which combines ghetto
enrichment with programs designed to encourage integration
of substantial numbers of Negroes into the society outside the
ghetto."

When I arrived in Los Angeles, racial tensions were not
quite as explosive as they had been a decade earlier. Nonetheless, they were entrenched across town. The arrival of Mexicans
and Central Americans in large numbers over the preceding
thirty years had further complicated the alliances and animosi-
ties that shaped local neighborhoods. In a study about the causes
of America's rioting, the urban economics scholars Edward
Glaeser and Denise DiPasquale observed that the 1992 riots
could be explained, in part, by the high unemployment among
young black men in the area. They also highlighted another
critical factor: ethnic diversity. From 1970 to 1990, the African American share of the population in South Central L.A. fell
from 80 percent to 45 percent, while Hispanics' share rose from
8 percent to 51 percent. "We are still far from understanding
why ethnic heterogeneity is so important in rioting behavior,"
they wrote. "But it does seem to be a central component of why
riots occur."

America's principal racial cleavage remains between blacks
and whites. Yet anybody arriving in Los Angeles today will recognize it is not the only divide. Black-brown gang conflict was
rampant when I lived there. Powerful Latino gangs terrorized
African Americans in an overt campaign of ethnic cleansing to
rid neighborhoods of blacks. Black-Latino riots broke out in
state prisons. Tensions played out on California's political scene,
where African American politicians struggled to preserve seats
in Congress, the California legislature, and municipal assem-

blies, even as the black share of the population shrank while Latino and Asian enclaves grew.

Even liberal scholars had a hard time accepting the brown into the American tent. In an essay on where Latinos fit in a multicultural America, the Latino scholars Albert Camarillo and Frank Bonilla noted how the prominent law professor Lance Liebman in the 1980s called "for a Supreme Court wise enough and ingenious enough to uphold legislative decisions that assist Blacks but refuse to uphold, because the justifications are weaker and the costs to the social fabric so great, extensions of those arrangements to other groups." Other groups meant people like me.

On the campaign trail in 2007, Barack Obama quoted Martin Luther King Jr. to a Hispanic conference, calling blacks and Latinos "brothers in the fight for equality." Perhaps one day. Blacks and Latinos across urban America still contemplate each other predominantly as competitors for scarce resources, economic, political, and social. In Southern California, any impetus for interethnic solidarity must vie with the competition for jobs and affordable housing.

Latino political operatives would sometimes vent to me about blacks being overrepresented in government jobs, while Hispanics were condemned to underrepresentation. African Americans, meanwhile, would complain about resources spent on teaching English to immigrants from Mexico.

Compton, a city tucked into the vast urban sprawl of Los Angeles's metropolitan area, maybe ten miles south of downtown, offers a telling story about how demographic change and ethnic animosity have shaped Southern California's history. Not that long ago, it was just about all white. Until the 1950s places like Compton, Lynwood, and Inglewood did not even allow blacks to reside within their boundaries. They protected their racial homogeneity from the African Americans arriving from

South Central Los Angeles and the American South by applying racial covenants to property titles and mortgages.

In 1948, the Supreme Court decided that restrictive real estate covenants were not enforceable by law. And realtors, who had been informal enforcers of racial exclusion, steering blacks away from white enclaves, turned around to fan the flames of white flight to the suburbs. They urged whites to sell and leave before the impending collapse in property values they predicted would occur once blacks became established in the neighborhood.

By 1960, about one-third of Compton's residents were black. They shared West Compton with a small enclave of Hispanics. Whites accounted for 60 percent of the population, mostly on the east side of town. Then the riots that broke out in the Watts neighborhood just north of the city border in 1965 persuaded these remaining whites to flee west. By 1970, 71 percent of Compton's population was African American. It became the first city west of the Mississippi River governed and administered by blacks.

Compton's racial mix would continue changing, however. In 1965, the Hart-Celler Immigration Act did away with national quotas that limited immigration visas mostly to people from northern European countries and pretty much barred immigrants from poor nations like Mexico. Immigration across the southern border jumped. In 1960, there were only 1.75 million people born in Mexico living in the United States. By 2000, they exceeded 21 million. Compton received a fair share. In 1990, blacks made up more than half of the city's residents. By 2000, when I arrived in Los Angeles, about 60 percent were Latino. The new mix produced a new variety of social and political tensions that belies the belief in a fraternity of the dispossessed.

Latino activists in Compton had no shortage of complaints against blacks, the black mayor, the all-black city council. The ordinance banning taco trucks and other outdoor vending carts smacked of outright discrimination, they said. All city jobs went to blacks. African Americans controlled the schools, the local chamber of commerce, and the Democratic Party machine. They showed no inclination to share. Latinos accused Mayor Omar Bradley of betrayal when, after being elected in 1993 with Hispanic support, he reneged on a promise to support a Latino to take his seat on the city council and backed a fellow African American instead.

Addressing the city's all-black council in 1998, a Latina activist evoked the history of black-white politics from the 1960s. "It was not that many years ago when black people were at this podium saying the same things of white folks," she said. "How could you forget?" But African American politicians would have none of this. Latinos had to be patient. They had to become citizens, register to vote, win by the rules. They didn't understand the cost borne by blacks in their struggle for emancipation and political representation.

Education provided perhaps the most obvious venue for tensions to flare. Latinos still made up the vast majority of Compton's school-age population, but African Americans controlled the school board. In 1990, Hispanic rights advocates complained that there were more than eight thousand children in Compton's public schools who spoke little or no English but only forty-six certified bilingual teachers. African American political leaders were unsympathetic.

"I have no respect for the language issue. This is America," said John Steward, a school board trustee. "Because a person does not speak English is not a reason to provide exceptional resources at public expense." Regarding Latinos' demand that Compton establish an affirmative action plan to hire more Hispanics for school district and city jobs, Steward retorted that affirmative action programs were established as reparations for black enslavement and were not "based on going back and forth across the border ten or fifteen times a year."

. . .

Black-brown tensions have burst into the open throughout the Southwest and beyond as the expanding Hispanic population has etched a new ethnic division on the national map, producing new sets of relative winners and relative losers around the country. "In environments where Latinos are economically advantaged relative to their black neighbors, blacks are more likely to harbor negative stereotypes about Latinos, to be reluctant to extend to Latinos the same policy benefits they themselves enjoy, and to view black and Latino economic and political interests as incompatible," wrote Claudine Gay, a professor of government and African American studies. "While the results suggest that diversity without conflict is possible, they make clear that the prospects for intergroup comity depend on some resolution of blacks' economic insecurities."

Indeed. On May 9, 2007, while George W. Bush's attempt at large-scale immigration reform was sailing toward its ultimate defeat in Congress, T. Willard Fair, president and chief executive of the Urban League of Greater Miami, addressed the Subcommittee on Immigration, Citizenship, Refugees, Border Security, and International Law of the Committee on the Judiciary of the House of Representatives. "The interests of black Americans are clear," he said. "No amnesty, no guest-workers, enforce the immigration law." Whatever the government did to help African Americans, "flooding the job market and overwhelming the public schools and other government services undermines all our efforts."

The oppression of blacks by the institutions of white America is America's defining sin. For four hundred years, blacks have been subjected to violence, discrimination, and mistreatment. Whites have devised specific policies to shunt them into ghettos and stunt their prosperity, only to turn around and preach to them about virtue. Still, the black-white divide is not the nation's only racial fault line. Hostility between blacks and Latinos or even whites and Latinos might not have spawned the sort of continued, institutionalized violence inflicted by whites upon blacks as a matter of daily routine. But it has decidedly contributed to the shaping of American institutions, further shaping the United States into a nation without empathy.

The demographer and urban planning scholar Dowell Myers believes that the right political messaging can ease ethnic rivalries. "Rapid demographic change is drawing new attention to the need for greater equity between race and ethnic groups," he writes. The white population is aging, too. Underscoring how the workers, taxpayers, and home buyers who will support the American economy into the future will be mostly people of color might persuade whites to buy into cross-racial solidarity.

And yet that's not the only available way to frame the future, Myers admits. Many whites prefer to understand America's demographic change as a threat to their dominance. What's more, America's people of color do not often see eye to eye.

To a Mexican American who had lived most of his life outside the U.S. borders, what perplexed me above all when I returned was how often race came up in everyday life, and the matter-of-factness with which Americans lived within their assigned ethnic box. I am a mongrel, the son of an Anglo father from Chicago—white, gray-green eyes, six feet tall—and a darker Mexican mother, who stands just over five feet and draws from a mixed pool of European and American Indian blood. I "read white," as Brent Staples, a former colleague on *The New York Times* editorial board, once told me. Working-class Mexicans call me *güero*, which translates loosely as "blondie." Growing up in Mexico City, where the correlation between skin color and privilege must be at least as strong as it is in the United States, I led a privileged existence. But in Mexico, as across most of Latin

America, racial identity is a much more fluid concept. It has little of the organizing power bestowed on it through American history.

Latin America is no stranger to ethnic conflict. There were hundreds of indigenous cultures spread across the continent when Europeans arrived in the sixteenth century to colonize and evangelize them, wiping many of them out. Brazil has a history of slavery more brutal even than America's. Nearly five million African slaves disembarked in Brazil between 1550 and 1875, over ten times as many as landed in the United States, according to the Trans-Atlantic Slave Trade Database.

The European colonizers of modern-day Latin America were as obsessed as anybody with racial classifications. They devised a complex taxonomy to split the population of New Spain into seven basic "castes." The spectrum ranged from Spaniards born in Spain through mestizos and mulattoes, of mixed European and either indigenous or African blood, to natives of the New World. They, and their many subdivisions, determined a clear pecking order of social, political, and economic privilege.

Still, today most people in Latin America understand themselves as racially mixed. Almost half of Brazilians define themselves as mixed race, or *pardos*, more than identify as white. The last time the Mexican census even asked about race was in 1921. Until the 2000 census, when it asked directly about indigenous identity, it kept track of such communities through language alone. José Vasconcelos, a politician and philosopher who was Mexico's first secretary of education, wrote in the 1920s that Mexicans were of the "Cosmic Race"—that which included all others.

After Latin American countries broke from Europe, ethnic affinities were eventually subsumed into an officially sanctioned mestizo kinship, part of a continent-wide strategy to build coherent nations out of a great variety of peoples. "The great mass of the population has some mixture of Indian blood," noted Henry

George Ward, the chargé d'affaires at the British consulate in Mexico from 1825 to 1827, shortly after the end of Mexico's war of independence from Spain. "Few of the middle classes—the lawyers, the *Curas*, or parochial clergy, the artisans, the smaller landed proprietors, and the soldiers—could prove themselves exempt from it; now that a connection with the Aborigines has ceased to be disadvantageous, few attempt to deny it."

It wasn't straightforward. It took until the early twentieth century for the idea of a mixed-race nation to overcome the whitening ideologies that had been prevalent over the previous hundred years. The mestizo identity, though, eventually became a prime tool for nation building, part of a narrative that downplayed racial and ethnic affinities to create homogeneous national populations. In the Square of the Three Cultures in Tlatelolco, near downtown in Mexico City, where the Aztec general Cuauhtémoc surrendered to the Spanish army led by Hernán Cortés on August 13, 1521, there's an inscription that reads, "It was neither victory nor defeat. It was the painful birth of the mestizo people that is the Mexico of today."

This is not to say that Latin America dealt with its racial divisions any better than the United States. While a state-sanctioned mestizo culture blurs racial divisions, it also allows political elites to deny racism even while depriving ethnic minorities of an identity. In Brazil and Guatemala the idea of an ethnically mixed nation has been used to resist affirmative action policies and ignore the cultural rights of minority groups. When the Zapatista guerrillas burst out of the jungle in the southeastern Mexican state of Chiapas in 1994, indigenous Tzeltales and Tzotziles led by the urban white subcommander Marcos, Mexicans seemed startled by the very existence of these impoverished indigenous groups subsisting on the margins of Mexican society, with few economic or political rights.

Still, nowhere in Latin America is race as routinely determinant of social and economic outcomes as it is in the United

States. In America, racial boundaries have been written into policies, laws, and contracts for hundreds of years. They are hard to breach even in love: In 2013, only one in sixteen marriages involved spouses of different races. In 1970, the share was one in a hundred. In sixteen states, interracial marriage was illegal until the Supreme Court found antimiscegenation laws unconstitutional in 1967.

The Senate Committee on Foreign Relations underscored America's different understanding of racial identity in its 1920 "Investigation of Mexican Affairs" pursuant to Resolution 106 to "investigate the matter of outrages on citizens of the United States in Mexico." Imagine, it asked, "a greater or lesser percentage of foreign blood, principally Spanish, mixed with this original 57 varieties of Indian blood, the Spanish blood not being renewed or restrengthened, but growing weaker from generation to generation, and one may dimly perceive the outlines of the racial problems of Mexico."

In the United States, efforts by the Census Bureau to incorporate "mixed race" Americans have aimed to determine a person's distance from whiteness. In the nineteenth century it also used classifications like "mulatto," as it did "quadroon" and "octoroon," which relied on a person's share of white blood. Immigrants from across the Rio Grande went from having their own "Mexican" race in 1930 to being classified as "white" from 1940 to 1970 to being allowed to pick whatever racial classification they preferred in the last three censuses. Some racial categories have relied on skin color. Others—like American Indian, Chinese, or Filipino—on provenance. Others still, like Hindu, on religion. "Asian or Pacific Islander," which encompasses a universe of billions of people of vastly different ancestries, culture, histories, religions, languages, and skin tones, has also been deemed a race.

In 2000 the Census Bureau tried to acknowledge mixed identities by allowing respondents to tick as many boxes as they wanted from the six options on its form: white, black, Asian, American Indian or Alaska Native, Native Hawaiian or other Pacific Islander, and Some Other Race. This added up to sixty-three possible racial identities: the six single races, fifteen possible combinations of two, twenty combinations of three, fifteen of four, six combinations of five, and one grand mix of all six categories: white–black–Asian–American Indian or Alaska Native–Native Hawaiian or other Pacific Islander–Some Other Race. Americans were not interested. Fewer than three out of a hundred ticked more than one option. Never mind that genetic testing suggests a great deal of intermixing between Americans of African and European descent. As understood by most Americans, the universe offers but one racial box.

The hard racial borders are particularly challenging for Latinos. Fewer than 5 percent of Hispanics tick more than one racial option. Two-thirds say they are white. More than a quarter can't even find their racial identity on the census form, ticking "Some Other Race" and then writing in "Mexican" or some such on the dotted line. In 2010, "Some Other Race" turned out to be the United States' third-largest racial category.

This drives demographers at the Census Bureau crazy. They have tried for years to nudge Latinos from this ambiguous "other" racial perch. They have considered eliminating the "other" option altogether, to shoehorn Hispanics into one of the recognizable racial boxes. They have argued that Hispanic ethnicity is not a race to justify including two separate questions on the census form. They have turned around to argue that "Hispanic" should be included as a clear-cut racial category, to force Latinos to declare a consistent allegiance. Battling for a racial taxonomy of society, they have taught us just how arbitrary the classification turns out to be.

Race in the United States has long been a wall. After the

brief era of Reconstruction following the Civil War, racial discrimination became embedded in legislation across the Jim Crow South, segregating blacks from whites across public places, including schools, restrooms, and restaurants, even drinking fountains. The antebellum rule that a drop of African blood turned an otherwise white person black—a convenient definition that freed slave owners from responsibility over the children they sired with their slaves—was written into law across the states of the former Confederacy from 1910 through the 1930s.

Over the last century, race has determined where you could live, whether you could get a loan, how you could serve in the military, and whether you could get a federal government job. The very fight against racial discrimination, culminating in the Civil Rights Act of 1964 and the Voting Rights Act a year later, reiterated race as America's most relevant social marker. It upheld its place as the variable around which to organize society. Its measurement is, to this day, a critical tool of governance.

I have not been a victim of America's racial violence. I've never been frisked by a cop or lost a job because of my skin tone. My Latino identity might even have helped me get jobs at the *Journal* and the *Times*, which likely saw me as a desirable minority to count toward their diversity goals and dilute their image as bastions of whiteness. I nonetheless allow myself to ask whether there might not be a better way to engage with America's multiracial, multicultural reality.

America can't just "get over" its racial divisions. The notion that race should no longer count—that universities and government agencies should forget about fostering racial diversity, that the census should stop measuring the thing—seems ridiculous in the face of persistent discrimination. A century and a half after the abolition of slavery and more than fifty years since the Civil Rights Act, America is rife with blatant racism. Against the hi-tech backdrop of contemporary society, it stands as a bloody stain of nostalgia for a brutal past. Brushing off race in the pursuit of social justice would detach the narrative of American inequity from its most important thread. It is no coincidence that the political Right is vociferously calling for a race-blind society. It is the same political alliance that opposed the civil rights agenda from the start.

Though giving a leg up to perennially marginalized ethnic minorities must remain a priority in the project to build a just society, building social policy around racial borders cannot be the ultimate objective. There is not one racial grievance in America but many. Crafting policy around them would slice the United States into a collection of protocols defining people's conflicting claims to power and resources. Understanding America as a set of exclusive ethnic bastions vying for their share of the pie would further undermine what America most lacks: social trust. Without it, Americans will never build a commonwealth of shared purpose, and the United States will remain something less than a nation.

Californians saw this coming first. In 1994, more than five million of them went to the polls to reelect the Republican governor, Pete Wilson, to another four-year term. By an overwhelming margin, they also passed Proposition 187, the "Save Our State" initiative meant to protect native Californians from the peril of immigrants streaming across the southern border. It barred illegal immigrants from welfare programs and other nonemergency services, including public education. It required people running social welfare programs to report people they suspected of being in the country illegally to immigration authorities.

The foreign born had mushroomed to nearly a quarter of California's population by then, up from less than 10 percent in 1970. Governor Wilson deployed Californians' incipient fear of this ethnic transformation to sway voters unhappy at his management of a deep, protracted recession. Older Hispanics across the state will still remember Wilson's campaign ad with its grainy image of Latinos running down a highway near a border crossing as a voice-over warns, "They keep coming." Wilson also sued the federal government under the Constitution's invasion clause, which requires the federal government to protect states from such unwelcome intrusions, for failing to stop an "invasion" of undocumented immigrants.

Just as black men were demonized across the South as a violent menace to society, Prop 187 deftly leveraged fears of "illegal aliens" to stoke white voters' fear. "If these trends continued, a Mexico-controlled California could vote to establish Spanish as the sole language of California," wrote Linda Hayes, Prop 187's Southern California media director in a letter to *The New York Times*, "10 million more English-speaking Californians could flee, and there could be a statewide vote to leave the Union and annex California to Mexico."

Prop 187 would eventually be stopped by a federal court, which determined that it infringed on the federal government's exclusive purview over immigration law. But Wilson's political strategy proved of enormous consequence. To this day, Republican operatives ruefully acknowledge that the governor's scorched-earth tactics probably doomed the GOP's chances of ever regaining power in a state where some three in ten eligible voters are Hispanic. Yet the initiative to save Californians from immigrants from across the border served as an inspiration two years later for the immigration chapter of President Clinton's federal welfare reform package.

Undocumented immigrants were already barred from federal aid programs for the poor. Welfare reform for the first time specifically restricted legal immigrants' access to these programs, including welfare as well as food stamps and health insurance. It also gave states new powers to deny benefits to noncitizen immigrants. For Clinton, who was trying to disentangle voters' understanding of the Democratic Party as the party of welfare, it amounted to a political no-brainer.

"Quite frankly, I do not think that when we're cutting benefits and cutting welfare for our citizens, I don't see why we should stretch and say that we have an obligation to those that aren't even citizens of our own country," explained Representative E. Clay Shaw, Republican of Florida. As the Texas Republican Bill Archer put it, "My ancestors, and most of our ancestors, came to this country not with their hands out for welfare checks." These were not arguments the president wanted to oppose. What's more, the Congressional Budget Office projected that the restrictions on noncitizens' eligibility for benefits would generate 44 percent of the $54 billion in welfare reform's projected savings during its first six years of implementation.

Politicians like Shaw would not have highlighted this, but the immigration provisions in welfare reform had another objective. By reducing the supposed magnetic draw of federal welfare programs on poor people from Mexico and points south, it would serve the immigration policy goal of improving the "quality" of the immigrants admitted. George Borjas, an economist who served as an adviser to Pete Wilson during his 1994 reelection effort, has often argued that the quality of immigrants has declined since the old days, when immigration law barred all but people of northern European stock. In his book *We Wanted Workers: Unraveling the Immigration Narrative*, Borjas argued that new arrivals from the south are not only less productive than immigrants of the past. They are sapping America's homegrown strength. "Imagine that immigrants do carry some baggage with them, and that baggage, when unloaded in the new environment, dilutes some of the North's productive edge," he wrote.

The case rests on a few glaring misconceptions. Welfare, to begin with, is not much of a magnet. Sure, in 1995 about a third of

Hispanics benefited from some form of federal aid for the poor, but they were overwhelmingly citizens. "It could be argued that the law superimposed welfare reform's larger goals—promoting work and marriage and reducing welfare use—on a population generally characterized by comparatively low welfare use, high work levels, and a significantly greater likelihood of living in intact families than the native-born poor," wrote Michael Fix, Randy Capps, and Neeraj Kaushal in an assessment of the law's impact. Moreover, there is no evidence of either immigrants' inferior quality or of their deleterious effect on America's abilities. Between 1970 and 2016, the share of immigrants with at least four years of college under their belt rose from 9 to 31 percent. Among all people in the United States over twenty-five years old, as a whole, the college completion rate increased from 11 to 35 percent. Like Pete Wilson's campaign strategy, the immigration chapter of welfare reform rested pretty much on bigotry.

Immigrants suffered the consequences. For instance, in Los Angeles County, approvals of welfare and Medicaid cases for legal residents fell by 71 percent in the two years before January 1998 while remaining flat for citizens, according to an analysis for the Citizens' Commission for Civil Rights. "These shifts in immigrant approvals occurred despite the fact that legal immigrants' eligibility for the benefits did not change in California," wrote Michael Fix and Wendy Zimmermann. "The results, then, can be read to suggest that welfare reform, along with related policy changes, is having a profound chilling effect on eligible immigrants' use of public services."

Years later, a study by the economists Marianne Bitler and Hilary Hoynes concluded that in the wake of the Great Recession following the collapse of the housing bubble in 2008, the American safety net had nothing to offer the children of immigrants, even though they were mostly citizens. The damage was not limited to immigrant parents and their American-born offspring. In turning a cold shoulder toward yet another group of "others," the American political system loosened the screws keeping the nation together by a further revolution.

It started as a backlash against Lyndon Johnson's War on Poverty. Racial resentment turned whites not only against welfare programs but against the very notion of government as an agent to help the marginalized. "The Nixon era, in fact, marks the moment when the boundaries of social citizenship—the line separating those with a right to social assistance from those without—were being redrawn," wrote the sociologist Cybelle Fox. Though this turn is usually understood in the context of white hostility toward African Americans, Latinos and immigrants also found themselves on the wrong side of the line.

Latinos started on the road to become an illegal population in the 1960s. Almost nine out of ten Mexicans who arrived in the United States from 1955 to 1965 came as legal guest workers under the bracero program, which was set up during World War II to prevent shortages of farmworkers as American men were sent off to war. Only 1 percent arrived illegally. After the bracero program was ended in the mid-1960s, the flow switched: more than five in ten Mexican immigrants arriving from 1985 to 1995 entered the United States without the proper authorization.

Mexicans, and Latinos more generally, gradually came to be portrayed as a menace to the nation. In the 1980s, President Ronald Reagan called unauthorized immigration a "threat to national security." Terrorists, he said, were just "two days driving time from Harlingen, Texas," on the Mexican border. In the mid-2000s, the archconservative Pat Buchanan—former adviser to the Republican presidents Nixon, Ford, and Reagan—came up with the idea of the "Aztlan Plot," a Mexican scheme to recover the territory Mexico lost to the United States in 1848. "If we do not get control of our borders and stop this greatest invasion in history, I see the dissolution of the U.S. and the loss of the American southwest," he said. The political scientist Samuel Huntington took up the argument with glee: "The persistent inflow of Hispanic immigrants threatens to divide the United States into two peoples, two cultures, and two languages."

Pushing large swaths of Hispanics into the shadows of illegality helped create a large new underclass of brown Spanish-speaking foreigners with no legal grounds to remain in the United States. They provided both a willing labor force for American corporations and a killer argument against public assistance for the poor.

And so it continues. President Trump chose the Mara Salvatrucha—a gang formed in the early 1980s in Los Angeles by the teenage children of Salvadoran refugees who fled that nation's civil war—to become the face of immigration's threat to American society. Never mind that, though brutal, MS-13, as it is also known, is pretty small—some 10,000 strong out of a total gang membership of 1.4 million, according to government estimates, scattered in loosely organized cells across the United States. Never mind that it is pretty much American grown. If anything, MS-13 exported violence from the United States back to Central America. Never mind that it only really poses an existential threat to other immigrant teens in L.A. and Long Island in New York.

As the president raised the alarm over supposed violence spilling over the border into the homes of American citizens, he also promised to protect them from immigrants' needs. The Trump administration has done its utmost to prevent Central American migrants from requesting asylum in the United States, including separating children from their parents at the border. It has launched raids to weed out undocumented immigrants in cities across the country. And it expanded the "Public Charge" rule enshrined in the 1996 welfare reform package. While that rule made it tough for immigrants who had received cash welfare to become permanent residents, Trump's version would count all sorts of public assistance against them—including Medicaid, food stamps, and housing subsidies. "Those seeking to immigrate to the United States must show they can support themselves financially," declared former Secretary of Homeland Security Kirstjen Nielsen, when she first outlined the proposed rule.

The final rule issued by the White House in August 2019 was immediately challenged in court. If it survives the challenge, foreigners who apply for visas or green cards could be turned down not only if they ever collected government benefits, but also if they have low incomes, little education, or even a shaky command of the English language—clear signs, the administration claims, that they will likely depend on welfare in the future.

Homeland Security estimated that 2.5 percent of eligible immigrants would drop out of public benefits programs because of the change—saving the federal government about $1.5 billion in taxpayer money. It noted that the new rule could lead to worse health outcomes, more use of emergency rooms, and a higher incidence of communicable diseases, not to mention an increase in poverty.

The reform could also change the nation's immigration mix, discouraging migrants from poorer countries and promoting a whiter, more European immigrant stock. What the Department of Homeland Security failed to acknowledge was how its efforts to further pare back access to America's threadbare social safety net to keep the lazy, violent interlopers out will weaken the country it supposedly secures.

The United States will soon find it needs more immigrants. Barring immigration, the American economy is all but condemned to shrivel. In 2018 international migration helped rural counties record their second straight year of growth after many years of decline, according to the census. An analysis of the data by Jed Kolko, chief economist of the job placement service Indeed, found that in the absence of international migration, 44 percent of the population would have been living in shrinking counties, instead of 27 percent. Ten large metros—including Miami, Boston, and San Francisco—would have lost population.

Depressed immigration is already weighing on the economy. Pia Orrenius and Madeline Zavodny estimated that one of the main reasons the American economy rebounded so sluggishly from the Great Recession was the slow growth in the labor supply, caused in part by weak immigration flows. America's prosperity is riding on nonwhite others. Immigration has slowed the decline of Rust Belt cities and towns. Immigrants added more than one million people between 2000 and 2015 to an otherwise fading Midwest. And yet America's politics remain poised to stop it.

Even before Pete Wilson came around, California was already on the front line of the political battle pitting hardworking taxpayers—honest, patriotic, white of course—against a moocher alien underclass. On June 6, 1978, two-thirds of the state's voters in a referendum approved Proposition 13, the "People's Initiative to Limit Property Taxation." At a stroke, they not only cut property taxes on homes, businesses, and farms but capped future raises and pretty much forbade the government to increase them again, requiring a majority of two-thirds of legislators in both houses to approve any changes.

In the first year under the new system, property tax collections dropped 52 percent to $4.9 billion. By 2011, the average real estate tax rate in California was 60 percent lower than when the law passed, putting the state in twenty-eighth place nationally in combined state and local property taxes, according to the Washington-based Tax Foundation. Abruptly deprived of money, cities and counties cast around for new sources of revenue, quickly lifting California's sales tax to the highest rate in the nation. And they relegated California's public education to mediocrity.

It's worth pointing out that if California were a country, it would be the fifth richest in the entire world. It is probably the most socially progressive state in the nation. Nonetheless, California's school finances started falling well behind the national average around 1980. Since Proposition 13 became law, the state slid from seventh place in terms of spending per pupil from kindergarten through twelfth grade to twenty-second place. Today it spends $6,849 per child, according to data from the census, less than half what schools spend, on average, in New York. For every $1,000 in personal income, California spends only $33.30 in its public school system, which puts it twelfth from the bottom among the nation's states. California's classrooms are the most crowded in the nation, with one teacher for every 23.4 students. And its scores are lagging. In 2015, California fourth graders ranked third from the bottom in the National Assessment of Educational Progress tests in both reading and math. Fewer than three in ten kids in the state scored at proficient or higher.

Proposition 13 amounted to a cross-generational "fuck you" to California's nonwhite future. Older Californians voting for Prop 13 felt they had already paid their fair share for the state's public goods. Why should they suffer increasing property taxes to pay for the education of others' kids? What gave the argument its political potency was ethnicity—a mix of nationality and language, skin tone, religion, and culture. California's old-timers were overwhelmingly white. The newcomers who were sending their children into the public school system were, by contrast, brown immigrants.

Between 1980 and 1990, California received 38 percent of all the new immigrants coming into the United States, accounting for more than half the state's population increase of six million over the decade. Most were short, Catholic, brown, Spanish-speaking Mexicans. Why spend on them? As Dowell Myers put it, "If services were declining in quality, that was too bad for the newcomers, because it was their fault! Established California residents shouldn't be asked to pay for new residents they had not welcomed."

This logic has come back to haunt the state, though. The spigot of immigration is now off. California's population is aging fast. There are fewer than five residents of working age for each senior. By 2030 there will be fewer than three. And they will be dumber. Today California sits with Texas at the very bottom of the scale of American educational attainment: only eight of ten adults finished high school. Already one in five Californians live in poverty—a rate substantially higher than the national average. Still, Californians seem to be content with what they have wrought. In 2008, on the thirtieth anniversary of Prop 13, the Field Research Corporation surveyed Californians about the legislation: 57 percent supported it, exactly the same share that voted for it in 1978.

Here's one reason they may not be concerned about public education's depleted finances: The non-Hispanic white share of the school-age population in California has shrunk since the turn of the century, from 35 to 26 percent, and many white native-born Californians are dropping out of the public school system and moving to private institutions instead. The share of non-Hispanic white kids in the state's public schools shrank even more, from 37 to 24 percent.

California's experience is a shot across the nation's bow. It has long been one of the richest states of the Union; fifth from the top in 2017, measured by its average household income. It also suffers the highest poverty rate of all states, however. Nineteen percent of Californians live below the poverty line, as measured by the census's broad Supplemental Poverty Measure, which includes the impact on poverty of taxes, welfare pro-grams, and the cost of living. California is fourth from the top in terms of income inequality, after New York, Connecticut, and Louisiana. As America follows California into a less white, more ethnically diverse future, the demographer Samuel Preston's prescient warning thirty-five years ago comes to mind. Regard-less of the skin color of America's children, the future prosperity of the country depends on them.

CHAPTER 5

The Suffering of White America

The term "American dream" speaks to me of something specific: my grandparents' house in Phoenix.

They were the kind of iconic working-class white Americans Norman Rockwell loved to paint: not extremely well educated; honest, by and large; hardworking. They had lived through the Great Depression in Chicago and moved southwest, where my grandfather got a job as an electrician on the Salt River Project and my grandmother worked as a librarian. Retired, on Social Security, they lived a frugal but hardly uncomfortable life.

They believed in family values. They put a lot of faith in God. And they were racist, in that vague, matter-of-fact way bred of custom rather than reflection. Though they loved my mother intensely, small and brown and Mexican though she was, a couple of times I heard my grandmother blurt out casually, "We just don't like black people."

Their house wasn't big—two bedrooms and one bath; there was a date tree in the yard out front, a driveway with an awning in the back. It was on the wrong side of the tracks, south and west from the money in Scottsdale. But it was relentlessly air-conditioned, with plush green carpeting from wall to wall and a complicated, never-to-be-messed-with sound system. The huge TV in the den, the eight-track deck, the double-wide fridge, the pickup truck and the Pontiac in the back—all of it spoke of a prosperity that seemed at odds with my understanding of a working-class life.

Phoenix was booming then, powered by a burgeoning electronics industry with rich government contracts. Sun City had opened its doors on the west side of town a few years before I was born, drawing retirees from all over the country and fueling a long-lasting construction boom. The Vietnam War had fattened the metro area's defense contractors working on government-funded projects.

I didn't see my grandparents often. My parents moved to Mexico when I was six, to be near my mother's family. But I visited most summers throughout my childhood. They would pack me off to Sunday school, where I once learned that the European Community—ten countries at the time and growing—somehow presaged the coming of the Antichrist. Then we would flee town to a trailer perennially parked at the Hawkeye trailer park in Sedona—not yet known for its chakras and spiritual vortices—in the heart of Red Rock country.

In Mexico, where I was growing up, retired electricians didn't get this life. Tucked in at night, in a bed that doubled as the trailer's dining room table, I couldn't but marvel at my grandparents' prosperity. This was not an America of broadly shared prosperity, I understand. Their standard of living was mostly unavailable to people of color. Yet from my perspective growing up in Mexico, surrounded by a sea of poverty, my grandparents' America amounted to a fundamentally superior world.

The United States is still much richer than Mexico. America's average GDP per head is three times as large as when I was born. It is more than five times Mexico's. But despite these gargantuan riches, the exemplary working-class America I experienced in my grandparents' trailer doesn't exist anymore.

In many respects, the United States today is a pariah, an outlier at the bottom of the industrialized world's ladder of well-being. It is a country where too many babies die before having a solid shot at life and too many men and women die of despair, where too many children are mothers and too many men are locked away. And if you think minorities are alone the victims of America's many pathologies, you might want to think again.

A black baby born today will live three and a half years less than a white baby. The maternal mortality rate among black mothers is more than three times that of white mothers. Black teens have babies at twice the rate of white teens. Still, in 2014, more than twelve white American women died of pregnancy-related causes for every 100,000 births, according to the Centers for Disease Control. That's more than four times the rate in the Netherlands, three times the rate in Germany, and almost six times the rate in Spain.

The average white American baby born in 2018 will die at least two years sooner, on average, than newborn Germans, Danes, Greeks, and Portuguese; at least three years sooner than babies in Korea, France, and Australia; and five years sooner than newborns in Japan. Poverty rates show a similar pattern. There are nearly twenty million poor non-Hispanic white Americans, almost twice as many as poor blacks. About half of them live in extreme poverty, with incomes lower than half the poverty line. While the poverty rate among people of color has been gradually declining, among non-Hispanic whites it is higher than in the early 1970s.

We like to blame globalization. But globalization struck everybody, the French and the Germans and the Canadians and the Japanese. American society—its hospitals and schools, its roads and middle-class homes—buckled alone, in a uniquely American way. The America that built the most prosperous working class the world had ever seen collapsed into a heap of pathologies simply due to a lack of empathy. The greatest irony is that while the black and the brown suffered most intensely from the fallout, the collapse in social trust wiped away the American dream of working-class whites too.

Public goods are the indispensable glue keeping societies together. Societies normally pay for them collectively because nobody would individually. Think universal health insurance or public education or unemployment insurance, or even firemen, cops, and public roads—they provide society-wide gains greater than the benefits to any individual. White Americans concluded that if public goods had to be shared across ethnic borders, with people of other races, they would rather not have them.

That's why the United States failed to build the safeguards erected in other advanced countries to protect those on the wrong side of wrenching economic and social change. Americans may hope to rationalize the omission as some sort of historical inevitability, the only natural choice for a self-reliant people bred on a rugged, ungoverned frontier. But their choice to leave those sinking to sink further has a darker parentage.

The beleaguered white workers who lashed out at the cosmopolitan elites and voted for Donald Trump in November 2016 are perhaps not old enough to remember this. But in 1961, at the fourth constitutional convention of the AFL-CIO in Miami, Martin Luther King Jr. offered their parents help. He foresaw many of the forces besetting the labor market, eliminating what were once good blue-collar jobs. If the labor movement would ally with blacks, he offered, their combined political power might help ensure that working men and women shared in the bounty to be created in America's future.

"In the next ten to twenty years automation will grind jobs into dust as it grinds out unbelievable volumes of production," the reverend told the overwhelmingly white crowd of delegates. "The political strength you are going to need to prevent automation from becoming a Moloch, consuming jobs and contract gains, can be multiplied if you tap the vast reservoir of Negro political power."

King lamented how unions had "contributed to the degraded economic status of the Negro." He reminded the AFL-CIO delegates how black voters had stood with organized labor, contributing to defeat right-to-work legislation in Louisiana even as it swept through other southern states in the 1940s and 1950s, starving unions of financing by preventing them from drawing mandatory dues. "Negroes are a solid component within the labor movement and a reliable bulwark for labor's whole program, and should expect more from it exactly as a member of a family expects more from his relatives than he expects from his neighbors," Dr. King said.

The AFL-CIO delegates gathered in Miami nonetheless rejected the offer. Louisiana became a right-to-work state in 1976. The grand alliance between black America and its working class envisioned by King was not to be. To be sure, unionized black workers make more than their non-union sisters and brothers. Research has found that wage discrimination by race is worse in non-union shops. Today, 12.6 percent of blacks are members of unions compared with 10.6 percent of whites. Yet after a campaign deeply stained by overt racial hostility, 43 percent of voters from union households bought into Donald Trump's agenda, according to exit polls. The GOP candidate might have won barely 8 percent of African American votes, but he delivered the party's best performance among union voters in more than twenty years. These white voters provide an explanation of why America was so uniquely unprepared for an age of furious change.

To be sure, the combined forces of globalization and automation delivered a powerful blow. China's entry into the market economy single-handedly killed 2.4 million American jobs from 1990 to 2007, according to the economists David Autor, David Dorn, and Gordon Hanson. It cut the wages of workers in industries competing with China's cheap manufactures. It knocked workers out of the labor force and pushed many of them onto the disability rolls. China's influence ricocheted across communities, sinking whole towns into depression. For decades, economists argued that jobs would undoubtedly emerge in other industries to mop up the workers displaced by incursions from the Asian juggernaut. They didn't come.

This has become a standard explanation for American voters' embrace of Donald Trump's promise to wall off the United States from the rest of the world. Add automation, which also ripped through manufacturing employment, and imports from Mexico and other developing nations that integrated into the production chain of multinational American businesses, and you can weave a story of ineluctable foreign forces driving the American worker into the ground.

When you look around at the experience of America's rich peers, however, you don't find the same story. Populism may also be on the rise on the other side of the Atlantic. But though European economies rely much more on international trade than the United States does, in Europe trade remains a fairly boring topic. It does not evoke anything like the angst it inspires on this side of the Atlantic. That's because Europe's extensive welfare state allows European workers to cope with the labor-market instability that is part and parcel of open trade.

The United States, too, could have acted to compensate workers whose jobs were lost and whose lives were dislocated. It could have built more generous unemployment insurance programs, spent on retraining, offered wage subsidies maybe, invested in infrastructure to create good jobs where others had been lost. But beyond some token efforts it did not. The United States spends about 0.24 percent of its gross domestic product to support people out of work, the least among countries in the OECD. The Trade Adjustment Assistance program for workers displaced by trade absorbs less than 0.004 percent of the nation's economic output.

Trade and technological progress make the country richer. The additional riches might not be equally shared across the board, but the government could redirect some of the gains to shield vulnerable communities from the downside of change. It might even give them a stake in progress too. The process is not particularly complicated. It requires taxing winners and investing the proceeds in programs that help the losers cope with their loss.

The classic study by Dani Rodrik notes that countries that trade more have bigger governments. It's part of a deal: business supports the welfare state in exchange for workers' support for open trade. The same might be said of technological change. Projections of the future impact of automation on the workforce are all over the map. One 2016 study by McKinsey & Company concluded that it would bump up to one-third of American workers out of their current occupational categories. A natural response might be to invest in retraining to help displaced workers acquire new skills for new jobs, as well as unemployment insurance and other supports for the workers suddenly deprived of employment.

A social safety net to protect the vulnerable offers many positive spillovers that benefit all citizens in society. Gareth Olds, an economist and data scientist, found in one study that the availability of food stamps increases entrepreneurship among poor families: they can afford to take more risks if they know they will be able to afford food. He also found that having access to the Child Health Insurance Program increased self-employment among poor families by 15 percent. In France, extended unemployment insurance boosted firm creation by 25 percent simply by allowing unemployed workers who started a business to keep their government benefits.

In *Wealth and Welfare States*, Irwin Garfinkel, Lee Rainwater, and Timothy Smeeding argue that "the primary reason why all rich nations have large welfare states" is that their broad economic and social benefits exceed their costs. The social safety net mitigates economic insecurity, promoting risk taking. Public education and health insurance also build and support productive human capital.

Consider health care: Treatment for substance abuse has been found to reduce crime; as drug use declines, so does drug-induced violence and violence associated with the drug trade. Theft to finance addictions declines too. Researchers at the University of Kentucky and Emory University concluded that increasing access to Medicaid reduces violent and property crime rates because poor addicts get more treatment. Jacob Vogler, a young economist seeking his PhD at the University of Illinois at Urbana-Champaign, estimated that the Affordable Care Act's Medicaid expansions resulted in cost savings of $13.6 billion just because of the reduction in crime.

By contrast, consider the high social cost of living in a country where the safety net has been left to wither. Across the world, countries with more robust systems of public support consistently best the United States across a range of straightforward measures of welfare: fewer dead babies, fewer dead mothers, longer life spans, lower poverty, better childcare, less addiction.

The American tragedy is that its political system was never able to stomach Rodrik's deal, largely because white America could not shake its understanding of social welfare as an undeserved gift to people of another race. Fewer than one in four whites accept they are the main beneficiaries of the welfare state. In a 2016 YouGov poll, two-thirds of whites said blacks take more from society than they give. Only 24 percent acknowledged the same for people of their own race. Just one in six whites said the government does a lot to help white people like themselves. Two-thirds said it does a lot to help blacks.

Every group shares this belief. Blacks and Hispanics believe the American government mostly helps whites, not people like themselves, according to the poll. People in both minority groups see themselves on the "giving" side of the "givers vs. takers" question, and put whites on the "takers" end. Whites' biases matter more, however. They hold political power.

FDR thought the only way he could build a safety net was by limiting its benefits to whites. Decades later, Lyndon Johnson proved him right: extending America's network of public assistance to the black and the brown cost him white support for a safety net of any kind. When the first black president of the United States tried to expand it by adding health insurance, a common feature across Europe for decades, the Republican Party—which by then had become the virtually exclusive domain of white voters from the South and rural America—set itself to stop him at all costs. To the untrained eye, Americans simply seem tightfisted. Reality, again, is darker.

More than 15 percent of American children live below the Census Bureau's supplemental poverty line, which counts the benefits of government programs on families' incomes. More than half live in families making less than twice the poverty rate. This is unheard of among rich countries. By international standards, which count as poor all those who draw less than one-half the income of families exactly in the middle of the spectrum, the United States suffers the fifth-highest child poverty rate among thirty-six countries in the OECD. That's higher even than Mexico's.

Spending on antipoverty programs has increased since the 1960s. In 1967, taxes and government transfers increased the share of children in poverty by 1 percentage point. By 2012, taxes and transfers moved about 11 percent of kids out of poverty. Today, the government adds $8,800 to the income of the poorest fifth of American households, raising them to $24,600 a year.

It is still clearly inadequate, though. By the OECD's count, the American government devotes under one-fifth of its gross domestic product to spending on "social" priorities like unemployment insurance, health benefits, and antipoverty programs. That puts it in the bottom half of countries in the grouping. Germans dedicate one-quarter of their GDP to such endeavors. The French devote almost a third of their economy to these tasks.

Whatever white Americans think, they are as a group the biggest beneficiaries of public spending on social programs. Tax credits and government assistance programs benefited 6.2 million whites without a college degree in 2014, compared with 2.8 million black Americans and 2.4 million Hispanics of similar educational backgrounds, according to the Center on Budget and Policy Priorities.

Under a definition of welfare that includes the earned income tax credit, a tax subsidy for workers with low earnings, and the child tax credit for low-income families with children, nearly four in ten working-class non-Hispanic white adults—people eighteen to sixty-four who are not in school and live in a household where nobody has a bachelor's degree—live with somebody who receives some government benefit.

White Americans may not fully realize it, but their vote against the black and brown welfare queens they charge with abusing the social safety net has left their struggling white brothers and sisters without a net to fall back on. Skimping on a system of social welfare that they viewed as an illegitimate handout to the black and the brown, they were undermining everybody in America.

The region of the Great Lakes was the cradle of the American industrial economy. From Minnesota through western New York into Pennsylvania and West Virginia, it made America's cars and dishwashers, its steel and chemicals. When new competitors deploying new technologies moved into their markets, many of the companies and the local economies they supported withered away. The young left. The middle-aged and the old, those least able to relocate or retool for a new world, stewed as the industrial-era prosperity they had come to believe their birthright faded away.

The share of working-age adults with bachelor's degrees across the region is well below the national average; in West Virginia, home to coal and chemicals, less than one in five adults over twenty-five have one. But the American economy now has few good jobs for high school graduates who didn't go to college. The typical worker in West Virginia, in the middle of the pay scale, makes only $14.79 an hour, $3 under the national median.

West Virginia is one of the whitest states in the nation: 95 percent of the population is neither Hispanic nor of color. It is the ultimate irony that West Virginians' suffering has been exacerbated by white voters' unwillingness to extend any sort of helping hand to blacks. They suffer one of the highest poverty rates in the country. More than a third of the state's children are on some form of public assistance—seven percentage points more than the national average.

Donald Trump campaigned in the state offering workers to turn the economy back in time and restore it to the presumed happy equilibrium of half a century ago, when West Virginians could go straight from high school to a job in the coal mines, steel mills, or chemical plants that dotted the state. But erecting tariffs on foreign steel, as President Trump did in his second year in office, can do nothing for the state's beleaguered workers.

What West Virginians need today are resources to contend with the furiously changing economy. The state has lost four in ten manufacturing jobs since the year 2000. Jobs in agriculture, mining, manufacturing, and construction—the traditional guy jobs that President Trump claims he can restore—make up less than a fifth of total employment, down from almost a fourth at the turn of the century.

West Virginia's main problem is that barely over a quarter of eighth graders in the state are proficient in reading and science; one in five meet that level in math. The state ranks tenth from the bottom in terms of high school completion among people over the age of twenty-four. Of those who finish high school, in 2018 only 28 percent took the SAT test to apply to college, less than the 36 percent nationwide average.

The biggest threat to America's future is what it is doing to its children. What West Virginia's children desperately need is public investment in their human capital. White Americans' effort to build a public education infrastructure designed to cut the nonwhite out is coming back to bite them.

Universal high school education was one of the single most important developments that set the United States apart, lifting it above its peers. By the early twentieth century, young Americans were much more educated than children in almost every European country, where education was still a preserve of the upper crust. Broad-based education gave Americans of lesser means the tools to prosper in an increasingly sophisticated economy, helping propel American prosperity beyond the wildest dreams of every other advanced country. As the labor economists Claudia Goldin and Lawrence Katz wrote in their book *The Race Between Education and Technology*, the U.S. education system "put the elite systems of Europe to shame."

In the years after the Civil Rights Act, public education proved essential to the emancipation agenda. Starting in the 1960s, schools all over the South were forced to desegregate by court order. By the 1970s, they were among the most integrated in the country. But racism proved hard to crack. Courts started releasing schools from desegregation orders around the turn of the century, ending the effort to integrate black, white, and Hispanic kids. When George W. Bush became president in 2001, 595 school districts across the country were under court-mandated desegregation orders, according to an analysis by

ProPublica. By the end of his administration the number had fallen to 380. The changes were justified under the argument that almost half a century after the Supreme Court mandated the end to educational segregation, the problem was pretty much solved. In any case, it was no longer a problem requiring court supervision. Schools resegregated as fast as they could.

In 1972, ProPublica found, only a quarter of black students in the South attended intensely segregated schools where at least nine out of ten students were racial minorities. In the school districts that have been released from desegregation orders since 1990, the share today is more than half. Scholars at the Brookings Institution concluded that in 2010 the average black student's public school had a white enrollment of less than 25 percent, down from around a third in 1980.

In 2014, Catherine E. Lhamon, the assistant secretary of education for civil rights during President Obama's second term, sent a "dear colleague" letter to states, school districts, and schools in which she underscored how fifty years after the Civil Rights Act desegregated the nation's schools, American education remained split by race and class.

Lhamon chronicled "chronic and widespread racial disparities in access to rigorous courses, academic programs, and extracurricular activities; stable workforces of effective teachers, leaders, and support staff; safe and appropriate school buildings and facilities; and modern technology and high-quality instructional materials." The shortchanged children are inevitably black and brown. States' and school districts' inability to provide enough resources to ensure a quality education across the board "further hinder[s] the education of students of color today."

Only about one in four blacks and one in five Hispanics over the age of twenty-five have at least a bachelor's degree. For non-Hispanic whites the share is one in three. The economists Martin Carnoy and Emma García found that black and Hispanic students who attend schools with mostly black and Hispanic kids are falling further behind those who attend more integrated schools.

Baltimore offers reason for pause. Its schools were never forced to integrate. Under pressure from the federal government to comply with the Civil Rights Act, in 1976 Baltimore sued, gained an injunction, and decided segregation was not its problem. So it built one of the most segregated school systems in the country. As white families fled to the suburbs or private schools, public education ended up serving mostly black kids: 92 percent of the students enrolled in Baltimore's public schools are people of color. It has served them badly. Some 4,000 students of the 6,500-strong class of 2004 managed to graduate from high school. Six years later, 434 had obtained a four-year college degree. Another 86 had finished a two-year program at a community college. For the rest, education failed.

There is a cost to shunting black and brown students to lower-performing schools, compounding their many deficits of opportunity. It is felt, intensely, in black and brown communities. What white Americans fail to acknowledge is that they too bear the cost. As William Frey argued in *Diversity Explosion*, these nonwhite kids are going to be called on to support the American economy.

Without access to a quality education, this nonwhite labor force will not have the wherewithal to support the many retired white boomers in our future. A worker in Baltimore with nothing but a high school certificate typically makes $28,496 per year. That's even less than the median earnings for high school graduates across the nation, of $29,815. It's hard to support a family on that kind of money. It is barely over the poverty line for a family of four. Segregated into lower-performing schools, America's future nonwhite workforce will be unlikely to generate the kind of tax revenues needed in coming decades to maintain the extra-large contingent of boomers in retirement.

The segregated school systems modeled around racial bias have failed the most vulnerable white students too. The sociologist Sean Reardon has documented how the academic achievement gap between the rich and the poor has grown bigger than that between blacks and whites. Fifty years ago, the black-white proficiency gap was one and a half to two times as large as the gap between a child from a family at the top ninetieth percentile of the income distribution and a child from a family at the tenth percentile. Today, the achievement gap between the poor and the rich is nearly twice as large as that between black and white children. The achievement gap that remains between whites and blacks or Latinos is mostly due to social class: African Americans and Hispanics are much more likely to be poor.

Higher education is increasingly the preserve of the elite. Only one in twenty Americans aged twenty-five to thirty-four whose parents didn't finish high school has a college degree, according to a 2014 analysis by the OECD. The average across twenty rich countries, it found, is almost one in four. Less than one in seven undergraduates at the most competitive colleges come from the poorer half of American families. The poor half mostly end up in community college. Sixty percent of students in community college come from families making less than $65,000 a year. In community college, their American dream mostly dies: One study by the Department of Education tracked students entering community college in 2004. After six years, one in three had obtained some degree, 18 percent were still at it, and 46 percent had dropped out.

Race gave inequity its first opportunity, underpinning the inevitable border that divided educational opportunity between the privileged and everyone else. It plowed a field between us and them upon which we could sow new dimensions of disparity.

· · ·

Disparity pinches intensely in places like Fall River, Massachusetts. This overwhelmingly white town lies barely fifty miles south of Boston, the bull's-eye of America's educational excellence, where students go to Harvard, Tufts, Brandeis, and the Massachusetts Institute of Technology. Five of the nine sitting justices on the Supreme Court studied at Harvard Law School.

In Fall River, however, the pedigree counts for little. Once the largest textile-producing center in the country, today Fall River suffers a 20 percent poverty rate. The typical household has an income of just over $39,000, a little over half the state average. More than four out of ten local children live in households receiving public assistance.

Few of them expect to make their way to Harvard or MIT. Less than 15 percent of adults over twenty-five have managed to get a bachelor's degree. More failed to finish ninth grade. Of those who make it into college, most will probably aim for a two-year associate degree at Bristol Community College. Odds are that only one in five will have gotten one within three years. Fewer than half will graduate.

Fall River offers a more accurate rendition of the state of American education than Harvard. The story starts before children experience their first day at school. As Jane Waldfogel, an expert on child and family well-being, reported in *Too Many Children Left Behind*, a book she co-authored with scholars from Canada, Britain, and Australia, poor children in the United States enter kindergarten more than a year behind their richer peers. They are seven times more likely to have been born to a teenage mother. Only half live with both parents, compared with 83 percent of the children of college graduates.

The children of less educated parents suffer higher obesity rates, have more social and emotional problems, and are more likely to report poor or fair health. Because they are much poorer, they are less likely to afford private preschool, let alone the extra lessons, tutors, music and art classes, and elite sports teams that richer, better-educated parents lavish on their children. Once they get into the public school system, they are shortchanged yet again.

George W. Bush's No Child Left Behind initiative demanded that schools focus on improving the performance of children on the bottom rung of the socioeconomic ladder. Barack Obama's Race to the Top aimed to turn around low-performing schools and pushed performance metrics to assess teachers and schools. In New York, Michael Bloomberg as mayor closed big public schools and encouraged smaller ones that could experiment with both the pedagogy and the curriculum. For decades Republicans have pushed vouchers for families to pay for parochial schools and opt out of the public system. Democrats and Republicans are championing charter schools, exempt from many of the laws and regulations binding public schools.

The experimentation, however, has done little to mitigate the most damaging feature of American education: its entrenched segregation. By allowing the most committed parents in underprivileged neighborhoods to escape from their schools, the solution has, to some extent, exacerbated education's inequality of opportunity.

The truth is, the only way to overcome these inequities is to build a society that truly invests in enhancing opportunity for everybody. Until then, public education will fail not just students of color but all those children who start a few steps behind. As noted in the 2013 OECD report, "Socioeconomic disadvantage translates more directly into poor educational performance in the United States than is the case in many other countries." In Fall River, four out of five people are white. About 45 percent of its white children live with a single parent. Public schools are failing them too.

Half a century ago, Americans were floored by Daniel Patrick Moynihan's assessment of the damage caused by economic upheaval to African American families. "We have shown a clear relation between male employment, for example, and the number of welfare dependent children," he wrote. "Employment in turn reflects educational achievement, which depends in large part on family stability, which reflects employment."

It is no longer a minority pathology. Almost three in four black babies and just over half of Hispanic children are born to single mothers. But so are a third of non-Hispanic white children. As Maria Cancian and Ron Haskins wrote in a study on low-income families, "It seems reasonable to conclude that nonmarital births will continue to swell the ranks of female-headed families for the foreseeable future."

Tupelo, Elvis Presley's birthplace in the northeastern corner of Mississippi, is ground zero of the American family's decline. There was a time when it offered more than rock-and-roll nostalgia. It had a specialty: upholstered furniture—the kinds of big, comfy recliners favored by mid-century American males. Then came the Chinese. Chinese imports of upholstered furniture and similar goods on which Tupeloans relied for a living soared. The local economy was devastated. Manufacturing employment has been slashed by 40 percent since 2001 in the surrounding Lee County. Overall employment has grown only 4.5 percent in nineteen years. Wages are up only 5 percent, after inflation. And the imploding job market took the family with it. By 2017, half of all children in Tupelo lived with a single parent.

The family is doing fine among well-heeled Americans. But for the roughly two-thirds of adults who never got a college degree, the institution has become pretty shaky. In 2012, more than eight in ten college-educated women between the ages of forty and fifty-five were married. Among white women in this age group holding at most a high school certificate, the marriage rate was closer to two-thirds. Among less educated black women it was less than half.

Less educated women are much more likely to be parenting alone. In 2010, 45 percent of white children and 75 percent of black children whose mothers had a high school degree or less lived with a single parent. Their lives will be extra tough. Almost half of children living with single mothers lived below the poverty line, four times the rate for kids living with married parents. Studies have found how boys raised by single moms in tough environments—without a male role model to look up to—are more likely to tune out as teenagers, fail at high school, never go to college, and repeat the pattern of deprivation of their dads.

As Moynihan recognized half a century ago, what broke the American family was the collapse of a labor market that had for decades enabled men with nothing more than a high school certificate to provide. At their peak in the 1960s and 1970s, four in ten white husbands and more than half of black husbands could be considered "working class," toiling for a decent wage in either manufacturing, construction, transportation, or utilities, Professor Cherlin wrote. By 2010, less than one in three had this kind of job.

Over the last thirty years, the wages of men with no more than a high school education plummeted by a fifth. In a society increasingly segregated by race, education, and income, where the well-to-do marry the equally prosperous, the less educated women who had to pick a mate from a pool of failed men chose instead to remain alone. After the traditional male-breadwinner working-class family buckled, Professor Cherlin noted, "nothing stable has replaced it."

Conservative advocates like to wrap these trends into a morality tale: Coddled by government welfare programs, American men decided the burdens of matrimony were too irksome to bear. Women on welfare, meanwhile, decided they didn't need a man when the state could provide. Predictably, the American political system doled out tough love to solve the problem.

President Clinton nixed the poor's entitlement to welfare, promising he would incentivize work, boost two-parent families, and reduce births out of wedlock. Years below, the government targeted noncustodial fathers as a source of money to reduce their children's burden to the public purse. In 1986, Congress passed the so-called Bradley Amendment, named after the Democratic senator and former basketball star Bill Bradley, which triggered automatic penalties for fathers who were overdue on their child support, regardless of their circumstances or ability to pay.

Since then, strict enforcement of child support has pushed many men into the gray economy, off the books. Young men have been subjected to wage garnishments and even prison to enforce child-support orders that can remain in place even when they lose their jobs or go to jail. Mothers and kids, meanwhile, have benefited little because more child support usually means a cut in public benefits. Court-ordered child support for women receiving public assistance goes to the state to offset state support.

What's been missing is a congruent response to Moynihan's core insight: the middle-class American family broke down because its economic underpinnings gave in. Policy should serve the goal "of enhancing the stability and resources of the Negro American family," he wrote so many years ago. Just scratch "Negro" from the sentence, and you have a great proposal for everybody.

This is not about morality. By any conventional standard, Tupelo should be pretty virtuous. After all, it is home to the American Family Association—formerly known as the National Federation for Decency—on the front line of the culture wars since 1977. Almost two-thirds of Tupeloans define themselves as religious believers. Tupelo's problem is about job opportunities.

Not to rub it in, but in France, too, the family is under stress. Marriage rates declined sharply over the last two decades. Unlike Americans, though, French mothers and fathers stuck together. In France, the child of an unmarried couple will probably grow up in a relatively secure financial environment with a cohabiting mom and dad. More than 76 percent of French children live with both parents. Less than 69 percent of American kids do.

France's choices reflect a different culture. It is more relaxed about cohabitation outside marriage. But more important, it has a more generous approach to social insurance and welfare. When French workers were clobbered by hi-tech globalization, the French government provided the economic undergirding for fragile families to survive. It spends about 3.7 percent of its gross domestic product on family benefits—including allowances for children, paid parental leave, and free childcare. This amounts to more than three times the share spent in the United States, according to OECD data.

In the United States, a single forty-year-old parent who has two kids, aged two and three, and makes two-thirds of the average wage will have to fork out more than her entire earnings to pay for childcare, according to an OECD analysis. In France, where the government guarantees universal childcare and sets rates to ensure affordability, that parent would pay only 5 percent of her wage.

Families at the bottom end of French society did a better job overcoming the economic shocks of the last quarter century simply because France's welfare state didn't let them fall that far. Taxes and government transfers reduce the poverty rate among French families by more than three-fourths, from 37 to about 8 percent. In the United States they shave it only modestly, from 27 to 18 percent.

Material support is critical to maintain the economic argument for mothers and fathers to stick together, and it remains critical when families nevertheless break apart. Only 15 percent of French kids living with a working single parent are poor. If the parent doesn't have a job, the share rises to just over one-third. In the United States, by contrast, poverty traps one out of three kids raised by a working single parent and over nine out of ten children with a nonworking single mom or dad. It's not hard to figure out who made the better choice.

It's not as if the French are happy with the taxes they pay. The *gilets jaunes* protests that shook France starting in 2018, sparked by a hike in gasoline taxes, were motivated by a sense among many French workers that their government institutions—a tax regime riddled with loopholes for the rich; deteriorating public services for working men and women like them—have broken with a social compact that promised increasing well-being for all.

Still, there is nothing in France like the uncompromising resistance in the United States to government and the services it provides. In France, tax revenues amount to over 46 percent of the nation's economic output. Government—federal, state, local—makes do, altogether, with 27 percent of GDP.

White Americans are hurting themselves in a variety of ways. Nowhere outside a war zone are there as many guns in circulation as in the United States. The National Rifle Association will argue that Americans' enthrallment with firearms is all about an ironclad belief in the Second Amendment. In truth, it owes a lot to racial mistrust. During the civil rights movement, when blacks started carrying guns to protect themselves from white extremists, and the cops, California's governor, Ronald Reagan, signed into law the Mulford Act, which prohibited carrying loaded guns in public. These days, whites are more than twice as likely as African Americans to own and carry guns, according to data from the Pew Research Center. They are more than twice as likely to reject gun control measures. Racism—often articulated as fear of black violence—counts among their main motivators. One study by researchers from Australia and Britain found that "symbolic racism"—expressed, for instance, by skepticism that slavery had made it harder for blacks to get ahead—explained much of whites' love for firearms. "Attitudes towards guns in many US whites appear to be influenced," they wrote, "by illogical racial biases."

The ultimate irony is that the whites who are arming themselves to protect themselves from some potential black violence are suffering most directly from America's abundance of guns. As Jonathan Metzl points out in his book *Dying of Whiteness*, gun suicides by whites skyrocketed from the late 1990s to the middle of the second decade of the twenty-first century, even as firearm homicides plummeted. By 2015, non-Hispanic whites accounted for more than 19,000 of the 20,779 suicides by firearm.

Consider, again, incarceration. There is little exceptional about Dearborn County, Indiana. Like much of rural America, this county twenty miles west of Cincinnati is relentlessly white. Over three-quarters of its fifty thousand or so residents track their ancestry to either Germany, Ireland, or England. Only 2.7 percent identify as people of color.

Dearborn is living the standard story of America's economic transformation. The typical household in the county takes in about $58,000—a little less than the national average. Less than one in ten of Dearborn's residents are poor. But like the rest of small-town America it is sliding inexorably behind, victim of economic forces sucking jobs and opportunity toward the large urban centers along the coasts.

Since 1990 the county has lost more than a fourth of its manufacturing jobs. Wages, on average, are a little lower than they were back then. Dearborn's population is not only shrinking but aging. Productivity, measured as the dollar value per worker of the county's economic output, has been declining at a pace of around 1.2 percent a year. Unsurprisingly, perhaps, many of the locals have taken to meth, prescription opioids, and heroin to relieve the pain.

The government's response? Dearborn puts more of its residents behind bars than any other county in the nation. About one in ten of Dearborn's adults are incarcerated or on probation. Far from the crime-infested urban enclaves of popular imagination, in which scary gangs of young blacks and Latinos rampage through the night, Dearborn has become the unlikely poster child for America's uncompromising strategy to deal with social dysfunction.

Primed to understand themselves as under siege by forces outside their control, white Americans will look upon Dearborn and ask where the world went wrong for them. Small towns will brew with resentment at the metropolitan elites who somehow deprived them of opportunity and at foreigners they fear might mooch off their taxes or take their jobs away. Few will acknowledge the responsibility of a white America that was unwilling to lend a hand to help Americans of another color and crafted a social strategy around throwing the losers in jail.

In the first decade of the twenty-first century, people in rural, suburban, and urban areas were all about equally likely to go to prison, according to an analysis in *The New York Times*. Today, people in small, overwhelmingly white rural counties are some 50 percent more likely to go to prison than people in urban America.

The damage of America's love affair with prison will reverberate down generations. More than half of all inmates have children who are minors. Those kids are almost five times more likely to be expelled or suspended from school than the children of free men and women. The economists Anna Aizer and Joseph Doyle Jr. found that putting minors in juvenile detention reduced their odds of graduating from high school and raised their odds of being imprisoned as adults.

Residents of neighborhoods with high incarceration rates are much more likely to suffer depression and anxiety, even among people who have never been to prison, according to a study of Detroit residents by researchers from Columbia University and Wayne State University. After a certain point a high incarceration rate will stoke criminality. Ex-cons return to their old neighborhoods having picked up undesirable behaviors in jail. Weighed down by a criminal record, unable to get a job, they are left with few choices but to hang out with their old buddies in crime.

Cons and ex-cons face legal restrictions on employment, access to social benefits like public housing, and eligibility for educational benefits. Some states remove parental rights and restrict civil rights, such as the right to vote, serve on juries, and hold public office. By putting such a large share of its upcoming workforce behind bars, the United States is condemning them, and itself, to failure.

Maybe one can hope that Americans can leave behind their characteristic racial hostility and work to build an inclusive society. In any event, they are more willing to extend a hand to the losers of economic change when they recognize themselves among the victims. The share of white babies born out of wedlock today is greater than that of black babies when Moynihan wrote his famous report. But nobody is saying that whites of loose morals are becoming enmeshed in a "tangle of pathology." As Ta-Nehisi Coates wrote, perhaps the term "pathology" "is something reserved for black people."

When crack cocaine gripped inner-city neighborhoods in the 1980s, Washington's response was a war on drugs. Over the next three decades, imprisonment rates for drug offenses multiplied by ten, to 143 per 100,000. This exceeds by half the average incarceration rate in western Europe for all crimes.

The main targets of the war, other than Mexicans and Colombians, were blacks. African Americans sell or indulge in illicit drugs about as often as whites, according to a report by the National Academies of Sciences. But 1.3 percent of black Americans were arrested for drug offenses in 2010, almost three times the rate for whites.

These days America faces another drug epidemic, but the addled this time around are mostly white. Growing numbers of middle-aged white men and, to a lesser extent, women are medicating themselves with opioids, graduating from prescription Oxycontin and fentanyl to heroin, which is cheaper. They often kill themselves along the way. Nearly thirty-five thousand people died from opioid overdoses in 2015.

The plight of working-class white America was put in stark relief by Anne Case and Angus Deaton. In a couple of seminal studies, the researchers found that death rates from suicide, alcohol and drug poisoning, alcoholic liver disease, and cirrhosis soared over the last quarter century among white Americans in their early fifties: to about 80 per 100,000 people, about double the average in other rich countries.

The death rate is rising principally among the less educated. In 2015 the drug, alcohol, and suicide mortality rate of non-Hispanic white men in their early fifties remained under 50 per 100,000 for those who had a bachelor's degree or more but soared to around 180 per 100,000 for those who had at most a high school certificate. In 1999, Case and Deaton wrote, a non-Hispanic white American aged fifty to fifty-four without a college degree had a 30 percent lower mortality rate than an African American of the same age and of any education level. By 2015 white Americans with no college were 30 percent more likely to die than blacks in that age-group. Similar mortality crossovers showed up between blacks and less educated whites in all age-groups from the late twenties to the early sixties.

Professors Case and Deaton call these deaths of despair.

"We propose a preliminary but plausible story," the researchers wrote, in which progressively worsening job opportunities for working-class whites with relatively low levels of education trigger an accumulation of disadvantages "in the labor market, in marriage and child outcomes, and in health." African Americans may die at a higher rate than whites, but they don't kill themselves as often. Roughly 26 out of every 100,000 non-Hispanic white Americans aged forty to fifty-nine kill themselves, according to government statistics. Among Latinos and blacks of this age, the suicide rate hovers around 7 per 100,000.

White workers without a college degree are killing themselves, in other words, because they have lost their claim on prosperity. In a recent study, economists Justin Pierce and Peter Schott found that death rates from suicides, drug overdoses, and other poisoning jumped in counties where jobs were most exposed to imports after the United States allowed China to enter the World Trade Organization. The death toll rose most notably among white men, who had dominated the best jobs in the manufacturing industries that were suddenly exposed to a steady stream of Chinese imports.

Critically, the policy response to this new crisis of addiction is proving different from the knee-jerk reaction to drugs that put so many black Americans in jail. The Senate is not about to appoint a new drug czar. The Drug Enforcement Administration isn't sending agents with arrest warrants into rural white communities. Politicians from the president on down are talking about a public health crisis, not a war.

In 2016, Congress passed the Comprehensive Addiction and Recovery Act, which would expand access to naloxone—the drug that can pull addicts back from the brink of overdose—as well as medications to combat addiction. Special drug courts have emerged around the country, offering addicts supervised rehabilitation.

Between 2011 and 2016, spending on Medicaid-covered prescriptions to treat opioid addiction and overdoses rose from under $400 million to over $900 million. Even as Republican senators were working to dismantle President Obama's expansion of health insurance over the fall of 2017, they called for tens of billions of dollars in federal funding to pay for drug rehabilitation programs in their states.

The question is whether this moment of white plight might teach white voters something about the importance of solidarity. The United States desperately needs to build the public goods other societies have put in place to shield their most vulnerable populations from the ravages of savage economic change. To build such a safety net requires overcoming a long tradition of racial mistrust, of racial fear, of racial condescension. It requires building an American dream that is open to everybody.

Phoenix has hit a rough patch in the last couple of decades. Its population has tripled since I was a kid, to 1.6 million. Its working class, though, hasn't prospered much. The income of the typical family has shrunk 10 percent since 2000. Phoenix's ethnic mix has changed: Whites "with Spanish surname" numbered 40,000 in 1960, less than one in ten city residents. Today Latinos account for over 40 percent of the population, and the share of non-Hispanic whites has shrunk by half. The latter are not very happy with this turn of affairs. In the twenty-four years up to 2016, residents of Maricopa County, where Phoenix lies, elected as sheriff Joe Arpaio, who during the last decade of his tenure embarked on a scorched-earth campaign against "illegal immigrants" that swept up anybody who looked Latino.

My grandparents' house was demolished in the 1980s to make way for the Red Mountain Freeway, stretching east toward Papago Park and the more affluent community of Scottsdale. The neighborhood has acquired a harsher edge. The child poverty rate hovers around 30 percent. Half the children in the zip code live with a single parent. Half rely on public assistance to make ends meet.

My grandparents died years ago. The economy on which they had built a life in a home with plush carpets, an eight-track, and a Pontiac in the back has fallen apart. From my vantage point as an American adult, the space once occupied by that house on the wrong side of the tracks speaks of America's failure.

CHAPTER 6

Tearing Ourselves Apart

The places that are shaping contemporary American politics aren't big cities like New York and San Francisco. They aren't the vanguard of American metropolises, at the frontier of technological progress. They are not seats of power. The story of American politics is being written in places like Macomb County, Michigan. Their tales share the distinct flavor of failure.

Stretching northeast from Detroit's suburbs, Macomb looks more like the past than the future. It is aging faster than the nation as a whole. It is relatively uneducated. Having relied for years on steady assembly jobs at the plants of General Motors, Ford, and Chrysler, open to anybody with a high school certificate, few of Macomb's workers bothered to go to college. Less than a quarter of the county's residents over twenty-five have a bachelor's degree. When the automotive industry embraced automation, replacing the good jobs it had once offered Macomb's modestly educated workers with machines, they discovered themselves ill-equipped for the new moment in the nation's economic history.

Since the turn of the century, Macomb has lost a third of its industrial jobs, as well as a quarter of its construction jobs. The county's new economy has offered no refuge to its displaced. Manufacturing, mostly putting cars together, is still the biggest employer, but according to an analysis by Macomb Community

College and the nonprofit Data Driven Detroit, three-quarters of the car industry's job postings require a bachelor's degree. More than four in ten health-care jobs also require completing four years of college. Across all industries, the share is half. Though Macomb is by no means poor—its families are still richer than the national average—it is getting there: the annual earnings of men working full-time have plummeted 22 percent since 2000.

Macomb remains notably homogeneous: 81 percent of its population is what the census calls non-Hispanic white. African Americans account for only 11 percent of county residents; Latinos for 2.4 percent. The locals, however, fondly recall the days when the county was much whiter: in the year 2000 more than nine out of ten residents in Macomb were white and not Hispanic.

Change is coming, though. Migrants from abroad have accounted for 60 percent of the county's population increase over the last six years. The demographic change has been so drastic that Macomb's majority white working class was more than willing to channel its anxiety over lost jobs and stagnant wages into a fear of demographic change and accept Donald Trump's invitation to blame their plight on someone else of darker skin. Having voted in two consecutive elections for the nation's first black president, in November 2016 they turned around and gave the county, and arguably the state of Michigan, to Trump. He won the county by 48,348 votes. His margin in the entire state was only 13,107.

After the election, stunned Democrats descended on Macomb to try to figure out what had just happened to a working class they had once thought of as their own. Democracy Corps, led by the veteran Democratic pollster Stan Greenberg, joined with the liberal Roosevelt Institute to perform focus groups with white men and women who defined themselves as Democrats or independents—they had voted for Barack Obama in 2008 or 2012—but had switched their allegiance to Trump. They uncovered a wealth of racial mistrust. Macomb's voters, they concluded, have "pretty powerful feelings about race, foreignness, and Islam that lead them to see white people as victims in a country feeling increasingly foreign to many of them."

The electoral swing was not subtle. I find it hard to wrap my head around how any voter could side with a thoughtful, African American intellectual with a profound grasp of policy and swerve, four years later, into the embrace of an anti-intellectual, old, white, racist demagogue. But the change underscores how abruptly white Americans' racial mistrust is reacting to new demographic realities.

Greenberg first polled in Macomb in 1985, when he was trying to figure out how a reliably Democratic suburb packed with loyal union members could have delivered a landslide to Ronald Reagan. He discovered a stark border of fear and mistrust between an aggrieved white "us" and a lazy black "them." The border had a place in geography too: Detroit's Eight Mile Road.

When he returned in 2008, however, blacks had been replaced as the object of white voters' contempt. The new targets were immigrants. "Detroit didn't come up. Nobody was blaming blacks," Greenberg told me. "Had I administered a test on racism, they would have scored badly, but racial relations were not central." Outsourcing was the enemy at the time; so was NAFTA.

By the time Trump declared his candidacy, Macomb's voters had settled on immigrants as the most important threat to their status. Trump's voters in Macomb—older, white, not Latino—could not fail to see that they are not the county's future. Were it not for migration, the county's population would be declining. In a time of shrinking economic opportunity, the anxiety generated by this demographic shift turned them decidedly inward.

Trump's discourse offered a thinly veiled promise that

whites could recapture a beloved old country where the good jobs were plentiful and the colored people were both scarce and powerless.

The nostalgia of Macomb's frazzled white voters is understandable. Their lives have become precarious. It is hardly surprising that they feel left behind by history. Yet their appetite for the easy answers offered by Trump—pitting an aggrieved white "us" against a foreign-sounding nonwhite "them"—offers few real solutions. Indeed, it augurs ill for any hopes that the United States could develop the generosity needed to build the collective response the nation's challenges call for.

Macomb offers a people clutched by fear of the other. The fear can be applied to blacks or to immigrants, to Muslims or simply to people who live in other countries. Whatever shape it takes, it does not leave much room for solidarity. It makes an ill fit for a country that is becoming less white with each passing year. With more economic disruption looming, increasing ethnic diversity will provide fresh kindling for the race-based, ethnically targeted, culturally framed hostility that has gripped the American political system. America's race-tinged politics have new depths to plumb.

Have you seen the Coca-Cola Super Bowl ad in which "America the Beautiful" is sung in a bunch of foreign languages? There are cowboys in it, but also people of color—Asians and Latinos, a street in some Chinatown, a woman in a head scarf. Many of Macomb's white men and women didn't buy it. "I just don't know why they can't all sing it in English, since it's America," said one respondent in the Democracy Corps focus group. When they heard Bobby Kennedy's legendary statement about America's "special burden to help black Americans make their way," many felt like the young American woman who answered, "Get over it. . . . Their own people sold them to us. Why don't they sue their own people?"

These attitudes have reshaped Macomb's politics over the

past half century. In 1960 it was the most Democratic suburban county in the country. John F. Kennedy won 63 percent of the vote there. Lyndon Johnson took 75 percent. But Democrats' embrace of civil rights—granting to blacks rights that had been held exclusively by whites—put an end to their dominance. In 1967, racial tensions in neighboring Detroit exploded into one of the nation's first urban race riots. In the 1970s, bitter disputes erupted over the busing of black children from poor urban schools into the whiter, more affluent schools in the suburbs. And Macomb's politics flipped. In 1972, Macomb embraced the Republican Party. In 1984 two-thirds of Macomb's voters turned out for Ronald Reagan.

In *Middle Class Dreams*, where Greenberg sets out to explain Reagan's landslide, Macomb's white voters are defined by their distaste for black America. "Blacks constituted the explanation for their vulnerability and for almost everything that had gone wrong in their lives," he wrote. When he asked the many white voters who had defected from the Democratic Party about Bobby Kennedy's take on America's responsibilities toward blacks, he got answers like "that's bullshit" and "no wonder they killed him."

The racial hostility of Macomb's disgruntled whites has lost some of its potency since the Reagan years, but only to a point. They might have voted for a black president in 2008 and 2012, but they were also voting against a specific enemy: an executive elite that was happy to outsource their jobs and replace them with robots and cheaper foreign workers. While the object of their fears might have shifted from blacks to Mexican immigrants, their mistrust of people of color remained as unassailable as ever. Preferential treatment of blacks "needs to stop," one woman told Greenberg's pollsters in 2016. "They have been given special preferences by getting in schools when they are not qualified just so that they can get the education, getting the job that they are not qualified for and everything else." An older woman in the focus group added, "We are now the ones that are the minority and they are the majority."

A guy called Steve told his story about how he was denied a so-called Bridge Card to access government benefits after losing a job at a Coca-Cola plant when he blew out his back. "We'd be at the grocery store, just looking at each other. How are we going to pay for all this and I'll see somebody with a basket full of stuff, loaded with—just overloaded—use a BRIDGE card wearing top of the line stuff, $500 purse and then they walk to an Escalade." Another guy, William, complained about struggling to get hot dogs for his kids while others used their government benefits card to get a porterhouse steak: "And I'm being told that I'm wrong or I'm racist or I'm not the . . . I'm privileged and that's what is wrong."

Race isn't Macomb's only dividing line. Mistrust can as easily be ignited by citizenship or language or religion. Mary said she was scared of the idea that the United States may become a majority-minority country because immigrants no longer take the trouble to assimilate American values. Another guy fumed at the immigrants in the Medicaid office who probably have access to food stamps. "I'm all for everybody having the American dream," he said. "But I feel that it's being taken away from a lot of people by people coming and taking advantage."

Building a coalition for a cohesive America, one that can overcome its ethnic dividing lines, will require freeing Macomb's pissed-off whites from the grip of race-based fear. From their perspective, though, the gains made by blacks and other racial minorities—equal legal rights, a shot at economic opportunity—have come directly out of their own hardworking hide. Many might have voted twice for a black president. They are nonetheless nostalgic for the country they lived in fifty years ago, when blacks had no shot at political power.

. . .

Big chunks of America share the pain of Macomb's blue-collar white voters. A poll by Ipsos and Reuters taken on the day of the presidential election found that 61 percent of Trump supporters said they felt like strangers in their own country, while 73 percent agreed with the idea that "more and more, I don't identify with what America has become."

They are troubled, fundamentally, by demographic change. Fifty years ago, non-Hispanic whites made up more than four-fifths of the population of the United States. Today their share has shriveled to less than two-thirds. On the "losing" side of these demographic shifts, working-class white voters embraced a candidate who promised to make their kind of America great again.

A few months before the election of 2016, Professors Autor, Dorn, and Hanson, together with the Swedish economist Kaveh Majlesi, released a study of the impact of trade on Americans' political preferences. They examined congressional votes in 2002 and 2010 in electoral districts that were the most exposed to China, where people tended to work in industries that competed directly with Chinese imports. These people were the most vulnerable to the surge in imports from China once it gained stable access to the American market after it was invited into the World Trade Organization. They were driven to extremes.

Voters in Republican congressional districts that recorded large increases in imports from China tended to replace moderate legislators with conservatives. Voters in Democratic districts exposed to the trade shock from China either turned to liberal Democrats of the Bernie Sanders persuasion or flipped to conservative Republicans directly. Race, unsurprisingly, made a difference: minorities tended to break to the liberal left when exposed to imports; whites, instead, broke toward the conservative right.

The realignment ultimately gave the presidency to a candidate who launched a trade war with China, barred many Muslim immigrants from the United States, and promised to both build a wall to stop Mexicans and others from entering the country and pull the United States out of the North American Free Trade Agreement. In a subsequent study, Autor and his colleagues applied their methodology to the nation's most closely contested states in the presidential election. They concluded that if the penetration of Chinese imports had grown only half as much as it did, the Rust Belt states of Michigan, Wisconsin, and Pennsylvania would have elected Hillary Clinton rather than Trump.

China alone didn't put Donald Trump in the White House. In research for the Democracy Fund Voter Study Group, John Sides found that attitudes about trade or government spending cannot account for voters' shift to the Republican Party between 2012 and 2016. Even those most opposed to more liberal trade were hardly more likely to vote for Trump than they were four years earlier to vote for the Republican hopeful Mitt Romney.

Rather, Sides found, voters were guided to Trump by their feelings about immigrants, black people, and Muslims. "No other factor predicted changes in white partisanship during Obama's presidency as powerfully and as consistently as racial attitudes," he concluded. The nation's first black president helped bring home an awareness to these voters that their days at the helm of political power were coming to a close.

China's rise played a role, for sure, offering a credible challenger to the United States' uncontested hold on global power. But the "China shock" shifting American attitudes wasn't just about lost jobs. "Both growing domestic racial diversity and globalization contributed to a sense that white Americans are under siege by these engines of change," noted the political scientist Diana Mutz. "White Americans' declining numerical dominance in the United States together with the rising status of African Americans and American insecurity about whether the United States is still the dominant global economic super-power combined to prompt a classic defensive reaction among members of dominant groups."

In 2015 non-Hispanic whites were a minority of the population in 24 of the nation's 100 largest metropolitan areas. That's 10 more than in 2010 and 19 more than in 1990. The trend is bound to accelerate. William Frey's book notes that between 2010 and 2030 the population of working age will lose fifteen million whites and gain twenty-six million from minority groups—mainly Latinos and Asians but also blacks. Non-Hispanic whites are projected to make up less than half the population of the entire country by the early 2040s, down from 85 percent fifty years ago.

Social psychologists have been studying how the sense of ethnic threat colors people's attitudes. Experiments by the social psychologists Jennifer Richeson and Maureen Craig found that white Americans who were informed that they will no longer be a majority of the population in a bit over two decades expressed more negative attitudes about Latinos, blacks, and Asian Americans and a more automatic pro-white and anti-minority bias. What's more, their politics shifted to the right.

Politically unaffiliated white Californians who were told about the state's growing Hispanic population were much more sympathetic to Republican positions than those who weren't exposed to information about their shrinking demographic footprint. This applied not just to views about race but also to race-neutral issues such as support for health-care reform. Whites who were informed about the demographic shift toward a more Hispanic America became more hawkish about defense spending. But if they were also reassured that white Americans would remain at the top of the heap despite the population dynamics, earning higher incomes and amassing more wealth than minorities, they did not embrace more conservative positions.

"These results suggest that rather than ushering in a more

tolerant future, the increasing diversity of the nation may instead yield intergroup hostility," wrote Craig and Richeson. Losing economic and demographic ground—in dead-end jobs at stagnant wages—blue-collar white Americans are shaping their political positions around their perception of racial threat and lashing out at a system that they have come to believe is rigged against them, the nation's rightful owners.

The world's liberal order is at stake. White Americans' ethnic fears are not only affecting domestic policy; they are reshaping their understanding of the United States' place in the world. Research by Mutz and her colleague Edward Mansfield suggests that racial mistrust is perhaps the most important determinant of people's feelings about globalization, broadly writ: whites who are prejudiced against other ethnic groups also tend to believe that the United States is superior to other countries and that it should refrain from engagement in world affairs. The more whites feel boxed in by rising minorities, the more they will distance themselves from other cultures.

The political scientist Shahrzad Sabet performed a nifty experiment to detect the impact of "us versus them" feelings on people's attitudes toward trade. People who believed the United States is superior to other countries, she found, were much more likely to accept more imports from another country if they were told this would benefit a company called "Gordon & Roberts" than if the company that would gain were named "Tuntyakore & Zideying." The second one was simply too alien. "Cultural distance from trading partners more than doubles the level of opposition to international trade," Sabet wrote.

The demographic threat to whites' dominant status at home is mixing in with the uncomfortable sense that the United States is no longer quite the preeminent global hegemon most Americans would like it to be. This is fueling a powerful bout of insecurity. In 2011, 38 percent of Americans endorsed the view that the United States "stands above all other countries in the world," according to a survey by the Pew Research Center. By 2014, the share was down to 28 percent. The drop has been most precipitous among Republicans. They are reacting by giving the cold shoulder to the entire postwar liberal order.

"For white Americans, the political consequences of racial and global status threat seem to point in similar directions with respect to issue positions," Mutz wrote: "opposition to immigration, rejection of international trade relationships, and perceptions of China as a threat to American wellbeing." President Trump's argument that the United States has been had by its trading partners, weakened by foreign trade, amounts in her view to an astute attempt to capitalize on the status threat experienced by his base of working-class white voters.

The analysis portends dark times for American politics, split between white voters set on protecting past prerogatives and lashing out at the forces of change, on the one hand, and a growing constituency of minorities who demand a say in setting the direction of the nation, on the other.

In 2014, midway through President Obama's second term, Ta-Nehisi Coates wrote a blockbuster essay in *The Atlantic* making the case for reparations from white Americans to the descendants of African slaves. He pointed out that generations of blacks continued to suffer from discrimination, often enforced and mandated by the state, long after slavery was abolished. Race-based oppression ranged from redlining of predominantly white neighborhoods to prevent black families from settling there, to the erection of a criminal justice system seemingly designed to remove black men from the streets.

This is not a brand-new idea. John Conyers, the veteran African American politician who represented parts of Detroit in the House from 1965 through 2017, introduced a bill calling to examine slavery and propose remedies back in 1989 and kept reintroducing it in every Congress since then. In 2019, several Democratic contenders for the presidency, including Senators Kamala Harris of California, Elizabeth Warren of Massachusetts, and Cory Booker of New Jersey and the former housing and urban development secretary Julián Castro, expressed their support.

The idea is not universally popular, though. A YouGov poll commissioned right after Coates's essay appeared found that whites disagreed pretty decisively with his prescription: Only 6 percent of white Americans, compared with 59 percent of blacks, agreed that the government should offer cash reparations to the descendants of slaves. Less than one in five whites—compared with almost two-thirds of blacks—agreed that the government ought to compensate slaves' descendants by offering them more education and job training. And only one in seven whites, compared with one in two blacks, agreed that slavery played a major role in blocking African Americans' success today. In 2016, a Marist poll asked the reparations question again. White support for reparations had increased to 15 percent.

The typical African American household makes only about 60 percent of what the typical white household takes in. The share of blacks in poverty is twice the share of whites. According to surveys by Pew, 70 percent of blacks think that discrimination is partly to blame. Only 36 percent of whites agree. Four in ten blacks say their blackness has stood in the way of success. Among less educated whites who have no more than a high school diploma, three-quarters claim their race has not provided them with any advantages in life.

It is perhaps unsurprising, then, that whites and minorities would disagree on what the government should do to heal the nation's socioeconomic ills. Almost two-thirds of white Americans would like the government to be smaller, raising fewer tax revenues and providing fewer services, a Pew survey found. By contrast, six out of ten blacks and seven out of ten Latinos would prefer the government to be bigger. In 2016 only 28 percent of white respondents told Gallup pollsters that the government had a major role in improving the social and economic status of blacks and other minorities, compared with almost two-thirds of blacks and Latinos. Three of four blacks and two of three Hispanics—but less than half of whites—favored affirmative action programs.

Race shapes Americans' views of the future. More than four in ten blacks believe the country will never make the changes needed to give blacks equal rights with whites, according to a Pew poll released a few months before Trump was elected president. Only one in twelve whites agreed with them. Six in ten white Republicans believe, in fact, that the country worries too much about race. Only a third believe more changes are needed to give blacks equal rights with whites.

Most white Americans think that the nation has done more than enough to expiate the sin of slavery, a belief that was exacerbated by Barack Obama's successful run for the White House. After his victory whites became much more likely to discount claims of racial discrimination, polls found. His success eroded whites' already weak support for affirmative action and other policies designed to favor racial minorities. If a black man could be elected president, they reasoned, the United States must have achieved racial equality; policies to balance the playing field were no longer needed. Instead, they concluded, something had to be done to prevent the playing field from tilting further against their interests.

If anything, demographic change will widen the gulf between white and nonwhite opinion. Consider that in the foreseeable future ethnic minorities are going to account for almost all of the nation's population growth. The only segment of the white population that is growing is over sixty. From 2000 to 2017, the white population under eighteen years old shrank in forty-three states, according to Frey's analysis. Were it not for minorities, America's younger cohorts would be shrinking.

This pattern is tailor-made for explosive battles over resources. Ruy Teixeira and Robert Griffin, researchers at the left-leaning Center for American Progress, report that 83 percent of Trump voters in 2016 believed minorities would put too much pressure on government resources. Called on to pay for the education of black, Latino, and Asian kids, white senior citizens are likely to dig in their heels.

Minorities are likely to rely more heavily on the public purse for some time. The sociologist Daniel T. Lichter suggests that if the demographic profile of poverty remains the same as it is today, by 2050 over 70 percent of America's poor will be minorities. Support for the safety net might also flip. Though they tend to be more supportive of government spending than non-Hispanic whites, this may not hold when working-age minorities realize that their payroll taxes are paying for older whites' Social Security and Medicare.

Can Americans overcome their racial mistrust to build a semblance of a cohesive society? To do so will require restoring empathy to that place in the American heart that has been colonized by loathing and fear.

Remember the book *The Emerging Democratic Majority?* Published in 2002, during President George W. Bush's first term, the analysis by Teixeira and the journalist John Judis made a big splash with its claim that demographic change would eventually deliver the government to Democrats pretty much forever. It predicted that the Republican base of white males would inevitably lose its power to determine control of the White House and Congress. Blacks, Hispanics, and other minorities—natural Democratic constituents—would inevitably tilt the balance the other way.

It is certainly not impossible that demographic change might transform America into a social democracy in the mold of western Europe by delivering a stable Democratic majority. In 2016, Teixeira and Griffin found, whites without a college degree cast only 42 percent of the national vote. That is almost twenty percentage points fewer than they did in 1992. At this pace, it is hardly far-fetched to predict a coalition of minorities achieving the electoral clout to impose their preference for higher taxes and a bigger government on a reluctant white minority.

Yet if the last election has taught us a lesson, it is that translating demographic change into political power will be anything but straightforward. Minorities have not shown much evidence that they can build the kind of stable cross-racial coalition that would be needed to rewrite the social contract. More critically, any attempt to leverage demographic clout to, say, beef up redistribution and build a more robust social safety net will be resisted by threatened whites as an illegitimate act of expropriation. These whites will be hanging on to political power for a good many years still.

The Chinese disruption of American politics might have run its course. The great global outsourcing of manufacturing production that gathered steam after China's entry into the World Trade Organization early this century appears to have reached a plateau. China is no longer the source of ultracheap labor it once was. The United States has probably already lost all the industrial jobs it had to lose. The manufacturing industries that remain are highly automated. There are fewer than thirteen million industrial jobs left in the country.

Still, it is premature to say America's populist outbreak is over. There are other economic disruptions awaiting over the horizon. The economist Frank Levy argues that even if artificial intelligence were to replace only a modest number of jobs—some truck drivers made redundant by self-driving trucks, some cashiers replaced by touch screen registers—it could nonetheless support a disproportionate populist backlash.

America's racial reconfiguration still has a long way to run. For all the references to the melting pot in American textbooks, for all the stories about an immigrant nation with a lady in New York harbor inviting the world's hungry masses in, the United States remains in the grip of its historical race-based antipathies. They have evolved. Racial politics are no longer solely about blacks and whites, and they are not confined to the South. But they are as powerful as ever. As the nation becomes browner with each passing year, whites' sense of dread of their demographic future will increase the power of race as a political force, deepening the nation's divides.

Before the 1965 Voting Rights Act gave blacks a shot at political power, whites in the South voted heavily Democratic.

It was June 11, 1963, when President Kennedy first proposed the civil rights bill on national television. Between April 6 and June 23 his support among southern whites measured by Gallup polls plummeted thirty-five percentage points, according to a study by the economists Ilyana Kuziemko and Ebonya Washington. The nation's racial partisan reorganization was under way. In 1960, all the senators from the eleven states of the former Confederacy were Democrats. In 2019, nineteen of the twenty-two were Republican.

Today, racial sorting has extended beyond the South, overwhelming other alliances to become the prime determinant of political allegiance. In 1992, white voters who had at most a high school education were more likely to favor Democrats over Republicans, according to polls by Pew, attached to the party by their links to organized labor. By 2016, though, they had flipped to the Republican Party by a margin of twenty-six percentage points.

Democrats have lost the white vote nationwide in presidential elections since the mid-1970s. In 2012 nonwhites made up about 45 percent of the votes for President Obama but only 11 percent of those for his Republican rival, Mitt Romney. Only one out of a hundred of Romney's voters were black.

American politics have become, first and foremost, about race. The Republican Party is today a vehicle for the political expression of white anxiety over demographic change. The Democratic Party, meanwhile, has all but given up on its traditional alliance with working-class white men. The racial sorting has reshaped politics into an existential battle between two radically distinct forces that offers next to no space for compromise.

The political scientists Michael Barber and Nolan McCarty have documented the rising ideological polarization in Congress starting in the 1960s. As conservative white southern Democrats switched parties, they drove the GOP further and further to the right, even as blacks in the South and Latinos in the West and the Northeast moved the Democrats in a liberal direction. As voters took sides, they bought into wholesale ideological packages rather than picking between policy positions. The conservative Republicans most rabidly opposed to the social safety net also tend to fervently oppose abortion, gun control, and gay marriage. Democrats, in turn, bought into a package that includes support for abortion rights and for renewable energy. Over time, moderate Republicans and centrist Democrats disappeared.

"As the public discourse around issues of social welfare, immigration, national security, and a whole host of other issues becomes highly racialized and explicitly hostile, the potential for open racial conflict may rise," noted Valentino, Neuner, and Vandenbroek. "As these negative attitudes toward racial out-groups become increasingly tightly tied to parties, polarization increases and gridlock and a lack of legislative compromise ensue."

Barber and McCarty argue that polarization has stymied the government's response to rising economic risks that are eroding the well-being of the working class. Globalization and technological change did not affect the United States alone. But Washington proved uniquely incapable of responding to mitigate their impact on the working class. While rich countries in western Europe deployed policies to protect their workers and slow the rise of inequality, successive governments in the United States just let market forces rip. When the dust settled on the 2016 election, Democrats not only had lost the presidency but ran only sixteen of fifty governorships. Republicans controlled both houses of Congress, while Democrats had the fewest House seats since the 1920s. Whites without a college degree, Democrats discovered, were really pissed off.

America's new politics of identity have turned the old notions of race-based privilege and oppression on their head. White Americans see themselves not as perpetrators of racial subjugation but as victims of a misguided campaign to redress overstated racial wrongs. They are more than willing to fight to take America back to when they could guiltlessly assert their privileges. Regardless of the merits of Coates's and others' case for compensation to redress centuries of oppression of black Americans, the argument not only is toxic to all the white "losers" of the nation's demographic change but further inflames an aggrieved constituency that is itching for a brawl.

It is hard to overstate the political challenge. A more cohesive America won't simply come about when minorities beat whites at the ballot box. The question is how to build a social compact that offers solidarity across ethnic lines. To start answering it, we must first change the conversation about what it is that ails us. The accountability debate—tallying crimes to establish historical debts—is important, I understand. But it hasn't much helped anybody. Instead, it has undercut the idea of a common ground on which we must all stand. It forgets that the most important question is not who owes what to whom but how to build a true commons across the racial divide.

As the political philosopher Danielle Allen pointed out in her essay "Toward a Connected Society," "In asking us to think about how in the present we should rectify past wrongs, it too dramatically shifts our attention from what should be our focus: how to build fair and just structures of opportunity in the present in the context of great demographic diversity."

It might sound ridiculous to argue that this requires soothing whites' fear, but the United States will not become a nation that tends to everybody without them. Presidential elections in the near future will be decided in counties like Macomb, white enclaves around the Rust Belt where displaced manufacturing workers are itching to punish somebody for their downfall. These white voters have not come to terms with the unassailable fact that they will soon be in a minority. They are not quite willing to accept that it would be best if they attained this status in a nation that guaranteed equal rights and opportunities to all. Increasingly, they think of themselves as the resistance.

While there may be a stable Democratic majority in America's future, built on the strength of minority voters, between now and then American politics will be consumed by whites doing their utmost to prevent the transformation. That will make for grim race relations and dead-end politics.

In 2016, 14 percent of Americans—including 12 percent of whites and 21 percent of blacks—said racial relations between the two groups were "very bad," according to Gallup. This is twice the share it recorded in 2001. Mistrust is growing among Latinos, too. Hispanics' view of relations between Latinos and whites is at its worst since 2005 and 2006, when the federal government and a variety of states tried to pass punitive legislation to crack down hard on undocumented immigrants.

Two-thirds of Americans—and three-quarters of African Americans—say the nation is riven by black-white conflict, polls by the Pew Research Center found. That is more than those who sense a clash between urban and rural dwellers, young and old Americans, and even the rich and the poor. In the face of such hostility, it will be hard to build a modern nation that can care for all Americans in the face of globalization and technological change.

Political incentives, in fact, suggest more political polarization is in the cards. Trump got to be president by overtly prodding the racial biases of working-class whites. Six months before the presidential election, a Pew poll recorded that 37 percent of African Americans and 41 percent of Latinos believed race relations were getting worse. By December 2017, just under a year into Trump's presidency, the pessimism had extended to 51 percent of blacks and 50 percent of Hispanics. Overall 60 percent of Americans thought Trump made race relations worse.

He has worked hard to exacerbate these tensions. He animates his base with periodic rants at immigrants bringing ills to the United States. He has offered subtle support for racial bigots like the white supremacists marching through Charlottesville, Virginia, in 2017. And he has appropriated much of their language, like when he invited four Democratic members of Congress—all women of color; all citizens—to leave the United States and "go back" to where they came from. Though he campaigned on a promise to restore the prosperity of the old blue-collar middle class, his policies hewed closely to the standard Republican playbook. He cut taxes and further limited government welfare. His attacks on the social safety net, on the ostensible grounds that it saps people's drive and encourages sloth, drew strength from the same mistrust that Friedrich Engels detected across the ethnic fault line that in nineteenth-century America divided Germans from Italians from Poles. By calling on government agencies to require that all recipients of government assistance get a job, President Trump was catering to blue-collar whites' belief that Uncle Sam routinely dips into their pockets to hand out their money to undeserving blacks.

But President Trump didn't build America's racial divide.

Ethnic hostility precedes his racist pitch for office. It precedes the presidency of Barack Obama, that fleeting moment when it appeared Americans could build an inclusive national project that breached the barrier of race but was ultimately snuffed out by the most toxic partisan warfare in generations. It precedes the administration of Bill Clinton, whom the African American author Toni Morrison dubbed the "first black president," who ended the poor's entitlement to government aid, scrapping assistance to people who didn't hold a job. The racial divide—breeding mistrust, standing in the way of an egalitarian society—is as old as the idea of an American nation. One of the capital questions to ask now is whether America's hi-tech postmodernity might yield a store of solidarity to overcome a wall built, bolstered, and refurbished over 250 years.

A universal basic income, Silicon Valley's favorite proposal for an imagined future when robots have taken over all but the most creative jobs, looks like a heavy lift for a political system still engrossed in arguments over whether the poor deserve to be helped. Even the rival proposal of guaranteed government jobs that would pay a living wage for able-bodied people to do, er, something faces a steep uphill slog to persuade a citizenry fundamentally hostile to taxation and redistribution.

The Trump administration even devised an argument to oppose the nation's remaining welfare programs. In the summer of 2018, the president's Council of Economic Advisers issued a report that deployed a few unorthodox assumptions to conclude there was little poverty to speak of in America. It measured poverty using data on consumption, which is more unreliable than the common approach based on income. It based its conclusions on a poverty definition derived from the cost of a basket of food in the 1960s, a measure most academics today consider outdated. The most unusual feature of the report was its implicit celebration of government aid, noting its critical importance in reducing poverty. This flatly contradicts Ronald Reagan's fabled assertion, long since become Republican orthodoxy, that the government fought a war on poverty and lost. It sits oddly in a report that, almost in the next sentence, promised to reduce the poor's "dependency" on government assistance by expanding the requirement that beneficiaries of aid first hold a job.

Could we learn from Europe? Writing about America's social dysfunction, I have often relied on the social democracies of western Europe as both a point of comparison and a source of inspiration. Few European countries are richer than the United States. Nowhere in Europe appears to be able to deliver the kinds of technological breakthroughs that come out of Silicon Valley. But as I pointed out earlier, most western European countries have built a consensus that values social well-being writ large. Across Europe health is considered, in effect, a human right, so European countries have built health-care systems to ensure it. Children's well-being is a valued priority, so European countries have developed a variety of programs to support families with kids. Many European governments also encourage employment among the poor. They manage to do so without resorting to the stigma righteously proffered by American welfare reformers. Instead, they provide training.

When it comes to building a new political regime, Europe, unfortunately, has little to offer the United States. If anything, influence seems to be propagating in the opposite direction: Europe's more inclusive political consensus is under siege by the same racial hostility that split America against itself. Social democracies built from the rubble of World War II in the middle of the twentieth century—when all Swedes were tall and blond, when virtually all the French were either Catholics or former Catholics—have proven too fragile to resist the burgeoning antipathy toward "others" who have begun to arrive in large numbers from Europe's old colonial outposts and elsewhere in the developing world. Muslims in Germany and Africans in Italy are igniting ethnic passions similar to those that have forever constrained the American state. They threaten to peel away at European social democracy and transform it into a project more like America's—streaked through with lines demarcating the end of "us" and the start of "them."

Right-wing "populist" parties have been gaining ground across Europe, largely powered by opposition to immigration among blue-collar Europeans. The Alternative für Deutschland gained 13 percent of the votes in the 2017 German election, up from just under 5 percent four years earlier, when it failed to meet the threshold to enter the Bundestag. In Britain, the UK Independence Party's share of the vote rose from 2.3 to 13 percent between 2005 and 2015. The Five Star Movement, which was founded just over ten years ago by a literal clown, walked into power in 2018 with a third of the Italian vote.

Marine Le Pen of the xenophobic National Front garnered one-third of the vote in the second round of the French presidential elections. The Swiss People's Party has also registered electoral gains, as have the Austrian Freedom Party, the Sweden Democrats, the Party for Freedom in the Netherlands, and the Danish People's Party. A report led by the political scientist Yascha Mounk for the Tony Blair Institute for Global Change concluded that the share of votes in European elections going to populist parties—those claiming to represent "the true will of a unified people against domestic elites, foreign migrants or ethnic, religious or sexual minorities"—rose from 8.5 percent in 2000 to 24.1 percent in 2017. As of 2017, fourteen European countries had populist politicians in government, twice as many as in 2000. While they are strongest in the former communist countries of the Soviet bloc, their share of the vote in western European countries also rose, from 4 to 13 percent, over the period.

The shift is motivated, first and foremost, by fear—often

irrational—of immigration. Three economists, Alberto Alesina, Stefanie Stantcheva, and Armando Miano, set out to measure attitudes toward immigrants across rich countries. Perhaps their most singular finding is that people generally have no clue as to how much immigration there is. Swedes think immigrants make up over a quarter of the population—some ten percentage points more than reality. The French believe 30 percent of the people living in France come from abroad, which is twice the immigrants' actual share. The same pattern holds in Britain, Italy, Germany, and, of course, the United States.

The overestimates are largest among the least educated, workers in low-skilled occupations with lots of immigrants, and those on the political right. They overstate the share of immigrants who are Muslim and understate the share of Christians. They underestimate immigrants' education and overestimate both their poverty rate and their dependence on welfare. Almost a quarter of French respondents, as well as nearly one in five Swedes, think the average immigrant gets twice as much government aid as native residents do. In no country is this true.

The exaggerated estimates serve a psychological purpose: they justify a drastic response. "People who are against immigration generate a sense of crisis," Professor Alesina told me. "They create a sense that 'This is a huge problem; we need a wall.'" The researchers found that just asking people about immigration reduced their support for income redistribution and the social safety net. "A major source of support for far-right parties in Europe has been the fear that immigration will erode welfare state benefits," noted Dani Rodrik in a major study of populism's emergence around the developed world, "a fear that is heightened in countries experiencing austerity and recession."

Europe's political realignment is by no means assured, but it is bringing European politics and policy more closely in line with those of the United States, shaped by in-group hostility toward the ethnic and cultural "other." In Britain, the European country that comes closest to sharing America's skepticism about government welfare, the pro-Brexit campaign exploited the fear that immigrants from poorer countries in the European Union were exploiting its welfare programs. Even the relatively generous Scandinavian countries are increasingly tying immigrants' access to safety net programs to learning the local language.

Denmark requires that "ghetto children," those born in one of twenty-five low-income, mostly Muslim immigrant neighborhoods, spend at least twenty-five hours a week separated from their families learning to be Danish, which includes learning to appreciate Christmas and Easter. Those who refuse will lose government benefits. In Germany, the AfD is pitching a "national social" political agenda. "The German social question of the twenty-first century," says the AfD leader Björn Höcke, is not about whether wealth is distributed from the rich to the poor or the old to the young but whether it is distributed from inside to outside Germany. The proposition, which is being appropriated by politicians on the left as well, is that redistribution is good, but only among Germans.

This kind of talk can bring back some bloodcurdling memories. Even if Europe's new political identity falls short of the murderous, racist populism that shaped its twentieth century, it does suggest that its experiment building a "social democracy," a society built on the assumption that "welfare"—health, education, well-being—is a human right that rich countries can afford, is at risk. Because immigration is only going to increase.

Europe, today, doesn't even have that many poor immigrants from distant cultures, compared with the United States. Over half of the working-age immigrants in the European Union are, in fact, other Europeans. Sixty-three percent of immigrants to the EU come from low-income nations, as defined by the OECD. In the United States, the comparable figure is 78 percent.

This will change. As economists Gordon Hanson and Craig McIntosh argued in a recent study, migration north across the

Mediterranean Sea is likely to explode in coming decades as poor and unstable African countries with bulging young populations send migrants to take the many jobs that Europe's aging populations will not be able to fill alone. Hanson and McIntosh predict that the stock of immigrants in Spain, the United Kingdom, and Italy will triple by 2040. Europe's politics will not take this in stride.

The political power of ethnic divisions raises some critical questions about the emergent world order. I agree with Dani Rodrik's belief in the value of social safety nets to provide insurance against economic upheaval. Societies offering robust social insurance—universal health care, adequate pensions, generous unemployment benefits, quality education and training—would be better able to cope with the inevitable dislocations wrought by technological progress and the globalization of production chains. Countries that protected their people from the downside of change, I'm pretty sure, would be in a better position to embrace it.

Yet a functioning social safety net has proven to be a poor antidote to a populist revolt. Indeed, generous public spending could bolster the argument for battening down the hatches against outsiders to protect one's own. One of the reasons the United States has been more relaxed than Europe about admitting immigrants of low skill is that it doesn't have much of a welfare state for the immigrants to "abuse." Europe's generous social safety net, by contrast, has provided arguments for the xenophobic insurrection.

Not everybody will agree that immigration will inevitably send European policy down an American path. As Rodrik points out, the nativist impulses underlying the current populist upheaval were likely provoked, to some extent, by the Great Recession. A slow, stumbling economic recovery across most of the rich industrialized countries of the West set off anxieties among working-class voters that were channeled by right-wing parties onto a xenophobic, nationalistic platform. In other words, the populist wave amounts to mass scapegoating. What may look like a racist or xenophobic backlash may have its roots in economic anxieties and dislocations.

This reading could offer some hope that as its economies return to growth, western Europe might snap back to its usual position in the spectrum of global governance—an example of the kind of society we could build if only we decided that exceptionally high rates of maternal and infant mortality, off-the-charts inequality, deep poverty, and imprisonment as a tool of social engineering are not good things to have. I am not convinced, though. Economic shocks may motivate some of the blood-and-soil rhetoric across a continent that knows these slogans well. Still, it would be foolish to ignore the shocks stemming from other social, cultural, and demographic changes—gender equality, changing norms governing sexual identity, rising environmental awareness, immigration.

New research in political science has come up with persuasive evidence that the populist upsurge across Western societies may have less to do with economic strains than with the kind of cultural competition brought about when new populations—ethnic minorities, immigrants, women, transsexuals—challenge the dominance of the traditional ruling group. Donald Trump's white voters are less motivated by the trade deficit than they are by the growing footprint of blacks, Latinos, and Asians threatening to take over their turf. They don't just want the manufacturing jobs of the 1950s back. They want the entire 1950s package, in which women were women, men were men, gays were banned, and minorities were, at best, a nuisance.

Similar cleavages appear on both sides of the Atlantic. "Less educated and older citizens, especially white men, who were once the privileged majority culture in Western societies, resent being told that traditional values are 'politically incorrect' if they have come to feel that they are being marginalized within their own countries," noted the political scientists Ronald Ingle-hart and Pippa Norris. "As cultures have shifted, a tipping point appears to have occurred."

The transition bodes ill for the survival of a welfare state based on some shared sense of national destiny. Asked to choose between a stronger social safety net—an insurance policy against the risks brought about by economic openness—and the protection against ethnic and cultural openness, including walls against immigrants, the exclusion of "others" from welfare benefits, and rules walling off alien cultural practices and norms, voters are turning to the latter. Against a background of relentless demographic change, where immigration pressures only build, the choice bodes ill for liberal democracy itself.

CHAPTER 7

The Future

Take a thirty-minute drive east across the Delaware River from Philadelphia, and you will reach the site of one of the most promising experiments in racial and socioeconomic integration in recent American history: the Ethel Lawrence Homes.

Blending into the tony suburban township of Mount Laurel, New Jersey, amid manicured lawns and multimillion-dollar houses, 140 fetching single-family homes stand out because of the families who live in them: they are neither white nor rich. Some make as little as $9,000 per year, less than half the poverty line for a family of three. Nine out of ten are either black or Latino. They can rent a one-bedroom home there for as little as $247 a month. It took an epic struggle over thirty years to get them there.

The tale, detailed in the wonderful *Climbing Mount Laurel*, coauthored by the sociologist Douglas Massey, starts back in the late 1960s, when a group of black residents worried about furious gentrification in town asked the local council to relax zoning rules that forbade building multifamily units and town houses so they could build thirty-six affordable garden apartments in the center of town. In October 1970, Mayor Bill Haines gave the council's response to a packed meeting at Jacob's Chapel AME church: no.

Ethel Lawrence, a schoolteacher who also happened to

belong to the local chapter of the NAACP, was one of the community leaders asking for the change. Her family had lived in Mount Laurel for seven generations. She lived there with her family of twelve in a dilapidated four-bedroom home. Instead of taking the mayor's advice to leave town, she became the lead plaintiff in a lawsuit that accused the town authorities of depriving her and her co-plaintiffs of their right to live in Mount Laurel, "solely on the basis of their economic status and, in effect, their race."

Between 1950 and 1970, Mount Laurel's population grew fourfold: thirteen thousand housing units had been built or planned in the last decade alone, but not one had been planned for low- and moderate-income families. In the two decades since 1950, nonwhites had declined from 10 percent to 2 percent of Mount Laurel's population, many of them forced to move to nearby Camden, an impoverished black enclave that itself was in decline due to the relocation of local businesses to places like Mount Laurel.

In effect, the plaintiffs charged, Mount Laurel was working to "maintain and further patterns of economic and racial segregation in the provision of housing, education and employment."

Lawrence and her co-plaintiffs won, twice. The first time, in 1975, the Supreme Court of New Jersey told Mount Laurel it had an obligation to help its low-income residents get housing. When that was mostly ignored, in 1983 the court broadened the rule: every town in New Jersey would have to provide a "fair share" of affordable housing. For good measure, the court added an enforcement mechanism: developers could sue municipalities to change zoning laws as long as they reserved a fifth of the development for moderate- and low-income homes.

The fight was not over. Local authorities fought tooth and nail what they viewed as the arrival of inner-city dysfunction on their doorstep. By the time the first Ethel Lawrence apartment was occupied, in late 2000, Lawrence was dead, but her victory may represent one of the most important landmarks in the effort to build a unified America.

Thousands of low-income, minority families have benefited from her effort, gaining a chance to move to neighborhoods beyond the ghettos reserved exclusively for the nonwhite and the poor. What came to be known as the "Mount Laurel doctrine" has led to the creation of forty thousand affordable housing units in New Jersey. Other states and municipalities have taken on the "fair share" concept to guide their housing policies.

The Mount Laurel win offers hope that transcends the confines of housing. The unprecedented intervention of the state of New Jersey to force the integration of its communities across boundaries of race and income offers America a glimpse at the kinds of policies that could help weave it more closely together as a nation.

The United States looks nothing like a melting pot, though it is a country made of people from everywhere. Whatever you look like or believe in, whether you are of old Irish stock, Jewish, a descendant of slaves, the child of Chinese immigrants, or a Mexican who just came across the border, you live in a country where most people are something else. The United States is unique among nations in this heterogeneity of provenance, culture, and ancestral experience.

Take Queensborough Community College, situated where the Long Island Expressway cuts through the Cross Island Parkway on the way from Manhattan to the Hamptons. About 15 percent of its students are non-Hispanic whites. Blacks, Hispanics, and Asians each account for a little under 30 percent. They come from around 130 countries and speak about seventy-nine languages among them.

Its track record is not bad by community college standards: about one in four students who enroll have an associate degree three years later, more than the national average. But what's striking about this place is its existence. This multiethnic multitude faithfully represents its underlying community in Queens, the most diverse county in the nation. The many-tongued buzz that floats above campus offers a taste of how people from all over the map—of diverse ethnicities and religions, languages and cultural practices—can integrate into something that can be called an American institution.

It is particularly disheartening, in light of this diversity, that Americans have built so many norms and institutions to privilege one subset of this miscellaneous assortment and shut out the rest: restrictions to reduce turnout among black and Latino voters; eligibility regulations to cut them from welfare rolls; zoning rules to keep them out of town.

Still, it bears remembering that the United States has probably done a better job than any other rich country in incorporating all the different people in its midst. The long-fought victory of the poor blacks and Puerto Ricans of Mount Laurel offers an example of how the country might self-correct. As the ethnic identity of the American population continues to meld, barriers designed in a time of more clear-cut racial definitions seem unlikely to hold. Maybe the United States even has a shot at forging a melting pot for real.

More immigrants than natives buy into the American dream. Seven out of ten think their kids will do better than they have, according to a report by the National Academies of Sciences, Engineering, and Medicine, compared with only half of the American born. Immigrants in the United States might be poorer than those living in Europe, and their wages may be lower, but many more have a job. Indeed, in the United States immigrants have higher employment rates than natives.

This is despite the fact that the United States has absorbed more immigrants from far-flung countries than most other developed nations. Fifteen and a half percent of the German population is foreign born, but over 70 percent of the foreigners come from other European countries. In Hungary, where Prime Minister Viktor Orbán has staked his leadership on a staunchly anti-immigrant platform, immigrants from outside Europe account for a vanishingly small share of the population. Even in Sweden, Europe's most inviting country, where immigrants account for 18 percent of the population, one-third of the foreigners were born in rich European countries in the OECD. Fewer than 10 percent of the population were born outside Europe.

By contrast, nearly 14 percent of people living in the United States were born outside its borders. The vast majority come from countries including Mexico and China where nobody cares about apple pie.

Perhaps Europe's secular values make the place tougher to crack for immigrants who are often deeply religious. The more ethnically and culturally homogeneous European nation-states lack the depth of experience the United States has in absorbing people from all over the map. As the sociologist Nancy Foner put it to me, "The United States does a better job at accepting immigrants as Americans in the making."

Solidarity might pin its hopes on this singular fact. As the United States draws more people of different colors and beliefs, the unfolding of new points of contact between diverse peoples could mitigate the racial hostility that has prevented the United States from becoming a nation that offers equal opportunity for all. The new colors on the map of America's heterogeneity could help bridge its starkest, most intractable ethnic division: that between blacks and whites.

Think of the "contact hypothesis" put forth in the 1950s by the American psychologist Gordon Allport: increasing contact between whites and minorities could promote familiarity and trust between the groups. Combine that with the more recent "buffering hypothesis," the idea that growing Hispanic and Asian populations could act as a buffer between whites and blacks, diminishing the salience of that most critical racial line. Then consider that adding hues to the American ethnic palette will, on its own, challenge the notion of "mainstream."

As the sociologist Richard Alba put it, whiteness in the United States has been a malleable concept. Newly arrived Irish, Italians, and eastern European immigrants were the excluded minorities of their day but were eventually included in the white American mainstream after they progressed up the socioeconomic ladder.

It was only fifty years ago that the Supreme Court struck down laws barring mixed-race marriages. By 2015, according to an analysis by the Pew Research Center, 17 percent of newly-weds married somebody of another race or ethnicity, one in ten babies living with both parents had parents who were of different races, and 6.9 percent of Americans were of mixed racial parentage. Over one in four Latinos and Asians marry outside their racial or ethnic group. So do almost one in five African Americans and over one in ten non-Hispanic whites. The Census Bureau projects that if current trends continue, the multiracial population will triple by 2060.

William Frey argues in *Diversity Explosion* that even the white-black racial barrier in marriage is softening. In 1980, for every thirty marriages between two African Americans there was one between white and black partners. By 2015, the ratio was one for every seven.

The very meaning of race is changing. Many kids who are classified as minorities by virtue of having a nonwhite parent see themselves as part of white America. They live very much as kids in white families do, in integrated neighborhoods rather than ethnic enclaves. Alba notes that families with a Hispanic mother and a non-Hispanic white father have pretty much the same income as families that are uniformly white.

The Census Bureau's announcement in 2015 that nonwhite babies outnumbered white ones relied on the one-drop rule, the understanding of race that became law in states across the Jim Crow South: one drop of minority blood makes a minority baby.

The social reality into which these babies are being born, however, no longer conforms to that definition. "In a society where racial and ethnic origins historically have confined Americans to different social strata, the mainstream has been long associated with the social spaces and cultural practices of white Americans," Alba argued. "That is now changing as the boundaries of the mainstream expand."

It would be reasonable to expect that the racial and ethnic barriers that have long stood in the way of American solidarity would soften as Americans' racial identities blurred. Noticeably, multiracial adults are more likely to support the social safety net than whites: 54 percent say government aid to the poor "does more good than harm, because people can't get out of poverty until their basic needs are met," according to a Pew survey. That is ten percentage points more than among the general public.

Nearly three out of four baby boomers, born from the end of World War II until the early 1960s, were white and non-Hispanic, according to Pew. Among millennials, born from 1981 through 1996, the share is down to 55 percent. As older cohorts fade into history, they will be replaced by younger Americans who not only are more ethnically diverse but also grew up in the more egalitarian culture that emerged from the civil rights movement of the 1960s. They experienced the election of a black American president in their formative years. They are marrying at higher rates outside their racial box.

Critically, most live more closely entwined with neighbors and friends from other racial and ethnic groups than Americans from any previous generation. As Paul Taylor noted in his book *The Next America*, millennials are "at ease with racial, ethnic, and sexual diversity." This proximity across ethnic and cultural divides could help build the common bond that the American experience has lacked for so long. Mount Laurel, replicated across the American landscape, might offer an antidote to America's poison.

Harvard psychologists have detected a decline of explicit and implicit racial bias over the last decade—including the kind of inchoate attachment of negative feelings to representations of other races that people keep hidden, lest they come across as racists. Donald Trump's ascent to the presidency, buoyed by a cohort of older white Americans drawn to his overt hostility toward people of color, seems to be pushing others in the opposite direction, startled perhaps by the president's narrow vision of America. In 2018, 52 percent of Americans polled by the General Social Survey believed that the government spends too little to improve the lot of blacks, up from 30 percent in 2014. Among whites, the share jumped from 24 to 45 percent. The increase was particularly steep among the young. In 2018, 57 percent of people aged eighteen to forty-nine thought the United States isn't spending enough to improve the living conditions of African Americans, compared to 44 percent of those over fifty.

This could deeply transform American politics, recasting it in the mold that Teixeira and Judis forecast so many years ago. In his 2019 book, *R.I.P. G.O.P.*, the Democratic pollster Stanley Greenberg forecast that 2020 will "shatter the Republican Party that was consumed by the ill-begotten battle to stop the New America from governing." Republicans' embrace of whites' resistance to a multiethnic nation would condemn the party to the political wilderness for a good many years.

Half a century ago, America proved its ability to change course, if only to prevent disaster. The country was up in flames, scorched by racial anger. In the first nine months of 1967, the Kerner Commission reported, there were 164 incidents where the police confronted African Americans on the streets in cities across the country. Eight were "major."

During a two-week stretch in July 1967, riots broke out in Newark, where truckloads of National Guardsmen and state troopers laid siege to the Hayes housing project under the dubious argument that they had heard sniper fire. Riots broke out in Detroit after a police raid on the "Blind Pig," an unlicensed, after-hours bar serving a black clientele. Ten thousand people rioted, and seven thousand National Guard and U.S. Army troops were deployed against them. Whole blocks burned. By the end, forty-three persons lay dead. More than seventy-two hundred were arrested, mostly black.

And somehow, from Detroit's ashes, the United States changed direction. Edward Glaeser of Harvard and Jacob Vigdor of the University of Washington tracked the data on residential segregation since the end of the nineteenth century through the first decade of the twenty-first. Segregation intensified through the first six decades of the twentieth century. The mass migration of African Americans from the South was met with stiff hostility by whites in the industrial enclaves of the Northeast and the Midwest, who fought to keep them out of their neighborhoods. In the 1950s, the typical urban African American lived in a neighborhood where the black share exceeded the citywide average by roughly sixty percentage points.

But starting somewhere in the 1970s, urban America's homogeneous neighborhoods gradually diversified. In 1980, the average white person lived in a neighborhood where 88 percent of the population was white. By 2010, she lived in a neighborhood with a 75 percent white share.

In 1960, the Census Bureau divided the metropolitan United States into 22,688 census tracts, or neighborhoods. More than one in five had zero black residents. In the half a century since then, the number of census tracts tripled to 72,531. The number of zero-black tracts declined to 424.

Changing demographics, to be sure, played a big part in this story—notably growing Hispanic and Asian communities in many cities. But like the long period of segregation before it, this half a century of desegregation was driven, primarily, by changes in government policy and law.

In *The Color of Law*, an exhaustive account of residential segregation in America, Richard Rothstein notes that residential neighborhoods in the nineteenth century were fairly integrated by race. But as blacks moved north, its cities deployed the law to keep them out.

When a prominent black lawyer moved onto a white block in Baltimore in 1910, the city enacted a zoning rule that banned blacks from buying homes in majority-white areas and vice versa. Similar ordinances were passed in Atlanta, Birmingham, Miami, Charleston, Dallas, Louisville, New Orleans, Oklahoma City, Richmond, St. Louis, and across the country.

In 1917, the Supreme Court ruled such blatant race-based zoning unconstitutional, so municipalities switched to economic zoning instead. Like Mount Laurel, city authorities would require that neighborhoods have only single-family homes or that homes have minimum lot sizes or square footage. The effect—keeping out poorer African Americans—was the same.

Overt racial segregation did not disappear. In 1926, the Supreme Court upheld covenants to ensure white homeowners could sell their homes only to other whites, on the grounds that they were private contracts and not government regulations. In some cities, blacks were allowed to work but forced to leave before sundown.

The federal government was a force for segregation from the start. Whites-only public housing had been around at least since Frederick Law Olmsted designed developments exclusively for whites who worked in defense plants during World War I. The 1949 Housing Act, pushed by President Truman to support public housing for servicemen returning from World War II, passed only after Democrats defeated an amendment barring segregation and racial discrimination in public housing.

The amendment had been introduced by Republicans as a poison pill: they knew no southern Democrat would vote for a bill with such provisions.

Alongside its many other acts of unfairness toward African Americans, the New Deal provided the most powerful push to shape a nation geographically segregated by race.

The Federal Housing Administration, launched in 1934 to promote homeownership by insuring mortgages for middle-income Americans, turned the United States into a nation of homeowners, dotting the suburbs with new housing developments. From the outset, the opportunity was limited to whites. It ended up sorting whites into the suburban landscape, while lower-income minorities packed segregated public housing in urban cores.

A manual by the FHA suggested to developers that the best financial bets, those most likely to be insured, were in places where highways or other natural boundaries could fence off communities and keep out "lower class occupancy, and inharmonious racial groups." Where children "are compelled to attend school where the majority or a considerable number of the pupils represent a far lower level of society or an incompatible racial element, the neighborhood under consideration will prove far less stable and desirable," the manual advised.

In 1940, the FHA denied insurance for a white development near a black community until the builder agreed to put up a half-mile-long concrete wall between the two. Across the country it outright refused to guarantee mortgages for integrated developments that housed blacks and whites.

Consider the town of Milpitas near San Jose, in what is now California's Silicon Valley. In 1953, when the Ford Motor Company decided to shutter its plant in Richmond, some fifty miles north, to relocate into a vast tract of land it had in the area, some

1,400 workers, including 250 blacks, needed to find a place to live.

Rothstein details how securing financing for a development that would house African Americans was its own nightmare, given the FHA's reluctance to underwrite integrated projects. Even when financing was ultimately secured, local authorities threw every available obstacle in the way. The town of Milpitas, which was quickly incorporated by its residents once Ford's plans were known, passed an ordinance to ban apartment buildings and allow only single-family homes.

When the developer sought to buy a lot in an unincorporated tract of Santa Clara County, the board of supervisors rezoned it for industrial use. When he found another lot in Mountain View, the town increased the minimum lot size from six thousand to eight thousand square feet. When a third patch of land was found, the developer of the adjacent, all-white Sunnyhills project persuaded the Milpitas sanitary district to jack up the fee for a sewer connection for the future integrated development and directly sued to stop it from using a drainage ditch.

By the time the integrated residential project was built, the Ford plant had been open for a year. Few blacks ever moved in. Black workers mostly carpooled a hundred miles round-trip from Richmond.

Economic and demographic forces, coupled with changes in federal housing policy and laws banning most forms of outright segregation, have gradually, painstakingly pushed the races closer together across the residential landscape.

In 1948 the Supreme Court ruled against using public resources to enforce the racial deed covenants that were commonly used to prohibit homeowners from selling or renting homes to African Americans. New York City officially banned housing discrimination in its 1957 fair housing practices ordinance, and the United States followed suit with the 1968 Fair Housing Act.

Federal funding for the large, segregated public housing projects that had arisen across urban America ended in the 1970s, replaced by federal vouchers to subsidize rents for those with low incomes. Hulking projects from Pruitt-Igoe in St. Louis to the Cabrini-Green towers in Chicago were demolished.

Vouchers allowed some low-income African Americans who had formerly been packed into segregated projects to move to more diverse areas. With easier access to federal mortgage guarantees, more African Americans could afford to move to the previously all-white suburbs.

It also happened that the great northward migration of African Americans reversed course. Many blacks left ghettos in the Northeast and the Midwest for less segregated cities in the Sunbelt that were also receiving large numbers of Latinos and Asians. By 2010, twenty of the most diverse metros in the country were in the South and the Southwest.

Altogether, Glaeser and Vigdor reported that in 657 out of 658 housing markets tracked by the Census Bureau, segregation was lower in 2010 than it was in 1970. By 2010, there were virtually no all-white neighborhoods in the country. African Americans lived in 199 out of every 200. As the "buffering hypothesis" would suggest, Asian and Latino newcomers did to some extent erode segregation between blacks and whites, somehow helping to bridge the nation's most contentious racial divide.

A study from Harvard's Joint Center for Housing Studies suggests that integration has continued to rise in recent years. In 2017, there were 21,104 "shared" neighborhoods in American cities, where at least a fifth of their residents were white and at least a fifth were from a community of color. That's over 400 more than at the turn of the century. Three in ten Americans live there, up from two in ten in 2000.

An assessment by Lichter and sociologists Domenico Parisi and Michael C. Taquino concluded that "if racial residential integration is a public policy goal, such results provide optimism about the future, especially as the United States becomes a majority-minority country by 2043."

To become as one, Americans must learn to live together, however. The task is actually more complex than how to build neighborly feelings. As Lichter points out, "Opportunities and preferences for interracial contact and affiliation will depend heavily on the prospect of upward socioeconomic mobility among today's minority children."

Economic convergence was critical to the integration of earlier "minority" cohorts. For the new immigrants who arrived from eastern and southern Europe, becoming white mainstream Americans required rising up the socioeconomic ranks. In the twenty-five years after World War II, Italians became white by catching up to other whites in education and socioeconomic attainment.

Rising income inequality amounts to a formidable challenge to integration. As Lichter notes, if nothing changes in the distribution of American prosperity, by 2050, seven in ten of America's poor will belong to an ethnic minority, driven by raw demographic change. That is a formidable wall to climb.

Still, residential integration could go a long way to close the income gap. Take Mount Laurel. Massey and his co-researchers took a look at how living enmeshed amid the affluent white country-club class affected the lives of the low-income African Americans in the Ethel Lawrence Homes. Comparing the fates of the lucky few who landed a home with those who failed to get one, they found that residents had substantially higher incomes years later. More of them had jobs. Their kids studied more and got better grades. And for all the fears that the raggedy new neighbors would depress property values in Mount Laurel, Massey and his coauthors found that property values were unaffected even in the neighborhoods that were nearest to the affordable housing development.

Segregation does not just stunt the progress of minorities.

A recent study by the Urban Institute in Washington found that both blacks and whites in less segregated neighborhoods are more likely to finish college. If Chicago could reduce its extremely high segregation—bringing it down to the median level of the hundred largest metros in the country—sixty-five thousand more white adults and eighteen thousand more blacks in the city would theoretically complete a bachelor's degree. What's more, the Urban Institute's projections suggest that in such a parallel universe in 2016 there would have been 533 homicides in the city rather than 762.

Evidence is mounting that reducing residential segregation is indispensable if we are to achieve some measure of equality of opportunity and tie every strand of America into a shared project.

In the 1970s the Supreme Court set off a vast natural experiment when it agreed with the American Civil Liberties Union that Chicago's approach to public housing, building projects only in areas with lots of minorities, amounted to racial discrimination. Rather than put projects in white neighborhoods, Chicago's Housing Authority stopped building public housing altogether. Instead, it distributed housing vouchers to seventy-five hundred African American families, allowing many of them to move to mostly low-poverty white neighborhoods.

More than a decade later, a study found that families who used their vouchers to move to low-poverty white suburbs fared much better than those who remained in segregated black neighborhoods in the city. Kids in families that moved to the suburbs were four times less likely to drop out of school and twice as likely to attend college.

Chicago's experience set off a wave of experimentation, most notably the Moving to Opportunity program in the early 1990s, launched in Bill Clinton's first administration. Poor, mostly black and Latino families in Baltimore, Boston, Chicago, Los Angeles, and New York were offered vouchers to move to better neighborhoods. In 2015, a careful analysis found the move generated hefty gains.

The evaluations, led by researchers at Harvard University's Opportunity Insights, found that children who moved to a better area before they turned thirteen were more likely to go to college and went to a better college than those who stayed behind. They made more money as adults and were less likely to become single parents. In one remarkable study, Raj Chetty, Nathaniel Hendren, and Lawrence Katz estimated that every year a child spent in a better neighborhood improved his or her adult outcomes.

Mobility, they concluded, is hard in impoverished segregated enclaves. Kids do best when they grow up in neighborhoods that are more integrated by income and race, suffer lower inequality and less violent crime, and have better schools and more two-parent households. The challenge is how to stop America's division into enclaves of poor and rich, to prevent the segregation of its living spaces into affluent preserves that minorities can never reach.

The most powerful means we know through which integrated communities might improve the lot of marginalized Americans, of course, is education. Funded mostly through local property taxes, which are usually higher in whiter, richer neighborhoods, schools have become one more tool in the toolbox of inequality. Bringing poor children of color into more affluent white schools would be a powerful counterbalance.

Consider Montgomery County, just outside Washington, D.C., in Maryland, one of the most affluent counties in the country. It has an inclusive housing policy that requires developers to build affordable homes. The county housing authority buys many of these units to rent to low-income families. According to a study commissioned by the Century Foundation, poor kids who attended low-poverty schools in the district closed much of the achievement gap in math with their richer peers. The research showed that the better neighborhood contributed to improve children's performances, the better schools accounting for about two-thirds of the gains.

Given the vast power of education to improve people's lot in life, it's hard to think of a more important decision than the Supreme Court's 1954 ruling in *Brown v. Board of Education of Topeka* in opening the American dream to disenfranchised blacks and other minorities.

The Court's direct ban on racial discrimination in southern schools might have had little immediate relevance in itself. The southern school districts that had previously discriminated by law simply adopted "freedom of choice" plans that put the onus on black families to enroll their children in white schools, an unappealing prospect given racial hostility at the time.

In 1971, the Court upped the ante. In the case of *Swann v. Charlotte-Mecklenburg Board of Education*, it ruled by unanimous decision that public schools in Charlotte, North Carolina, and the county of Mecklenburg in which it sits could require pupils to be bused outside their residential neighborhoods in order to achieve racially balanced enrollment and equal educational opportunity for blacks and whites.

Few school districts desegregated willingly nonetheless. Most did not enact significant desegregation plans until they were forced to by either court order or the threat of litigation. If it were not for the NAACP—suing school systems left and right—desegregation might have remained but a stunted dream.

The results were ultimately impressive, though. In 1968, 78 percent of African American students in the South were in acutely segregated schools, where minorities accounted for at least 90 percent of the student body. By 1972, only 25 percent of southern black students were in such segregated schools, the lowest share in the country.

Then the Supreme Court took school desegregation beyond the South. In 1973, in *Keyes v. School District No. 1, Denver, Colorado*, it ruled against de facto segregation in northern school systems too. A failure to provide equal educational opportunity to all students, regardless of race, color, or national origin, it decided, amounted to "intentional state action" in violation of the equal protection clause of the Fourteenth Amendment.

By the middle of the 1970s, hundreds of school districts were subject to court-ordered desegregation plans. Gary Orfield, an education policy expert, notes that by 1980 only about one-third of black students attended apartheid schools with next to no white students, roughly half the share of 1968. Integration even made inroads in the Northeast, where desegregation was most effectively resisted.

Buffalo in upstate New York, home to a large African American community that had arrived chasing defense industry jobs from 1940 to 1970, did next to nothing to desegregate its schools until it had to. In 1971, the student body in twenty out of ninety-six schools in the public school system was at least 90 percent black. Twenty schools were at least 90 percent white.

So the NAACP sued. Buffalo's subsequent desegregation plan closed ten schools and transformed neighborhood black schools into specialized magnet schools that would interest white students too. By 1981, over fourteen thousand children, almost 30 percent of Buffalo's students, were being bused—white kids to schools in black communities, black students to white schools. In 1985, *The New York Times* ran a front-page piece under the headline "School Integration in Buffalo Is Hailed as a Model for U.S." Black children got their best shot in decades at the American dream.

The economist Rucker Johnson looked at the effects of desegregation by following the lives of children born between

1945 and 1968, many of whom were in school during the desegregation era following *Brown*.

He concluded that desegregation plans implemented from the 1960s to the 1980s decidedly improved the quality of schools attended by blacks and increased their educational attainment. Black children who entered elementary school after desegregation was mandated averaged more than 1.5 additional years of education than those who experienced a segregated education and were 30 percent more likely to graduate from high school. What's more, black students who benefited from desegregation had higher incomes as adults—earning over 30 percent more than those educated in the segregated era. They also had better health and suffered lower rates of incarceration. The lifetime odds of black Americans being thrown in prison or jail were a quarter lower for those who went through school after desegregation.

"How many generations does it take to reverse the ills of segregation?" Johnson asks in his book *Children of the Dream*. "The evidence in this book says just one." What's more, Johnson detects no adverse impact on whites: the charge that allowing poor blacks into prosperous white schools would erode the quality of white kids' education proved to be baloney.

America's twentieth century is paved with worthwhile efforts to breach the barrier of racial animus and build an integrated country. From the Civil Rights Act to its sister, the War on Poverty, from school desegregation to the more modest victories in Mount Laurel, a century worth of experimentation has yielded a formidable arsenal of tools to build a more inclusive society.

Just over a decade ago, David Rusk, the veteran urban policy expert, gave a speech before the National Inclusionary Housing Conference. At the time, he said, almost 5 percent of the population of the United States lived in communities that had inclusionary zoning rules mandating mixed-income housing as a part of new developments. Then he ran a what-if scenario:

Almost 22 million homes were built in the hundred largest metropolitan areas between 1980 and 2000. If they had all had inclusionary zoning mandates, builders would have added 2.6 million affordable homes, covering 40 percent of the affordable housing need. If, like Montgomery County, housing authorities could purchase many of these units to rent to poor families, urban segregation by income in these metros would have fallen by more than a third.

Even in Philadelphia, an acutely segregated city with high concentrations of poverty, segregation would have declined by 19 percent. Cities with fewer poor people, like Las Vegas, would have become entirely integrated. Socioeconomic integration would go a long way in ending segregation by race.

In Denver, Rusk argued, a metro-wide inclusionary zoning policy combined with policies to achieve economic parity between the schools in its seventeen school districts would drive school segregation by income—which correlates fairly tightly with segregation by race and ethnicity—down to levels lower than in some of the world's most egalitarian societies, like Sweden or the Netherlands.

Moving poor kids of color en masse to rich white neighborhoods is not going to happen, of course, regardless of what the Moving to Opportunity experiment found. Nonetheless, the accumulated evidence of how integrated neighborhoods improve the future prospects of disadvantaged children offers a clear approach for policy makers to address entrenched inequality.

Hundreds of municipalities have enacted inclusionary zoning programs in which developers are given incentives to set aside homes for low-income families. Massachusetts, Texas, Nevada, and Mississippi are reshaping tax credits to provide incentives for builders who develop housing for low-income families in low-poverty, high-opportunity neighborhoods. Inspired by the Moving to Opportunity findings, several large metros are looking into ways to use housing vouchers to encourage low-income families to move to better neighborhoods.

The federal government spends $20 billion a year on the Housing Choice Voucher program. More than 80 percent of the vouchers are used in moderate- or high-poverty neighborhoods. Ten percent of these families live in neighborhoods with poverty rates above 40 percent. Housing authorities, including in Minneapolis, Seattle, Houston, and Cook County, Illinois, are encouraging beneficiaries to move to low-poverty areas. They are providing counseling, helping with moving costs and the like, and offering incentives to landlords in good neighborhoods to accept low-income tenants on vouchers. We have the policy tools we need to build a more integrated society. The question is, will we use them?

As I noted before, young Americans are more familiar with people from other ethnicities and cultures. They are marrying across boundaries, stitching integration into family structures. Growing Asian and Hispanic populations are transforming racial politics that were for so long determined by the bitter conflict across the black-white divide.

Will we go all the way? Will we overcome the ethnic mistrust that has stunted our development as a society and build a country with a sense of solidarity that works for whites and blacks and Asians and Latinos, transcending racial divides? To become as one, with a common national and cultural identity, we must tackle the ingrained tribal logic with which we have organized the world. Yet for every inch we move toward the goal of a cohesive society, we seem to slip back two.

Despite the desegregation that spread across urban America since the 1970s, despite the growing cohorts of young people of color, the mixed marriages, the multiple efforts and experiments to integrate Americans across the racial divide, the odds still look pretty long. Daniel Lichter put it rather tersely: the empirical literature "offers few guarantees that growing racial diversity will lead to a corresponding breakdown in racial boundaries."

Racial politics may well become more forbidding as the white population shrinks and minority populations grow. This could reshape the political map in troubling ways. Rural America—staunchly conservative, economically stagnant, over-whelmingly white—is likely to maintain control of the Senate for a good long while, despite its flagging population. In the House, by contrast, the more prosperous and ethnically diverse urban America will prevail. Gridlock is baked into our demography.

Whites might learn to share physical and social spaces and interact as coequals with minorities. Then again, they might not. Blacks and Latinos may never overcome their reciprocal mistrust as they compete for limited resources. Alliances are up for grabs.

A research paper by political scientists from Harvard, Stan-ford, and the Massachusetts Institute of Technology suggests that the arrival of 1.5 million African Americans from the South into northern cities at the beginning of the twentieth century helped "whiten" the millions of European immigrants who had arrived there since 1850. Italians, Poles, and Jews, racially ambiguous until then, were invited into the white mainstream.

Maybe Latinos and Asians will be invited into American whiteness, cleaving the nation's racial identity between blacks and "nonblacks." Or, as President Trump appears to want, the racial battle lines will be drawn between whites and nonwhites. America's multitude of ethnic identities might make for a con-flict on many fronts. Integration is only one option. In my view, it is not the most likely.

Consider again the attempts to desegregate American schools. Sixty years after *Brown*, you might expect schools across the country would be pretty integrated places, yet American schools have resegregated. Orfield found, for instance, that the proportion of black students attending predominantly minority schools rose from 63 percent in 1988 to 73 percent in 2005. In the South, less than a quarter of black children go to integrated schools, where at least half the students are white. That's about half the share that did so in 1989 and roughly the same share that did in 1968.

The arrival of Hispanic immigrants and their children contributed to increasing segregation in American schools. Black schoolchildren's exposure to white schoolchildren declined, to some extent, because whites' share of the population did. Still, the flight of white families from cities to the suburbs created a split between white and minority school districts, even as segregation inside school districts declined.

What is most disheartening about the ultimately failed campaign to integrate public education is that despite the early successes America stopped trying. Between 1990 and 2010, hundreds of districts forced by court order to establish desegregation plans were released from court oversight. The Supreme Court lost its integrationist zeal.

In *San Antonio Independent School District v. Rodriguez*, in 1973, the Court ruled that vast funding disparities—some predominantly minority districts raised less than 7 percent as much, per pupil, as what was available for students in mostly white schools nearby—did not violate the equal protection clause of the Fourteenth Amendment.

In *Milliken v. Bradley* a year later, it ruled by five votes to four that Detroit did not have to bus students across the lines dividing its fifty-three school districts to mitigate interdistrict segregation. If the district lines had not been drawn with racial intent, school districts did not have to integrate with each other.

"No single tradition in public education is more deeply rooted than local control over the operation of schools," wrote Chief Justice Warren E. Burger for the majority. Taking the other side, Justice Thurgood Marshall offered a pointed dissent: "In the short run, it may seem to be the easier course to allow our great metropolitan areas to be divided up each into two cities—one white, the other black—but it is a course, I predict, our people will ultimately regret."

In *Parents Involved in Community Schools v. Seattle School District No. 1*, in 2007, the Court further outlawed the use of students' race in shaping voluntary school assignment plans, making it harder for districts to voluntarily desegregate. So it is that one of the most powerful, promising policies to extend prosperity across America's racial boundaries fizzled.

In the decade after *Brown*, schools became consistently more integrated than the neighborhoods in which they sat. But the pattern flipped as desegregation orders were gradually dropped. Buffalo's desegregation order, for instance, ended in 1995. By 2010, 44 percent of the black students in town went to schools where at least nine out of ten children were nonwhite, five times as many as in 1989. John Kucsera and Gary Orfield noted in a report for the Civil Rights Project that by 2010 the typical black student in Buffalo attended a school where 73 percent of students were poor, more than double the poverty rate in the typical white school.

The latest fad in education is for affluent communities to secede from the school districts their children share with poor minority kids from across the tracks. Not all succeed. Early in 2018 a federal appeals court rejected the efforts by Gardendale, a suburb of Birmingham, Alabama, where whites account for 78 percent of the population and the poverty rate is 7 percent, to secede from the larger Jefferson County school district, which is 55 percent nonwhite and 22 percent poor. The three-judge panel ruled that Gardendale's efforts were meant to prevent having poor black kids bused into their schools.

Decisions like this are rare, though. One hundred twenty-eight communities have tried to secede from their district from the turn of the century to 2019, according to a report by EdBuild, an advocacy group pushing for equitable funding for public schools. Seventy-three of the secession efforts succeeded. And funding gaps between white and nonwhite schools persist. EdBuild estimates that school districts with mostly minority students get $23 billion less than predominantly white districts. In Illinois, school districts that serve the most students of color have to make do with about 18 percent less, $2,573 per pupil, than the schools with the smallest share of minorities, according to a study of the 2015 school year by the Education Trust. In Texas and New York the deficit hovers around 10 percent.

Thirty states have explicit policies allowing for school district secessions. Only six require a consideration of the impact of the split on racial and economic diversity or equality of opportunity for different groups of students. In twenty-one states there is no provision that keeps communities from seceding in order to cordon off local wealth. Just four consistently require a majority vote of approval specifically from the members of the community being left behind.

More typical than the case of Gardendale is what happened to the clutch of predominantly white suburbs in Shelby County, Tennessee, which pushed to become independent school districts in order to avoid sharing their tax revenues with the overwhelmingly black schools in the county seat of Memphis.

After a judge ruled against the secession plan, the Tennessee legislature simply amended state law to allow it to happen. According to EdBuild, 67 percent of the population of the splinter districts are white and only 11 percent are poor. In the district they left behind, whites account for 8 percent of the population, and over a third of the students live below the poverty line.

There is a cost to this. Rucker Johnson, who fleshed out the economic and social gains stemming from school integration, also calculated the costs of turning our back on that goal. He found that a 15 percent increase in school segregation during six of the twelve years of public education reduced a black child's educational attainment by one-quarter of a year, trimmed her chances of going to college by seven percentage points, and cut her wages as an adult by 7 percent. Meanwhile, a white kid who was not exposed to minority children at school was more likely to have only white friends, live in an all-white neighborhood as an adult, and embrace conservative politics.

The irreducible truth is that white Americans would rather not share the fruits of their privileges. It is a banal truth, even. Resting our hopes on some hypothesis that living close together will help people develop more harmonious relations across racial and ethnic divides seems foolhardy. So does the belief that the young, who are educated at schools where poor minorities sit alongside other poor minorities, where whites never see over the racial wall, will prove eager to build an integrated nation overcoming America's racial divisions.

A recent study by researchers at Tufts University, funded by the Russell Sage Foundation, concluded that white millennials may be slightly more liberal than older whites but their views on race are closer to those of older whites than those of nonwhite millennials. They "are hardly immune to the power of race to shape their attitudes."

Drawing data from two national surveys in 2012 and 2016, they found that just over a quarter of white millennials agreed with the proposition that white people in the United States have certain advantages because of the color of their skin, twenty percentage points less than the share of nonwhites of any age. Less than one in ten millennial whites strongly support affirmative action programs; about one in three strongly oppose them—the exact reverse of the pattern of minority respondents.

This is consistent with other studies. A survey by researchers at the GenForward project at the University of Chicago found that nearly half of white millennials believe that discrimination against whites has become as big a problem as discrimination against blacks and other minorities, a view that is shared by only a quarter of Hispanics, Asians, and African Americans.

A study of white high school seniors from 1976 to 2000 by sociologists Tyrone Forman and Amanda Lewis found that students in the more recent cohorts were more likely to agree that it isn't their business if minorities are treated unfairly.

The findings "offer a corrective to popular narratives that tell us that young Americans will usher in a more racially harmonious era," noted the researchers Deborah J. Schildkraut and Satia A. Marotta. "As the nation's population is becoming ever more diverse, whites are reacting by closing ranks around the group, identifying more strongly as white, and having that identification become a more prominent influence over their political beliefs."

Indeed, young whites are just as likely as their older peers to adopt conservative positions when they are faced with the fact that their ethnic group, narrowly defined, will be in the minority within a quarter century or so. The question is, what happens if millennials prove no more inclined to extend the benefits of American citizenship across racial divides? Faced with increasing ethnic diversity, the young might double down on the proposition that an American should stand on his or her own two feet, alone.

"Should we instead place our hopes for greater racial unity on the subsequent generation, which is going to be more diverse still?" asked Marotta and Schildkraut. The problem is that by the time we get to Generation Z, what victories we have achieved in the pursuit of a shared destiny might have all but unraveled.

They are already beginning to slip away. The desegregation of America's neighborhoods is still an unfinished task. Even as we have outlawed overt segregation by race, the nation's biggest, most productive cities are undergoing furious segregation by income, fueled by fast-paced gentrification that is pushing low-income communities of color farther and farther out.

As the economists Veronica Guerrieri and Alessandra Fogli pointed out in a recent study, this pattern of residential segregation is exacerbating income inequality. Rich, mostly white new residents arriving in formerly poor communities of color may pay more taxes to fund better schools. But they also kick out the former poor residents who can no longer afford the rent. Layered on top of income inequality, residential segregation adds another obstacle for low-income urban communities—mostly made up of people of color—to get ahead. Guerrieri and Fogli titled their paper "The End of the American Dream?"

There are, to be sure, many more "shared" neighborhoods across the country, where substantial white populations coexist with minority groups. But the black-white color line seems as intractable as ever. In 1990 the average black resident lived in a neighborhood where only 34 percent of the population was white. Twenty years later, she lives in a neighborhood where whites amount to 35 percent. Meanwhile, the average white lives in a neighborhood where only 8 percent of the neighbors are black. That's up from 5 percent in 1980.

Whites are still offering intense resistance to residential integration. Three thousand seven hundred and sixty-four neighborhoods that counted as integrated in 2000, with a substantial share of white and minority residents, had resegregated by the period between 2011 and 2015, according to a study by Harvard's Joint Center for Housing Studies, 2,627 of them resegregated because whites left and their share of the population fell below 20 percent.

Meanwhile, the growth of the Hispanic population is resegregating many metropolitan areas. Forty-three percent of the neighborhoods that were considered integrated in 2000 had become Hispanic destinations in 2011 to 2015.

Like the segregation between school districts set off when

each district was forced to integrate, rising residential integration within cities seems to be spurring segregation between them. The current moment of neighborhood diversity is starting to look like a temporary phenomenon occurring in the transition between two homogeneous states. We seem on our way to a nation just as intensely segregated but at a larger scale, along different lines. Rather than white and black neighborhoods, we must choose between black and white cities.

I can't envision much boundary-breaking solidarity emerging from this America. White racial isolation is the kind of configuration that produces a divisive figure like Donald Trump. Black isolation will feed the age-old prejudices that have stunted the development of a state invested in the social welfare of all.

Neither of these choices leads to a United States where the state in question is configured to stand by every one of its citizens.

Acknowledgments

I have grappled with my American identity for years. I am undoubtedly American like my father, just as I am as Mexican as my mother. But though I was born and lived the first six years of my life in the United States, I have long had some trouble defining myself as of this place. Unlike many Americans, I believe that this country, in the pursuit of its interests, has done unspeakable damage to multitudes of powerless people around the world.

High school made me Mexican. It was the place where I built my first stable sense of social belonging. It happened to be in Mexico, in a context that was decidedly on the left side of the Cold War. I was educated among the children of exiles, expelled from countries all over Latin America by right-wing military regimes supported by the United States.

In middle school we celebrated the United States' defeat in Vietnam, that exemplary story of a small nation defending its independence against the most powerful nation on earth. We protested America's support for Augusto Pinochet's genocidal regime in Chile. We demonstrated against the American invasion of Grenada, its murderous meddling in El Salvador, and its inane blockade of Fidel Castro's Cuba. In 1979, at the age of sixteen, I visited Managua to celebrate the triumph of the Sandinista revolution.

For all my contempt for the United States' many interventions in other countries' affairs, however, I also felt a strong sense of admiration for what the United States had built at home. Raised amid Mexico's blatant inequities—papered over with slogans about the rights of the people—I couldn't but accept that the American social contract was better. Indeed, it seemed superior to anything I had seen anywhere else in the world. The United States might be a paranoid thug. But like no other country I knew, it had somehow succeeded in offering ordinary people a true shot at prosperity. I understood this up close. My grandparents were among them.

Then, in the late 1990s, I returned to live here.

I am less critical, today, of American foreign policy. Now I know the Soviet Union was just as thuggish a bully. I have come to understand the Cold War was not over different visions for the world but, like any other war, over power. I accept that the left side of it also packed genocidal repression. I still think America's defeat in Vietnam was a positive development, tempering its imperial overreach. But I have overcome my Manichaean reflex to comprehend the world as clearly divided between right and wrong.

I have also lost my admiration, however. While I have been living in the United States for the last twenty years, my appreciation for America's social contract has been replaced by a gnawing, frustrating question that just won't let go: How could a country this rich provide such a crap deal to so many of its people? American politicians take pride in offering a cold shoulder to their fellow citizens. They mock deprivation as justice, a reward for idleness or other shortcomings. And deprived American voters help put these politicians back in office, again and again.

My grandparents, I now understand, lived the exception, not the rule. They achieved their prosperity through a narrow window of opportunity—within a few decades after World War II. The question I've been asking myself, from which this book emerges, is why did it close when countless Americans were still on the outside? Just as I realized that the Soviets weren't the good guys, so too I came to realize that America's exceptional social contract was, in fact, never meant for everybody.

This winding preamble is to acknowledge the Centro Activo Freire as a central character in my story. This small, unorthodox high school in Mexico City, strained between its commitment to critical inquiry and its uncritical embrace of left-side-of-the-Cold-War dogma, was first to alert me about America's contradictions. The CAF, as it was known, challenged me to explore where the United States was right—if only to confront the relentlessly anti-American orthodoxy at school—as well as where it was decidedly wrong.

In the many years since then, countless others have contributed to my understanding of the American conundrum. I must thank my editors at *The Wall Street Journal*—above all Jonathan Friedland, my bureau chief in Los Angeles—who gave me the priceless opportunity to explore how Hispanic America interacted, not always felicitously, with America's other communities. At *The New York Times*—this vast university—I learned from many teachers: from Tom Redburn, my cantankerous, encyclopedic editor, whose critical eye invariably improved my writing; from David Leonhardt, my gifted colleague, whose talent to transform the most complex ideas into the clearest writing I never ceased to admire; from Larry Ingrassia, who invited me to write the Economic Scene column so many years ago, essentially granting me carte blanche to explore the world. Not least, I must thank all the economists and sociologists, psychologists and historians, who over these many years so generously gave me their time. Guiding me patiently through their research, they provided me with the best education I could ever have hoped for. Every insight in this book draws from their work.

I would like to believe *American Poison* came to me, that I just needed to write it. Yet deep-seated though my frustration with America's broken social contract may be, I would never have landed on this idea without the help of others. Zoë Pagnamenta, my agent and dear friend, has somehow always believed there are books worth writing within me. Her patient, soft-spoken encouragement through many iterations of my thinking was essential for this book to be. So too were the observations of my friend Cressida Leyshon, one of the sharpest editors I have ever met. *The New Yorker* is lucky to have her. Cressida helped me think through how my original idea about America's failures might be best understood embedded in the historical process that made us this way. I have people to thank on the other end of the journey as well. Sheldon Danziger from the Russell Sage Foundation provided an invaluable intellectual backstop, drawing from his boundless grasp of the scholarly literature to point out gaps in my understanding of the research. Margaret Simms of the Urban Institute made priceless comments, generously deploying her deep understanding of the intersection of race, poverty, and inequality to sharpen my rendering of the American social contract. Hilary McClellen, who fact-checked the manuscript, saved me from embarrassment countless times. I am grateful for her careful eye.

Of course I must thank Jonathan Segal, my editor at Knopf, who accompanied me for the full ride, offering words of advice and support every step of the way. Jon and I have been having lunch for years, sharing life stories, throwing ideas back and forth. He helped steer my thoughts from an inchoate critique of American social policy into a specific condemnation of the racist underpinnings of our warped welfare state. Once the manuscript was done, he applied his eye to tighten the weaker bits and clarify the murkier corners of my thinking. He did it on paper, with a pencil; no use for the trickery of Microsoft Word.

Above everything I must thank my family. My mother, Male (Mah-leh), an overflowing source of inspiration, taught me humility and how to challenge the limits to what I know. Snigdha, my partner, proposed laughter to mediate my relationship with the world. She has worked hard to teach me joy. Mateo, my boy, and Uma, my girl, remind me every day of the raw joy of living. They emit the kind of blinding light we draw only from those we love. There were dark moments in this writing. Uma, Mateo, Snigdha, and my mom helped me overcome the darkness.

Bibliography

Acharya, Avidit, Matthew Blackwell, and Maya Sen. "The Political Legacy of American Slavery." *Journal of Politics* 78, no. 3 (July 2016): 621–41.

Acs, Gregory, Rolf Pendall, Mark Treskon, and Amy Khare. "The Cost of Segregation: National Trends and the Case of Chicago, 1990–2010." Urban Institute, March 2017.

Aigner, Peter-Christian. "What the Left and Right Both Get Wrong About the Moynihan Report." *Atlantic*, April 16, 2014.

Aizer, Anna, and Joseph J. Doyle. "Juvenile Incarceration, Human Capital, and Future Crime: Evidence from Randomly Assigned Judges." *Quarterly Journal of Economics* 130, no. 2 (May 2015): 759–803.

Alba, Richard. "The Likely Persistence of a White Majority: How Census Bureau Statistics Have Misled Thinking About the American Future." *American Prospect*, January 11, 2016.

Albright, Len, Elizabeth S. Derickson, and Douglas S. Massey. "Do Affordable Housing Projects Harm Suburban Communities? Crime, Property Values, and Property Taxes in Mt. Laurel, New Jersey." *City Community* 12, no. 2 (June 2013): 89–112.

Alesina, Alberto, Reza Baqir, and William Easterly. "Public Goods and Ethnic Divisions." *Quarterly Journal of Economics* 114, no. 4 (November 1999): 1243–84.

Alesina, Alberto, Reza Baqir, and Caroline Hoxby. "Political Jurisdictions in Heterogeneous Communities." NBER Working Paper No. 7859, August 2000.

Alesina, Alberto, Arnaud Devleeschauwer, William Easterly, Sergio Kurlat, and Romain Wacziarg. "Fractionalization." NBER Working Paper No. 9411, December 2002.

Alesina, Alberto, and Paola Giuliano. "Preferences for Redistribution." NBER Working Paper No. 14825, March 2009.

Alesina, Alberto, and Edward Glaeser. *Fighting Poverty in the US and Europe*. Oxford: Oxford University Press, 2004.

Alesina, Alberto, Edward Glaeser, and Bruce Sacerdote. "Why Doesn't the US Have a European-Style Welfare System?" NBER Working Paper No. 8524, October 2001.

Alesina, Alberto, and Eliana La Ferrara. "Participation in Heterogeneous Communities." NBER Working Paper No. 7155, June 1999.

Alesina, Alberto, Armando Miano, and Stefanie Stantcheva. "Immigration and Redistribution." NBER Working Paper No. 24733, October 2018.

Alesina, Alberto, Elie Murard, and Hillel Rapoport. "Immigration and Preferences for Redistribution in Europe." NBER Working Paper No. 25562, February 2019.

Alexander, Michelle. *The New Jim Crow*. New York: New Press, 2012.

Allen, Danielle S. "Toward a Connected Society." In *Our Compelling Interests: The Value of Diversity for Democracy and a Prosperous Society*, edited by Earl Lewis and Nancy Cantor. Princeton, N.J.: Princeton University Press, 2016.

Almond, Douglas, Kenneth Y. Chay, and Michael Greenstone. "Civil Rights, the War on Poverty, and Black-White Convergence in Infant Mortality in the Rural South and Mississippi." MIT Department of Economics Working Paper No. 07-04, December 2006.

Anderson, Carol. *White Rage: The Unspoken Truth of Our Racial Divide*. New York: Bloomsbury, 2016.

Appelbaum, Binyamin, and Robert Gebeloff. "Even Critics of Safety Net Increasingly Depend on It." *New York Times*, February 11, 2012.

Argys, Laura M., Andrew I. Friedson, M. Melinda Pitts, and D. Sebastian Tello-Trillo. "Losing Public Health Insurance: TennCare Disenrollment and Personal Financial Distress." Federal Reserve Bank of Atlanta Working Paper No. 2017-6, August 2017.

Asen, Robert. "Nixon's Welfare Reform: Enacting Historical Contradictions of Poverty Discourses." *Rhetoric and Public Affairs* 4, no. 2 (Summer 2001): 261–79.

Ashok, Sowmiya. "The Rise of the American 'Others': An Increasing Number of Respondents Are Checking 'Some Other Race' on U.S. Census Forms, Forcing Officials to Rethink Current Racial Categories." *Atlantic*, August 27, 2016.

Austin, John, and Britany Affolter-Caine. "The Vital Center: A Federal-State Compact to Renew the Great Lakes Region." Brookings Institution Metropolitan Policy Program, 2006.

Autor, David, David Dorn, and Gordon Hanson. "When Work Disappears: Manufacturing Decline and the Falling Marriage-Market Value of Young Men." NBER Working Paper No. 23173, January 2018.

Autor, David, David Dorn, Gordon Hanson, and Kaveh Majlesi. "Importing Political Polarization? The Electoral Consequences of Rising Trade Exposure." NBER Working Paper No. 22637, September 2016.

Ayscue, Jennifer B., Greg Flaxman, John Kucsera, and Genevieve Siegel Hawley. "Settle for Segregation or Strive for Diversity? A Defining Moment for Maryland's Public Schools." Civil Rights Project, April 2013.

Bailey, Martha J., and Sheldon Danziger, eds. *Legacies of the War on Poverty*. New York: Russell Sage Foundation, 2013.

Baldassare, Mark, Dean Bonner, Alyssa Dykman, and Lunna Lopes. "Proposition 13: 40 Years Later." Public Policy Institute of California, June 2018.

Balderrama, Francisco, and Raymond Rodriguez. *Decade of Betrayal: Mexican Repatriation in the 1930s*. Albuquerque: University of New Mexico Press, 2006.

Baldwin, Kate, and John D. Huber. "Economic Versus Cultural Differences: Forms of Ethnic Diversity and Public Goods Provision." *American Political Science Review* 104, no. 4 (November 2010): 644–62.

Barber, Michael, and Nolan McCarty. "Causes and Consequences of Polarization." In *Solutions to Political Polarization in America*, edited by Nathaniel Persily, 15–58. Cambridge, U.K.: Cambridge University Press, 2015.

Bayer, Patrick, and Kerwin Kofi Charles. "Divergent Paths: A New Perspective on Earning Differences Between Black and White Men Since 1940." BFI Working Paper No. 2018-45, July 2018.

Berman, Ari. "The GOP War on Voting." *Rolling Stone*, August 30, 2011.

Bernstein, David E. "Racism, Railroad Unions, and Labor Regulations." *Independent Review* 5, no. 2 (Fall 2000): 237–47.

Betts, Julian R., and Robert W. Fairlie. "Does Immigration Induce 'Native Flight' from Public Schools into Private Schools?" *Journal of Public Economics* 87, no. 5–6 (May 2003): 987–1012.

Bitler, Marianne, and Hilary W. Hoynes. "Immigrants, Welfare Reform, and the U.S. Safety Net." NBER Working Paper No. 17667, December 2011.

Bobo, Lawrence D., and Camille Z. Charles. "Race in the American Mind: From the Moynihan Report to the Obama Candidacy." *Annals of the American Academy of Political and Social Science* 621 (January 2009): 243–59.

Bobo, Lawrence D., and Vincent L. Hutchings. "Perceptions of Racial Group Competition: Extending Blumer's Theory of Group Position to a Multiracial Social Context." *American Sociological Review* 61, no. 6 (December 1996): 951–72.

Bondurant, Samuel R., Jason M. Lindo, and Isaac D. Swensen. "Substance Abuse Treatment Centers and Local Crime." NBER Working Paper No. 22610, September 2016.

Borjas, George. *We Wanted Workers: Unraveling the Immigration Narrative*. New York: W. W. Norton, 2016.

Boustan, Leah Platt. "Was Postwar Suburbanization 'White Flight'? Evidence from the Black Migration." *Quarterly Journal of Economics* 125, no. 1 (2010): 417–43.

Bradbury, Bruce, Miles Corak, Jane Waldfogel, and Elizabeth Washbrook. *Too Many Children Left Behind: The U.S. Achievement Gap in Comparative Perspective.* New York: Russell Sage Foundation, 2015.

Brueggemann, John. "Racial Considerations and Social Policy in the 1930s." *Social Science History* 26, no. 1 (Spring 2002): 139–77.

Buchanan, Suzy. "Tensions Mounting Between Blacks and Latinos Nationwide." *Intelligence Report*, Southern Poverty Law Center, July 27, 2005.

Camarillo, Albert M. "Cities of Color: The New Racial Frontier in California's Minority-Majority Cities." *Pacific Historical Review* 76, no. 1 (February 2007): 1–28.

Cancian, Maria, and Ron Haskins. "Changes in Family Composition: Implications for Income, Poverty, and Public Policy." *Annals of the American Academy of Political and Social Science* 654, no. 1 (July 2014): 31–47.

Card, David, and Jesse Rothstein. "Racial Segregation and the Black-White Test Score Gap." *Journal of Public Economics* 91, no. 11–12 (December 2007): 2158–84.

Carnoy, Martin, and Emma García. "Five Key Trends in U.S. Student Performance." Economic Policy Institute, January 12, 2017.

Cascio, Elizabeth, Nora Gordon, Ethan Lewis, and Sarah Reber. "Paying for Progress: Conditional Grants and the Desegregation of Southern Schools." NBER Working Paper No. 14869, April 2009.

Case, Anne, and Angus Deaton. "Mortality and Morbidity in the 21st Century." *Brookings Papers on Economic Activity* (Spring 2017): 397–476.

———. "Rising Morbidity and Mortality in Midlife Among White Non-Hispanic Americans in the 21st Century." *PNAS* 112, no. 49 (2015): 15078–83.

Chae, David H., Sean Clouston, Mark L. Hatzenbuehler, Michael R. Kramer, Hannah L. F. Cooper, Sacoby M. Wilson, Seth I. Stephens-Davidowitz, Robert S. Gold, and Bruce G. Link. "Association Between an Internet-Based Measure of Area Racism and Black Mortality." *PLoS ONE* 2, no. 4 (2015).

Charlesworth, Tessa E. S., and Mahzarin R. Banaji. "Patterns of Implicit and Explicit Attitudes: I. Long-Term Change and Stability from 2007 to 2016." *Psychological Science* 1, no. 19, 2019.

Cherlin, Andrew J. *Labor's Love Lost: The Rise and Fall of the Working-Class Family in America.* New York: Russell Sage Foundation, 2014.

Chetty, Raj, Nathaniel Hendren, and Lawrence F. Katz. "The Effects of Exposure to Better Neighborhoods on Children: New Evidence from the Moving to Opportunity Experiment." *American Economic Review* 106, no. 4 (2016): 855–902.

Chmielewski, Anna K., and Sean F. Reardon. "Patterns of Cross-National Variation in the Association Between Income and Academic Achievement." *AERA Open* 2, no. 3 (2016): 1–27.

Clear, Todd R. "The Effects of High Imprisonment Rates on Communities." *Crime and Justice* 37, no. 1 (2008): 97–132.

Clemans-Cope, Lisa, Marni Epstein, and Genevieve M. Kenney. "Rapid Growth in Medicaid Spending on Medications to Treat Opioid Use Disorder and Overdose." Urban Institute, June 2017.

Clemens, Michael A., Carlos Gutierrez, and Ernesto Zedillo. *Shared Border, Shared Future: A Blueprint to Regulate US-Mexico Labor Mobility.* Report of the Center for Global Development Working Group on Innovations in Bilateral Cooperation to Regulate US-Mexico Labor Mobility in the 21st Century, 2016.

Clemens, Michael A., Ethan G. Lewis, and Hannah M. Postel. "Immigration Restrictions as Active Labor Market Policy: Evidence from the Mexican Bracero Exclusion." *American Economic Review* 108, no. 6 (June 2018): 1468–87.

Coates, Ta-Nehisi. "The Black Family in the Age of Mass Incarceration." *Atlantic*, October 2015.

———. "The Case for Reparations." *Atlantic*, June 2014.

———. "Other People's Pathologies." *Atlantic*, March 2014.

Cohen, Cathy J., Matthew Fowler, Vladimir E. Medenica, and Jon C. Rogowski. "The 'Woke' Generation? Millennial Attitudes on Race in the US." GenForward University of Chicago Report, October 2017.

Committee on Foreign Relations, U.S. Senate. *Investigation of Mexican Affairs.* Vol 2. Washington, D.C.: Government Printing Office, 1920.

Commons, John R., et al. *History of Labour in the United States.* 1918. Washington, D.C.: Beard Books, 2000.

Congressional Budget Office. *Immigration and Welfare Reform.* Washington, D.C.: Congressional Budget Office, 1995.

Contrera, Jessica. "They Are Poor, Sick, and Voted for Trump. What Will Happen to Them Without Obamacare?" *Washington Post*, March 11, 2017.

Costa, Dora L., and Matthew E. Kahn. "Cowards and Heroes: Group Loyalty in the American Civil War." *Quarterly Journal of Economics* 118, no. 2 (May 2003): 519–48.

Craig, Maureen A., and Jennifer A. Richeson. "Majority No More? The Influence of Neighborhood Racial Diversity and Salient National Population Changes on Whites' Perceptions of Racial Discrimination." *RSF: The Russell Sage Foundation Journal of the Social Sciences* 4, no. 5 (August 2018): 141–57.

Craig, Maureen A., Julian M. Rucker, and Jennifer A. Richeson. "The Pitfalls and Promise of Increasing Racial Diversity: Threat, Contact, and Race Relations in the 21st Century." *Current Directions in Psychological Science* 27, no. 3 (2018): 188–93.

———. "Racial and Political Dynamics of an Approaching 'Majority-Minority' United States." *Annals of the American Academy of Political and Social Science* 677, no. 1 (2018): 204–14.

Cutler, David M., Edward L. Glaeser, and Jacob L. Vigdor. "The Rise and Decline of the American Ghetto." *Journal of Political Economy* 107, no. 3 (June 1999): 455–506.

Davies, Gareth, and Martha Derthick. "Race and Social Welfare Policy: The Social Security Act of 1935." *Political Science Quarterly* 112, no. 2 (Summer 1997): 217–35.

Department of Homeland Security. "Inadmissibility on Public Charge Grounds." *Federal Register*, October 10, 2018.

DiIulio, John J. "Prisons Are a Bargain, by Any Measure." *New York Times*, January 16, 1996.

DiJulio, Bianca, Mira Norton, Symone Jackson, and Mollyann Brodie. *Kaiser Family Foundation/CNN: Survey of Americans on Race.* Kaiser Family Foundation, November 2015.

DiPasquale, Denise, and Edward L. Glaeser. "The Los Angeles Riot and the Economics of Urban Unrest." *Journal of Urban Economics* 43, no. 1 (January 1998): 52–78.

Du Bois, W. E. B. "Statement on the Denial of Human Rights to Minorities in the Case of Citizens of Negro Descent in the United States of America and an Appeal to the United Nations for Redress." National Association for the Advancement of Colored People, 1947.

Duncan, Greg J., and Richard J. Murnane, eds. *Whither Opportunity? Rising Inequality, Schools, and Children's Life Chances.* New York: Russell Sage Foundation, 2011.

Duncan, Greg J., and Anita Zuberi. "Mobility Lessons from Gautreaux and Moving to Opportunity." *Northwestern Journal of Law and Social Policy* 1, no. 1 (Summer 2006).

EdBuild. "Fractured: The Breakdown of America's School Districts." June 2017.

Edin, Kathryn G., and H. Luke Shaefer. *$2 a Day: Living on Almost Nothing in America.* New York: Houghton Mifflin Harcourt, 2015.

Edsall, Thomas B. "Making the Election About Race." *New York Times*, August 27, 2012.

Eiermann, Martin, Yascha Mounk, and Limor Gultchin. "European Populism: Trends, Threats, and Future Prospects." *Tony Blair Institute for Global Change Report*, December 29, 2017.

Enos, Ryan D. "What the Demolition of Public Housing Teaches Us About the Impact of Racial Threat on Political Behavior." *American Journal of Political Science* 60, no. 1 (January 2016): 123–42.

Ezcurra, Roberto, and Andrés Rodríguez-Pose. "Does Ethnic Segregation Matter for Spatial Inequality? A Cross-Country Analysis." CEPR Discussion Papers 11913, March 17, 2017.

Fahle, Erin M., and Sean F. Reardon. "How Much Do Test Scores Vary Among School Districts? New Estimates Using Population Data, 2009–2015." Stanford Center for Education Policy Analysis Working Paper No. 17-02, September 2017.

Falk, Gene. "Temporary Assistance for Needy Families (TANF): Size and Characteristics of the Cash Assistance Caseload." Congressional Research Service, Washington, D.C., January 29, 2016.

Farley, Reynolds. "Identifying with Multiple Races: A Social Movement That Succeeded but Failed?" In *The Changing Terrain of Race and Ethnicity*, edited by Maria Krysan and Amanda E. Lewis. New York: Russell Sage Foundation, 2004.

———. "The Kerner Commission Report Plus Four Decades: What Has Changed? What Has Not?" PSC Research Report No. 08-656, September 2008.

Featherman, David L., and Maris A. Vinovskis, eds. *Social Science and Policy Making: A Search for Relevance in the Twentieth Century*. Ann Arbor: University of Michigan Press, 2001.

Figlio, David N., and Deborah Fletcher. "Suburbanization, Demographic Change, and the Consequences for School Finance." NBER Working Paper No. 16137, June 2010.

Finklea, Kristin. "MS-13 in the United States and Federal Law Enforcement Efforts." Congressional Research Service, Washington, D.C., August 20, 2018.

Fischel, William A. "An Economic History of Zoning and a Cure for Its Exclusionary Effects." *Urban Studies* 41, no. 2 (February 2004): 317–40.

Fix, Michael, ed. *Immigrants and Welfare: The Impact of Welfare Reform on America's Newcomers.* New York: Russell Sage Foundation, 2009.

Fix, Michael, and Wendy Zimmermann. "The Legacies of Welfare Reform's Immigrant Restrictions." Urban Institute, August 1998.

Foner, Eric. "The Meaning of Freedom in the Age of Emancipation." *Journal of American History* 81, no. 2 (September 1994): 435–60.

———. *Reconstruction: America's Unfinished Revolution, 1863–1877.* New York: Harper & Row, 1988.

Foner, Nancy, and Richard Alba. *Strangers No More: Immigration and the Challenges of Integration in North America and Western Europe.* Princeton, N.J.: Princeton University Press, 2015.

Foner, Nancy, and George M. Fredrickson, eds. *Not Just Black and White.* New York: Russell Sage Foundation, 2004.

Fordham, Benjamin O., and Katja B. Kleinberg. "How Can Economic Interests Influence Support for Free Trade?" *International Organization* 66, no. 2 (Spring 2012): 311–28.

Forman, Tyrone A., and Amanda E. Lewis. "Beyond Prejudice? Young Whites' Racial Attitudes in Post–Civil Rights America, 1976 to 2000." *American Behavioral Scientist* 59, no. 11 (2015): 1394–428.

Fouka, Vasiliki, Soumyajit Mazumder, and Marco Tabellini. "From Immigrants to Americans: Race and Assimilation During the Great Migration." HBS Working Paper No. 19-018, August 2018.

Fox, Cybelle. "The Changing Color of Welfare? How Whites' Attitudes Toward Latinos Influence Support for Welfare." *American Journal of Sociology* 110, no. 3 (November 2004): 580–625.

———. *Three Worlds of Relief: Race, Immigration, and the American Welfare State from the Progressive Era to the New Deal.* Princeton, N.J.: Princeton University Press, 2012.

———. "Unauthorized Welfare: The Origins of Immigrant Status Restrictions in American Social Policy." *Journal of American History* 102, no. 4 (March 2016): 1051–74.

Fox, Cybelle, and Thomas A. Guglielmo. "Defining America's Racial Boundaries: Blacks, Mexicans, and European Immigrants, 1890–1945." *American Journal of Sociology* 118, no. 2 (September 2012): 327–79.

Frey, William. *Diversity Explosion: How New Racial Demographics Are Remaking America*. Washington, D.C.: Brookings Institution Press, 2018.

Fryer, Roland G., Jr., and Steven D. Levitt. "Understanding the Black-White Test Gap in the First Two Years of School." *Review of Economics and Statistics* 86, no. 2 (May 2004): 447–64.

Fuetsch, Michelle. "Latino Aspirations on Rise in Compton: Demographics: Latinos Stream into the Area. Some Say the Black-Run City Is Hostile to Their Needs." *Los Angeles Times*, May 7, 1990.

Gay, Claudine. "Seeing Difference: The Effect of Economic Disparity on Black Attitudes Toward Latinos." *American Journal of Political Science* 50, no. 4 (October 2006): 982–97.

Gilens, Martin. *Why Americans Hate Welfare: Race, Media, and the Politics of Antipoverty Policy*. Chicago: University of Chicago Press, 1999.

Gilliam, Franklin D., Jr. "The 'Welfare Queen' Experiment: How Viewers React to Images of African-American Mothers on Welfare." *Nieman Reports*, June 15, 1999.

Glaeser, Edward, and Jacob Vigdor. "The End of the Segregated Century: Racial Separation in America's Neighborhoods, 1890–2010." Manhattan Institute Civic Report No. 66, January 2012.

Goldfield, Michael. "Race and the CIO: The Possibilities for Racial Egalitarianism During the 1930s and 1940s." *International Labor and Working-Class History* 44 (Fall 1993): 1–32.

Goldin, Claudia, and Lawrence F. Katz. *The Race Between Education and Technology*. Cambridge, Mass.: Belknap Press, 2010.

Gordon-Reed, Annette. "America's Original Sin: Slavery and the Legacy of White Supremacy." *Foreign Affairs*, December 12, 2017.

Grabar, Henry. "Who Gets to Live in Fremont, Nebraska? A New Costco Plant Could Save the Town—by Bringing Hundreds of Immigrants to the Only Place in America That Passed a Law to Keep Them Out." *Slate*, December 6, 2017.

Greenberg, Stanley B. *Middle Class Dreams: The Politics and Power of the New American Majority*. New York: Crown, 1995.

Greenberg, Stanley B., James Carville, Andrew Baumann, Karl Agne, and Jesse Contario. "Back to Macomb: Reagan Democrats and Barack Obama." Democracy Corps, December 12, 2008.

Greenberg, Stanley B., and Nancy Zdunkewicz. "Macomb and America's New Political Moment: Learning from Obama-Trump Working Class Voters in Macomb and Democratic Base Groups in Greater Detroit." Democracy Corps, May 7, 2018.

Greenberg, Stanley B. *R.I.P. G.O.P.: How the New America Is Dooming the Republicans*. New York: Saint Martin's Press, 2019.

Greenhouse, Steven. *Beaten Down, Worked Up: The Past, Present, and Future of American Labor*. New York: Knopf, 2019.

Greyser, Linda L., et al. *Fall River Public Schools: District Leadership and Resource Management Evaluation Report*. Massachusetts Department of Elementary and Secondary Education, March 2009.

Griffin, Robert, and Ruy Teixeira. "The Story of Trump's Appeal: A Portrait of Trump Voters." Democracy Fund Voter Study Group, June 2017.

Guerrieri, Veronica, and Alessandra Fogli. "The End of the American Dream? Inequality and Segregation in US Cities." University of Chicago Booth School of Business Working Paper, 2018.

Guerrieri, Veronica, Daniel Hartley, and Erik Hurst. "Endogenous Gentrification and Housing Price Dynamics." NBER Working Paper No. 16237, October 2012.

Hahn, Heather, Laudan Y. Aron, Cary Lou, Eleanor Pratt, and Adaeze Okoli. "Why Does Cash Welfare Depend on Where

You Live? How and Why State TANF Programs Vary." Urban Institute, June 2017.

Hamill, Pete. "The Revolt of the White Middle Class." *New York*, April 1969.

Hamilton, Dona Cooper. "The National Association for the Advancement of Colored People and New Deal Reform Legislation: A Dual Agenda." *Social Service Review* 68, no. 4 (December 1994): 488–502.

Hannah-Jones, Nikole. "School Segregation, the Continuing Tragedy of Ferguson." ProPublica, December 19, 2014.

———. "Segregation Now." ProPublica, April 16, 2014.

Hanson, Gordon, and Craig McIntosh. "Is the Mediterranean the New Rio Grande? US and EU Immigration Pressures in the Long Run." *Journal of Economic Perspectives* 30, no. 4 (Fall 2016): 5–82.

Hatzenbuehler, Mark L., Katherine Keyes, Ava Hamilton, Monica Uddin, and Sandro Galea. "The Collateral Damage of Mass Incarceration: Risk of Psychiatric Morbidity Among Nonincarcerated Residents of High-Incarceration Neighborhoods." *American Journal of Public Health* 105, no. 1 (January 2015): 138–43.

Heilbrunn, Jacob. "The Moynihan Enigma." *American Prospect*, July–August 1997.

Herbert, Bob. "In America: A Sea Change on Crime." *New York Times*, December 12, 1993.

Hero, Rodney, and Morris Levy. "The Racial Structure of Economic Inequality in the United States: Understanding Change and Continuity in an Era of 'Great Divergence.'" *Social Science Quarterly* 97, no. 3 (September 2016): 491–505.

———. "The Racial Structure of Inequality: Consequences for Welfare Policy in the United States." *Social Science Quarterly* 99, no. 2 (June 2018): 459–72.

Hero, Rodney, Morris Levy, and Brian Yeokwang An. "It's Not Just Welfare: Racial Inequality and the Local Provision of Public

Goods in the United States." *Urban Affairs Review* 54, no. 5 (September 2018): 833–65.

Hero, Rodney, and Robert R. Preuhs. "Immigration and the Evolving American Welfare State: Examining Policies in the U.S. States." *American Journal of Political Science* 51, no. 3 (July 2007): 498–517.

Hill, Herbert. "The Problem of Race in American Labor History." *Reviews in American History* 24, no. 2 (June 1996): 189–208.

———. "Racism Within Organized Labor: A Report of Five Years of the AFL-CIO, 1955–1960." *Journal of Negro Education* 30, no. 2 (Spring 1961): 109–18.

Hochschild, Arlie. *Strangers in Their Own Land: Anger and Mourning on the American Right*. New York: New Press, 2016.

Hollinger, David A. "Obama, Blackness, and Postethnic America." *Chronicle of Higher Education*, February 29, 2008.

Hopkins, Daniel J. "The Diversity Discount: When Increasing Ethnic and Racial Diversity Prevents Tax Increases." *Journal of Politics* 71, no. 1 (2009): 160–77.

House Budget Committee. *The War on Poverty: 50 Years Later*. Washington, D.C.: House Budget Committee, 2014.

Hungerman, Daniel M. "Race and Charitable Church Activity." *Economic Inquiry* 46, no. 3 (July 2008): 380–400.

Hussey, Laura S., and Shanna Pearson-Merko. "The Changing Role of Race in Social Welfare Attitude Formation: Partisan Divides over Undocumented Immigrants and Social Welfare Policy." *Political Research Quarterly* 66, no. 3 (September 2013): 572–84.

Inda, Jonathan Xavier. *Targeting Immigrants: Government, Technology, and Ethics*. Malden, Mass.: Blackwell, 2006.

Inglehart, Ronald, and Pippa Norris. "Trump and the Populist Authoritarian Parties: The Silent Revolution in Reverse." *Perspectives on Politics* 15, no. 2 (June 2017): 443–54.

Jackson, C. Kirabo, Rucker C. Johnson, and Claudia Persico. "The Effects of School Spending on Educational and Economic Outcomes: Evidence from School Finance Reforms." NBER Working Paper No. 20847, January 2015.

Jacobson, Jessica, Catherine Heard, and Helen Fair. "Prison: Evidence of Its Use and Over-use from Around the World." Institute for Criminal Policy Research, 2017.

Jäntti, Markus, Gerald Jaynes, and John E. Roemer. "The Double Role of Ethnic Heterogeneity in Explaining Welfare-State Generosity." Cowles Foundation Discussion Paper No. 1972, December 2, 2014.

Johnson, Kevin R. "The Forgotten Repatriation of Persons of Mexican Ancestry and Lessons for the War on Terror." *Pace Law Review* 26, no. 1 (Fall 2005).

Johnson, Rucker C. "Long-Run Impacts of School Desegregation & School Quality on Adult Attainments." NBER Working Paper No. 16664, September 2015.

Johnson, Rucker C., and Alexander Nazaryan. *Children of the Dream: Why School Integration Works*. New York: Basic Books, 2019.

Judis, John B., and Ruy Teixeira. *The Emerging Democratic Majority*. New York: Scribner, 2002.

Kahlenberg, Richard D. "An Economic Fair Housing Act." Century Foundation, August 3, 2017.

Katznelson, Ira. *When Affirmative Action Was White: An Untold History of Racial Inequality in Twentieth-Century America*. New York: W. W. Norton, 2005.

Kaufmann, Franz-Xaver. "The Idea of Social Policy in Western Societies: Origins and Diversity." *International Journal of Social Quality* 3, no. 2 (Winter 2013): 16–40.

Kearney, Melissa S., Benjamin H. Harris, Elisa Jácome, and Lucie Parker. "Ten Economic Facts About Crime and Incarceration in the United States." Hamilton Project Policy Memo, May 1, 2014.

Keller, Josh, and Adam Pearce. "A Small Indiana County Sends More People to Prison than San Francisco and Durham, N.C., Combined. Why?" *New York Times*, September 2, 2016.

Kelley, Robin D. G. "Building Bridges: The Challenge of Organized Labor in Communities of Color." *New Labor Forum*, no. 5 (Fall–Winter 1999): 42–58.

Kennedy, David M. *Freedom from Fear: The American People in Depression and War, 1929–1945*. New York: Oxford University Press, 2005.

Kesler, Christel, and Irene Bloemraad. "Does Immigration Erode Social Capital? The Conditional Effects of Immigration-Generated Diversity on Trust, Membership, and Participation Across 19 Countries, 1981–2000." *Canadian Journal of Political Science* 43, no. 2 (June 2010): 319–47.

Kinder, Donald R., and Allison Dale-Riddle. *The End of Race? Obama, 2008, and Racial Politics in America*. New Haven, Conn.: Yale University Press, 2012.

Kinder, Donald R., and Cindy Kam. *Us Against Them: Ethnocentric Foundations of American Opinion*. Chicago: University of Chicago Press, 2009.

Kolko, Jed. "How Much Slower Would the U.S. Grow Without Immigration? In Many Places, a Lot." *New York Times*, April 18, 2019.

Kucsera, John, and Gary Orfield. "New York State's Extreme School Segregation, Inequality, Inaction, and a Damaged Future." Civil Rights Project, UCLA, March 2014.

Kuziemko, Ilyana, and Ebonya Washington. "Why Did the Democrats Lose the South? Bringing New Data to an Old Debate." *American Economic Review* 108, no. 10 (2018): 2830–67.

Lacy, Dean. "Moochers and Makers in the Voting Booth: Who Benefits from Federal Spending, and How Did They Vote in the 2004 Through 2012 Presidential Elections?" *Public Opinion Quarterly* 78, no. S1 (2014): 255–75.

Lash, Cristina L. "Making Americans: Schooling, Diversity, and Assimilation in the Twenty-First Century." *RSF: Russell Sage Foundation Journal of the Social Sciences* 4, no. 5 (August 2018): 99–117.

Lause, Mark A. "The American Radicals & Organized Marxism: The Initial Experience, 1869–1874." *Labor History* 33, no. 1 (1992): 55–80.

Lazonick, William, Philip Moss, and Joshua Weitz. "The Equal Employment Opportunity Omission." Institute for New Economic Thinking Working Paper No. 53, December 2016.

Lee, Jennifer, and Frank D. Bean. "Reinventing the Color Line: Immigration and America's New Racial/Ethnic Divide." *Social Forces* 86, no. 2 (December 2007): 561–86.

Lee, Woojin, and John E. Roemer. "Racism and Redistribution in the United States: A Solution to the Problem of American Exceptionalism." *Journal of Public Economics* 90, no. 6–7 (August 2006): 1027–52.

Lee, Woojin, John E. Roemer, and Karine van der Straeten. "Racism, Xenophobia, and Redistribution." *Journal of the European Economic Association* 4, no. 2–3 (April–May 2006): 446–54.

Levin, Josh. "The Welfare Queen." *Slate*, December 19, 2013.

Levy, Frank S. "Computers and Populism: Artificial Intelligence, Jobs, and Politics in the Near Term." *Oxford Review of Economic Policy* 34, no. 3 (Fall 2018): 393–417.

Lhamon, Catherine E. "Dear Colleague Letter: Resource Comparability." Department of Education Office for Civil Rights. Washington, October 1, 2014.

Lichter, Daniel T. "Integration or Fragmentation? Racial Diversity and the American Future." *Demography* 50, no. 2 (April 2013): 359–91.

Lichter, Daniel T., Domenico Parisi, and Michael C. Taquino. "Spatial Segregation." Stanford Center on Poverty and Inequality, 2015.

Lieberman, Robert C. "Race, Institutions, and the Administration of Social Policy." *Social Science History* 19, no. 4 (Winter 1995): 511–42.

———. *Shifting the Color Line: Race and the American Welfare State.* Cambridge, Mass.: Harvard University Press, 2001.

Lieberman, Robert C., and John S. Lapinski. "American Federalism, Race, and the Administration of Welfare." *British Journal of Political Science* 31, no. 2 (April 2001): 303–29.

Lindert, Peter H. "What Limits Social Spending?" *Explorations in Economic History* 33 (1996): 1–34.

Link, Michael W., and Robert W. Oldendick. "Social Construction and White Attitudes Toward Equal Opportunity and Multiculturalism." *Journal of Politics* 58, no. 1 (February 1996): 149–68.

Logan, John R. "The Persistence of Segregation in the 21st Century Metropolis." *City Community* 12, no. 2 (2013).

———, ed. *Diversity and Disparities*. New York: Russell Sage Foundation, 2014.

Logan, John R., and Charles Zhang. "Global Neighborhoods: New Pathways to Diversity and Separation." *American Journal of Sociology* 115, no. 4 (January 2010): 1069–109.

Lopez, Mark Hugo, Ana Gonzalez-Barrera, and Gustavo López. "Hispanic Identity Fades Across Generations as Immigrant Connections Fall Away." Pew Research Center, December 20, 2017.

Lowrey, Annie. "Are Immigrants a Drain on Government Resources?" *Atlantic*, September 28, 2018.

Luttmer, Erzo F. P. "Group Loyalty and the Taste for Redistribution." *Journal of Political Economy* 109, no. 3 (2001).

Mansfield, Edward D., and Diana C. Mutz. "Support for Free Trade: Self-Interest, Sociotropic Politics, and Out-Group Anxiety." *International Organization* 63, no. 3 (Summer 2009): 425–57.

Marois, Michael B., and James Nash. "California Schools Suffer Under Proposition 13 Tax Cap's Chaos." *Bloomberg*, July 12, 2011.

Martinson, Robert. "Can Corrections Correct? The Paradox of Prison Reform—II." *New Republic*, April 8, 1972.

———. "The 'Dangerous Myth': The Paradox of Prison Reform—I." *New Republic*, April 1, 1972.

———. "The Meaning of Attica: The Paradox of Prison Reform— III." *New Republic*, April 15, 1972.

———. "Planning for Public Safety: The Paradox of Prison Reform—IV." *New Republic*, April 29, 1972.

———. "What Works? Questions and Answers About Prison Reform." *National Affairs* (Spring 1974).

Massey, Douglas S. "The New Latino Underclass: Immigration Enforcement as a Race-Making Institution." Stanford Center on Poverty and Inequality, April 2012.

Massey, Douglas S., Len Albright, Rebecca Casciano, Elizabeth Derickson, and David N. Kinsey. *Climbing Mount Laurel: The Struggle for Affordable Housing and Social Mobility in an American Suburb*. Princeton, N.J.: Princeton University Press, 2013.

Massey, Douglas S., and Nancy A. Denton. *American Apartheid: Segregation and the Making of the Underclass*. Cambridge, Mass.: Harvard University Press, 1993.

Massey, Douglas S., Jorge Durand, and Karen A. Pren. "Explaining Undocumented Migration to the U.S." *International Migration Review* 48, no. 4 (Winter 2014): 1028–61.

Massey, Douglas S., and Karen A. Pren. "Unintended Consequences of US Immigration Policy: Explaining the Post-1965 Surge from Latin America." *Population and Development Review* 38, no. 1 (2012): 1–29.

———. "Origins of the New Latino Underclass." *Race and Social Problems* 4, no. 1 (2012): 5–17.

Mayda, Anna Maria, and Dani Rodrik. "Why Are Some People (and Countries) More Protectionist than Others?" *European Economic Review* 49, no. 6 (August 2005): 1393–430.

McCarty, Nolan, Keith T. Poole, and Howard Rosenthal. *Polarized America: The Dance of Ideology and Unequal Riches*. Cambridge, Mass.: MIT Press, 2006.

McIlwain, Charlton D., and Stephen M. Caliendo. "Mitt Romney's Racist Appeals: How Race Was Played in the 2012 Presidential Election." *American Behavioral Scientist* 58, no. 9 (2014): 1157–68.

Memoli, Michael A., and Kathleen Hennessey. "Tea Party Express Spokesman Resigns After Racist Blog Post." *Los Angeles Times,* July 24, 2010.

Mettler, Suzanne. *The Government-Citizen Disconnect.* New York: Russell Sage Foundation, 2018.

Metzl, Jonathan M. *Dying of Whiteness: How the Politics of Racial Resentment Is Killing America's Heartland.* New York: Basic Books, 2019.

Mins, Leonard E., ed. "Engels to Sorge, Marx-Engels Correspondence." *Science and Society* 2, no. 3 (1938).

Moore, Peter. "Overwhelming Opposition to Reparations for Slavery and Jim Crow." YouGov, June 2, 2014.

Moyers, Bill D. "What a Real President Was Like." *Washington Post,* November 19, 1988.

Moynihan, Daniel Patrick. "It Will Shame the Congress." *New York Review of Books,* October 19, 1995.

———. *The Negro Family: The Case for National Action.* Washington, D.C.: U.S. Department of Labor, Office of Policy Planning, March 1965.

Murray, Charles. *Coming Apart: The State of White America, 1960–2010.* New York: Crown, 2013.

Mutz, Diana C. "Status Threat, Not Economic Hardship, Explains the 2016 Presidential Vote." *Proceedings of the National Academy of Sciences* 115, no. 19 (2018).

Myers, Dowell. "California Futures: New Narratives for a Changing Society." *Boom: A Journal of California* 2, no. 2 (2012): 37–54.

———. *Immigrants and Boomers.* New York: Russell Sage Foundation, 2007.

———. "Mutual Benefits and Equity amid Racial Diversity: A Generational Strategy for Growing a Broader Base of Support for Social Equity." *Journal of Planning Education and Research* 35, no. 33 (2015): 369–75.

Myers, Dowell, and Morris Levy. "Racial Population Projections and Reactions to Alternative News Accounts of Growing Diversity." *Annals of the American Academy of Political and Social Science* 677, no. 1 (2018): 215–28.

Myles, John, and Jill Quadagno. "Political Theories of the Welfare State." *Social Service Review* 76, no. 1 (March 2002): 34–57.

Myrdal, Gunnar. *An American Dilemma: The Negro Problem and Modern Democracy*. New York: Harper & Brothers, 1944.

Nathan, Richard P. "A Retrospective on Richard M. Nixon's Domestic Policies." *Presidential Studies Quarterly* 26, no. 1 (Winter 1996): 155–64.

National Emergency Council. *Report on Economic Conditions of the South*. [Washington, D.C.]: [Government Printing Office], 1938.

Neal, Derek, and Armin Rick. "The Prison Boom and the Lack of Black Progress After Smith and Welch." NBER Working Paper No. 20283, July 2014.

New York Times. "N.A.A.C.P. Asserts Reagan Budget Profits the Rich at Expense of Poor." April 14, 1981.

O'Brien, Kerry, Walker Forrest, Dermot Lynott, and Michael Daly. "Racism, Gun Ownership, and Gun Control: Biased Attitudes in US Whites May Influence Policy Decisions." *PLoS ONE* 8, no. 10 (2013).

OECD. *Doing Better for Families*. Paris: OECD, 2011.

———. *Lessons from PISA for the United States: Strong Performers and Successful Reformers in Education*. Paris: OECD, 2011.

———. *Settling in 2018: Indicators of Immigrant Integration*. Paris: OECD, 2015.

Olds, Gareth. "Entrepreneurship and Public Health Insurance." Harvard Business School Working Paper No. 16-144, May 2016.

———. "Food Stamp Entrepreneurs." Harvard Business School Working Paper No. 16-143, May 2016.

Orfield, Gary. "Reviving the Goal of an Integrated Society: A 21st Century Challenge." Civil Rights Project, UCLA, January 2009.

Orfield, Gary, Erica Frankenberg, Jongyeon Ee, and John Kuscera. "Brown at 60: Great Progress, a Long Retreat, and an Uncertain Future." Civil Rights Project, UCLA, May 15, 2014.

Orfield, Gary, and Chungmei Lee. "Historic Reversals, Accelerating Resegregation, and the Need for New Integration Strategies." Civil Rights Project, UCLA, August 2007.

Orrenius, Pia, and Madeline Zavodny. "The Potential Role of Immigration in the US Labor Market." Migration Policy Institute Discussion Paper (unpublished), October 11, 2018.

Owens, Ann, Sean F. Reardon, and Christopher Jencks. "Income Segregation Between Schools and School Districts." Stanford Center for Education Policy Analysis Working Paper No. 16-04, May 2016.

Parisi, Domenico, Daniel T. Lichter, and Michael C. Taquino. "The Buffering Hypothesis: Growing Diversity and Declining Black-White Segregation in America's Cities, Suburbs, and Small Towns?" *Sociological Science* 2 (March 2015): 125–57.

Perlman, Selig. *History of Labor in the United States, Part 6: Upheaval and Reorganization*. New York: Macmillan, 1921.

Pew Research Center. "America's Immigration Quandary." March 30, 2006.

———. "King's Dream Remains an Elusive Goal; Many Americans See Racial Disparities." August 22, 2013.

———. "Multiracial in America: Proud, Diverse, and Growing in Numbers." June 2015.

———. "On Views of Race and Inequality, Blacks and Whites Are Worlds Apart." June 27, 2016.

Pierce, Justin R., and Peter K. Schott. "Trade Liberalization and Mortality: Evidence from U.S. Counties." Finance and Economics Discussion Series No. 2016-094. Washington, D.C.: Board of Governors of the Federal Reserve System, 2016.

Plaut, Victoria C. "Diversity Science: Why and How Difference Makes a Difference." *Psychological Inquiry* 21, no. 2 (April–June 2010): 77–99.

Porter, Eduardo. "Census Expands Race Options but Some Still Feel Left Out." *Wall Street Journal*, March 2, 2001.

———. "Growing Minority Groups Will Likely Face Lawsuits over Redistricting." *Wall Street Journal*, March 14, 2001.

———. "Hispanics Seek Increased Representation, and Republicans Are Very Eager to Help." *Wall Street Journal*, April 2, 2001.

———. "Latin Love of Lard Revives the Shunned Shortening." *Wall Street Journal*, June 15, 2001.

———. "Liz Claiborne Aims to Cash In on Craze for All Things Latino." *Wall Street Journal*, August 9, 2001.

———. "New 'Got Milk?' TV Commercials Try to Entice Hispanic Teenagers." *Wall Street Journal*, December 28, 2001.

Porter, Eduardo, and Karl Russell. "Migrants Are on the Rise Around the World, and Myths About Them Are Shaping Attitudes." *New York Times*, June 20, 2018.

Poterba, James. "Demographic Structure and the Political Economy of Public Education." NBER Working Paper No. 5677, July 1996.

Preston, Samuel H. "Children and the Elderly: Divergent Paths for America's Dependents." *Demography* 21, no. 4 (November 1984): 435–57.

Putnam, Robert D. *Bowling Alone: The Collapse and Revival of American Community*. New York: Simon & Schuster, 2000.

———. "*E Pluribus Unum*: Diversity and Community in the Twenty-First Century: The 2006 Johan Skytte Prize Lecture." *Scandinavian Political Studies* 30, no. 2 (June 2007): 137–74.

Quadagno, Jill. *The Color of Welfare: How Racism Undermined the War on Poverty*. New York: Oxford University Press, 1996.

———. "Race, Class, and Gender in the U.S. Welfare State: Nixon's Failed Family Assistance Plan." *American Sociological Review* 55, no. 1 (February 1990): 11–28.

Quint, Howard H. *The Forging of American Socialism*. Indianapolis: Bobbs-Merrill, 1964.

Rafael, Steven, and Michael A. Stoll. *Why Are So Many Americans in Prison?* New York: Russell Sage Foundation, 2013.

Reardon, Sean F., Elena Tej Grewal, Demetra Kalogrides, and Erica Greenberg. "Brown Fades: The End of Court-Ordered School Desegregation and the Resegregation of American Public Schools." *Journal of Policy Analysis and Management* 31, no. 4 (Fall 2012): 876–904.

Reardon, Sean F., Demetra Kalogrides, and Kenneth Shores. "The Geography of Racial/Ethnic Test Score Gaps." Stanford Center for Education Policy Analysis Working Paper No. 16-10, March 2018.

Reardon, Sean F., and Ann Owens. "60 Years After Brown: Trends and Consequences of School Segregation." *Annual Review of Sociology* 40 (2014): 199–218.

Reardon, Sean F., and Ximena A. Portilla. "Recent Trends in Income, Racial, and Ethnic School Readiness Gaps at Kindergarten Entry." Stanford Center for Education Policy Analysis Working Paper No. 15-02, June 2016.

"Recent Legislation: Welfare Reform—Treatment of Legal Immigrants—Congress Authorizes States to Deny Public Benefits to Noncitizens and Excludes Legal Immigrants from Federal Aid Programs—Personal Responsibility and Work Opportunity Reconciliation Act of 1996, Pub. L. No. 104-193, 110 Stat. 2105." *Harvard Law Review* 110, no. 5 (March 1997): 1191–96.

Reich, Steven A. "Organized Labor and the Civil Rights Movement: Lessons from a Troubled Past." *New Labor Forum* 18, no. 3 (Fall 2009): 60–70.

Report of the National Advisory Committee on Civil Disorders. Washington, D.C., 1968.

Reynolds, Preston P. "The Federal Government's Use of Title VI and Medicare to Racially Integrate Hospitals in the United States, 1963 Through 1967." *American Journal of Public Health* 87, no. 11 (1997): 1850–58.

Richards, Meredith P. "The Gerrymandering of School Attendance Zones and the Segregation of Public Schools: A Geospatial Analysis." *American Educational Research Journal* 51, no. 6 (December 2014): 1119–57.

Rodrik, Dani. *The Globalization Paradox: Democracy and the Future of the World Economy.* New York: W. W. Norton, 2011.

———. "Populism and the Economics of Globalization." *Journal of International Business Policy* (2018).

Roediger, David. "Labor in White Skin: Race and Working-Class History." In *Towards the Abolition of Whiteness: Essays on Race, Politics, and Working Class History.* New York: Verso, 1984.

Rothstein, Richard. *The Color of Law: A Forgotten History of How Our Government Segregated America.* New York: Liveright, 2017.

Rothwell, Jonathan T. "Racial Enclaves and Density Zoning: The Institutionalized Segregation of Racial Minorities in the United States." *American Law and Economics Review* 13, no. 1 (Spring 2011): 290–358.

Rothwell, Jonathan T., and Douglas S. Massey. "Density Zoning and Class Segregation in U.S. Metropolitan Areas." *Social Science Quarterly* 91, no. 5 (December 2010): 1123–43.

Rugh, Jacob S., and Douglas S. Massey. "Segregation in Post–Civil Rights America: Stalled Integration or End of the Segregated Century?" *Du Bois Review: Social Science Research on Race* 11, no. 2 (2014): 205–32.

Sabet, Shahrzad. "What's in a Name? Isolating the Effect of Prejudice on Individual Trade Preferences." American Political Science Association 2013 Annual Meeting Paper, August 27, 2013.

Salvatore, Nick. "Workers, Racism, and History: A Response." *New Politics* (Summer 1987): 22–26.

Schaffner, Brian F., Matthew MacWilliams, and Tatishe Nteta. "Understanding White Polarization in the 2016 Vote for President: The Sobering Role of Racism and Sexism." *Political Science Quarterly* 133, no. 1 (Spring 2018): 9–34.

Schildkraut, Deborah J., and Satia A. Marotta. "Assessing the Political Distinctiveness of White Millennials: How Race and Generation Shape Racial and Political Attitudes in a Changing America." *RSF: Russell Sage Foundation Journal of the Social Sciences* 4, no. 5 (2018): 158–87.

Schrag, Peter. *Not Fit for Our Society: Nativism and Immigration.* Berkeley: University of California Press, 2010.

Schram, Sanford F., and Joe Soss. "A Public Transformed? Welfare Reform as Policy Feedback." *American Political Science Review* 101, no. 1 (February 2007): 111–27.

Schram, Sanford F., Joe Soss, and Richard C. Fording, eds. *Race and the Politics of Welfare Reform.* Ann Arbor: University of Michigan Press, 2003.

Schwartz, Heather. *Housing Policy Is School Policy: Economically Integrative Housing Promotes Academic Success in Montgomery County, Maryland.* New York: Century Foundation, 2010.

Schwartz, Mildred A. *Trends in White Attitudes Toward Negroes.* Chicago: National Opinion Research Center, 1967.

Shapiro, Doug, Afet Dundar, Jin Chen, Mary Ziskin, Eunkyoung Park, Vasti Torres, and Yi-Chen Chiang. *Completing College: A State-Level View of Student Attainment Rates.* Herndon, Va.: National Student Clearinghouse Research Center, 2015.

Shapiro, Doug, Afet Dundar, Xin Yuan, Autumn T. Harrell, and Phoebe Khasiala Wakhungu. *Completing College: A National View of Student Attainment Rates—Fall 2008 Cohort.* Herndon, Va.: National Student Clearinghouse Research Center, 2014.

Shaw, Theodore. "On the Sesquicentennial of the Fourteenth Amendment." *Poverty and Race*, April–June 2018.

Sides, John. "Race, Religion, and Immigration in 2016: How the Debate over American Identity Shaped the Election and What It Means for a Trump Presidency." Democracy Fund Voter Study Group, June 2017.

Simon, Jonathan. *Governing Through Crime: How the War on Crime Transformed American Democracy and Created a Culture of Fear.* New York: Oxford University Press, 2007.

Sitkoff, Harvard. *A New Deal for Blacks: The Emergence of Civil Rights as a National Issue.* Vol. 1, *The Depression Decade.* Oxford: Oxford University Press, 1979.

Smelser, Neil J., William Julius Wilson, and Faith Mitchell, eds. *America Becoming: Racial Trends and Their Consequences.* Vol. 1. Washington, D.C.: National Academies Press, 2001.

Sommers, Benjamin D. "State Medicaid Expansions and Mortality, Revisited: A Cost-Benefit Analysis." *American Journal of Health Economics* 3, no. 3 (2017): 392–421.

Sommers, Benjamin D., Katherine Baicker, and Arnold M. Epstein. "Mortality and Access to Care Among Adults After State Medicaid Expansions." *New England Journal of Medicine* 367 (September 2012): 1025–34.

Sommers, Benjamin D., Atul A. Gawande, and Katherine Baicker. "Health Insurance Coverage and Health—What the Recent Evidence Tells Us." *New England Journal of Medicine* 377 (August 2017): 586–93.

Sorge, Friedrich Adolph. *Socialism and the Worker.* Pamphlet published by the Social Democratic Federation in Britain, 1904.

Soss, Joe, Richard C. Fording, and Sanford F. Schram. *Disciplining the Poor: Neoliberal Paternalism and the Persistent Power of Race.* Chicago: University of Chicago Press, 2011.

Spader, Jonathan, and Shannon Rieger. "Patterns and Trends of Residential Integration in the United States Since 2000." Joint Center for Housing Studies of Harvard University Research Brief, September 2017.

Spitzer, Scott. "Nixon's New Deal: Welfare Reform for the Silent Majority." *Presidential Studies Quarterly* 42, no. 3 (September 2012): 455–81.

———. "Nixon's Northern Strategy: Welfare Reform and Race After the Great Society." APSA 2009 Toronto Meeting Paper, 2009.

Stephens-Davidowitz, Seth. "The Cost of Racial Animus on a Black Candidate: Evidence Using Google Search Data." *Journal of Public Economics* 118 (2014): 26–40.

Sturm, Jan-Egbert, and Jakob de Haan. "Income Inequality, Capitalism, and Ethno-linguistic Fractionalization." CESIFO Working Paper No. 5169, January 2015.

Syms, Deirdre, and Kurt Metzger. "The New Macomb County." Macomb Community College and Data Driven Detroit, December 2012.

Tabellini, Marco. "Gifts of the Immigrants, Woes of the Natives: Lessons from the Age of Mass Migration." Harvard Business School BGIE Unit Working Paper No. 19-005, April 3, 2019.

Tarazi, Wafa W., Cathy J. Bradley, Harry D. Bear, David W. Harless, and Lindsay M. Sabik. "Impact of Medicaid Disenrollment in Tennessee on Breast Cancer Stage at Diagnosis and Treatment." *Cancer* 123, no. 17 (September 2017): 3312–19.

Taylor, Paul. *The Next America: Boomers, Millennials, and the Looming Generational Showdown*. New York: PublicAffairs, 2014.

Telles, Edward, and Denia Garcia. "Mestizaje and Public Opinion in Latin America." *Latin American Research Review* 48, no. 3 (2013): 130–52.

Tello-Trillo, Sebastian D. "Effects of Losing Public Health Insurance on Healthcare Access, Utilization, and Health Outcomes: Evidence from the TennCare Disenrollment." Conference Paper of the Association for Public Policy Analysis and Management, November 2016.

Tesler, Michael. *Post-Racial or Most-Racial? Race and Politics in the Obama Era*. Chicago: University of Chicago Press, 2016.

———. "The Spillover of Racialization into Health Care: How President Obama Polarized Public Opinion by Racial Attitudes and Race." *American Journal of Political Science* 56, no. 3 (July 2012): 690–704.

Thomas, Jesse O. "Will the New Deal Be a Square Deal for the Negro?" *Opportunity: Journal of Negro Life*, October 1933.

Tienda, Marta, and Norma Fuentes. "Hispanics in Metropolitan America: New Realities and Old Debates." *Annual Review of Sociology* 40 (2014): 499–520.

Torben, Andersen M., et al. "Economic Policy and the Rise of Populism—It's Not So Simple." In *EEAG Report on the European Economy 2017*, 50–66. Munich: CESifo Group, 2017.

Traub, James. "The Criminals of Tomorrow." *New Yorker*, October 27, 1996.

Travis, Jeremy, Bruce Western, and Steve Redburn, eds. *The Growth of Incarceration in the United States: Exploring Causes and Consequences*. Washington, D.C.: National Academies Press, 2014.

Trounstine, Jessica. "Segregation and Inequality in Public Goods." *American Journal of Political Science* 60, no. 3 (July 2016): 709–25.

Turner, Sarah, and John Bound. "Closing the Gap or Widening the Divide: The Effects of the G.I. Bill and World War II on the Educational Outcomes of Black Americans." *Journal of Economic History* 63, no. 1 (March 2003): 145–77.

U.S. Commission on Civil Rights. *An Assessment of Minority Voting Rights Access in the United States: 2018 Statutory Enforcement Report*. Washington, D.C., 2018.

Uslaner, Eric. *Segregation and Mistrust: Diversity, Isolation, and Social Cohesion*. Cambridge, U.K.: Cambridge University Press, 2012.

Valentino, Nicholas A., Fabian Guy Neuner, and L. Matthew Vandenbroek. "The Changing Norms of Racial Political Rhetoric and the End of Racial Priming." *Journal of Politics* 80, no. 3 (November 2016).

Valentino, Nicholas A., and David O. Sears. "Old Times There Are Not Forgotten: Race and Partisan Realignment in the Contemporary South." *American Journal of Political Science* 49, no. 3 (July 2005): 672–88.

Vigdor, Jacob, and Jens Ludwig. "Segregation and the Black-White Test Score Gap." NBER Working Paper No. 12988, March 2007.

Vogler, Jacob. "Access to Health Care and Criminal Behavior: Short-Run Evidence from the ACA Medicaid Expansions." November 14, 2017.

Wagner, Alex. "America's Forgotten History of Illegal Deportations." *Atlantic*, March 6, 2017.

Ward, Henry George. *Mexico in 1827*. London: Henry Colburn, 1828.

Waters, Mary C., and Marisa Gerstein Pineau, eds. *The Integration of Immigrants into American Society*. Washington, D.C.: National Academies Press, 2015.

Wen, Hefei, Jason M. Hockenberry, and Janet R. Cummings. "The Effect of Medicaid Expansion on Crime Reduction: Evidence from HIFA-Waiver Expansions." *Journal of Public Economics* 154 (October 2017): 67–94.

Western, Bruce. "Poverty, Politics, and Crime Control in Europe and America." *Contemporary Sociology* 40, no. 3 (2011): 283–86.

Wheaton, Sarah, and Michael Shear. "Blunt Report Says G.O.P. Needs to Regroup for '16." *New York Times*, March 18, 2013.

White House Council of Economic Advisers. "Economic Report of the President." Washington, D.C., January 1964.

———. "Expanding Work Requirements in Non-cash Welfare Programs." Washington, D.C., July 2018.

Whitehurst, Grover J., Richard V. Reeves, and Edward Rodrigue. "Segregation, Race, and Charter Schools: What Do We Know?" Brookings Center on Children and Families, October 2016.

Wilkins, Clara L., and Cheryl R. Kaiser. "Racial Progress as Threat to the Status Hierarchy: Implications for Perceptions of Antiwhite Bias." *Psychological Science* 25, no. 2 (2014): 439–46.

Williams, Joan C. *White Working Class: Overcoming Class Cluelessness in America*. Boston: Harvard Business Review Press, 2017.

Williams, Joan C., and Heather Boushey. "The Three Faces of Work-Family Conflict: The Poor, the Professionals, and the Missing Middle." University of California Hastings College of the Law and Center for American Progress, January 2010.

Wilson, William Julius. *When Work Disappears: The World of the New Urban Poor*. New York: Vintage, 1997.

Woolhandler, Steffie, and Himmelstein, David U. "The Relationship of Health Insurance and Mortality: Is Lack of Insurance Deadly?" *Annals of Internal Medicine* 167, no. 6 (2017).

Wright, Lawrence. "One Drop of Blood." *New Yorker,* July 24, 1994.

Wu, Li-Tzy, George E. Woody, Chongming Yang, Jeng-Jong Pan, and Dan G. Blazer. "Racial/Ethnic Variations in Substance-Related Disorders Among Adolescents in the United States." *Archives of General Psychiatry* 68, no. 11 (2011): 1176–85.

Yotam, Margalit. "Lost in Globalization: International Economic Integration and the Sources of Popular Discontent." *International Studies Quarterly* 56, no. 3 (2012): 484–500.

Young, Clifford. "It's Nativism: Explaining the Drivers of Trump's Popular Support." Ipsos Public Affairs, September 2016.

Yu, Corine M., and William L. Taylor, eds. *The Test of Our Progress: The Clinton Record on Civil Rights.* Washington, D.C.: Citizens' Commission on Civil Rights, 1999.

Zangwill, Israel. *The Melting-Pot.* New York: American Jewish Book Company, 1921.

Zubrinsky, Camille L., and Lawrence Bobo. "Prismatic Metropolis: Race and Residential Segregation in the City of the Angels." *Social Science Research* 25, no. 4 (1996): 335–74.

Index

A NOTE ABOUT THE AUTHOR

Eduardo Porter writes about economics for *The New York Times*, where he was the Economic Scene columnist from 2012 to 2018. He began his career in journalism nearly three decades ago in Mexico. Since then he has reported from Tokyo, London, and São Paulo, Brazil. Porter joined *The Wall Street Journal* in 2000, writing from Los Angeles. He joined the *Times* in 2004 and served on its editorial board from 2007 to 2012. Porter is the author of *The Price of Everything* (2011). He has a partner, a daughter, and a son. He lives in Brooklyn.

A NOTE ABOUT THE TYPE

This book was set in Janson, a typeface long thought to have been made by the Dutchman Anton Janson, who was a practicing typefounder in Leipzig during the years 1668–1687. However, it has been conclusively demonstrated that these types are actually the work of Nicholas Kis (1650–1702), a Hungarian, who most probably learned his trade from the master Dutch typefounder Dirk Voskens. The type is an excellent example of the influential and sturdy Dutch types that prevailed in England up to the time William Caslon (1692–1766) developed his own incomparable designs from them.

Composed by North Market Street Graphics,
Lancaster, Pennsylvania

Printed and bound by Berryville Graphics,
Berryville, Virginia